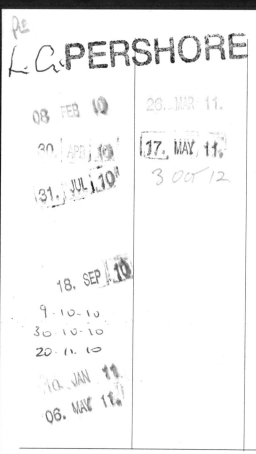

My Story, My Life

VAL DOONICAN

THE COMPLETE AUTOBIOGRAPHY

My Story, My Life

BOOKS

First published in Great Britain in 2009 by
JR Books, 10 Greenland Street, London NW1 0ND
www.jrbooks.com

A catalogue record for this book is available from the British Library.

ISBN 978-1-906779-61-0

1 3 5 7 9 10 8 6 4 2

Printed and bound in Great Britain by the MPG Books Group

Since this volume covers my whole life so far, I would like to dedicate its contents firstly to both my wonderful families, old and new, and secondly to the entire cast of my story. Words can't really say what a privilege it has been to spend my long working life in the company of so many interesting, talented and 'fun' people. The unique pleasure of sharing music and songs with the great stars that I'd previously admired from afar, is something for which I am deeply grateful.

Acknowledgements

To my dear wife Lynn who has put up with my 'workaholic' life for the past forty-seven years; our two special daughters Sarah and Fiona, without whose skills and devotion this volume may not have seen the light of day; the late Sir Bill Cotton Jnr who trusted me with my first television series 'way back in 1964'; TV Producers/Directors John Ammonds and Yvonne Littlewood MBE; agents/managers Eve Taylor and Bernard Lee; my 'music-man' Roger Richards; personal assistant Peggy Birkenhead (she of the 'green folder') and, of course, her successor Pat Turvey; but, above all, those millions of theatregoers, record buyers and television viewers whom I've never met but who have made such an enormous contribution to my life's work. My thanks to all of them.

Val Doonican, a Tribute, by Terry Wogan

I know what you're thinking: it's the Irish Murphyia, huddling together for warmth…you're wrong. I'd be a life-long fan of Val Doonican, even if he came from Cork. Now, I don't know whether he emerged from his Waterford chrysalis a fully-fledged entertainer, but when I saw him first on stage with the Four Ramblers in Dublin in the early sixties, he was well on his way: willowy, blond, handsome, with a smile you could see in the 'gods', which is where I was seated. For some reason, I didn't put together the voice on the radio that sang 'Donnelly's Sausages For You' with him, until one morning some years later, a boy broadcaster myself by then, I heard your man on the BBC Light Programme with a show so full of relaxed charm, easy music and fun, that any eejit could tell that it had 'Here Comes the Biggest Musical TV Star of the Decade' written all over it. And so it was…I've had the privilege and pleasure to know Val D, to appear on his show and to play golf with him. He is everything, and more, than you'd expect. And still, to my eyes, the willowy, blond, handsome star whose smile lit up that theatre in Dublin, all those years ago…

My Story, My Life

Prologue

One evening, back in the early 1970s, my wife Lynn and I found ourselves at Cap Ferrat near Cannes. We were in the company of some very distinguished guests at the house of a Hollywood legend. White-gloved butlers served us sumptuous food and wine and the conversation was sparkling.

I should say that this was by no means the level of grandeur we were used to, so let me explain how we came to be there. At that time, my television series was in its 10th year and professionally speaking, things were going fine. We had come to enjoy exotic holidays in such locations as Barbados and Jamaica and had made some special friends along the way. Among them were the film director Ken Annakin and his partner Pauline. (At the time of writing this, news of Ken's passing has just been announced.) Following our Caribbean holidays, we had met up several times in London. Then, to our delight, Ken asked us to spend a week with them at their lovely home in the South of France.

After a couple of days visiting places of interest, Ken announced over morning coffee: 'Oh, by the way. We've been invited to a dinner party by some friends tomorrow night, if that's all right with you.'

The next evening we set off and were soon turning into the front drive of a luxurious house. Its back lawn reached down to the water, where beautiful boats were moored ready for their owners. Ken tapped my arm. 'You go over and ring the bell.' I obeyed and climbed the few steps to the doorway, but never got as far as ringing the bell. The door suddenly opened and a welcoming voice and outstretched hand greeted me. 'Hello, old chap. How nice to meet you. Do come in.' It was David Niven. He was very much in the public eye at the time, promoting his best-selling autobiography *The Moon's a Balloon*.

I can't remember exactly what was on the menu that evening, but the company and conversation were pure joy. Our host's storytelling was spellbinding. With the meal long finished, we sat in David's study. More champagne arrived and our host settled himself cross-legged, 'yoga-style', on the floor and yet more reminiscences were shared. Ken encouraged me to talk about my childhood days back in Ireland. A background that couldn't have been further removed from where I found myself that evening.

When, eventually, we said our farewells and thanks, David accompanied us to our car. He shook my hand. 'By the way, old chap,' he said, 'I loved those stories. Do write them down. Remember that when you finally go, they will go too, and that would be a real shame. At least you could leave them to your grandchildren.'

A week later, Lynn and I were back at home and picking up the threads of normal life. Inspired by our French trip I got myself a pretty hefty notebook and slowly began to re-live my childhood days, my family and friends – in fact, anything from that far-off era. I was amazed by my powers of recall. I had no previous experience of taking on a task like this, but kept telling myself it was just for my grandchildren (though I wasn't expecting any to come along for many years). I wrote long hand as computers weren't a household object in those days. I managed to jot down several pages most days when I wasn't at work. These I gathered together and at regular intervals, sent them off to my assistant, Peggy (Pegs), where they were tidied up, typed and filed away in what she referred to as 'Val's green folder'.

I was, of course, getting on with my stage and TV work and wasn't taking much notice of how much material was building up in Pegs' little workroom. The weeks became months and we developed a pretty professional routine of 'getting on with it'.

One morning at the end of a long phone call, Pegs casually said, 'I must say, you're doing really well with your writing project. Have you any idea how much you have jotted down so far?' I was aware of the little dent in my right-hand middle finger as a result of holding my pen. I knew it was a lot. 'I did a rough tot-up the other evening,' she said 'and would you believe, it's over 60,000 words?'

I was due to appear on the Parkinson show about that time and from what I can remember, we had planned to talk about golf. (I had played for many years, but Michael was a recent convert.) My fellow guests on the show that evening were the delightful writer and broadcaster Arthur Marshall and the Scottish jazz singer Annie Ross. Sitting in the green room, I listened as Arthur discussed his latest memoir about his life as a teacher. After this, Annie Ross talked about her life in the USA including a visit to the home of the legendary Mae West.

When eventually it was my turn, I joined the threesome and quite to my surprise, Michael opened with the line, 'And when are you going to write a book about your life, Val?' I was taken aback, but Michael encouraged me to speak of what it was like to lose my father while still in my early teens. I genuinely feared that recounting such sad times might be a bit 'hearts and flowers' and I had no wish to impose that on other members of my family.

The reaction to that appearance was quite remarkable. People rang me; others stopped me in the street. Most surprising of all was the news that a publisher had approached my business manager asking if they could look at my 'green folder'. The publisher was Elm Tree Books, whose parent company Hamish Hamilton published David Niven's own *The Moon's a Balloon*. It really seemed too good to be true.

The publishers sent a charming editor to visit me. She told me that they didn't want to change the manuscript much, as it sounded 'just as if I was relating the story to friends'. I also agreed to do some illustrations as painting and drawing has been a lifelong hobby.

The Special Years was published in 1980 and, I'm pleased to say, was met with great enthusiasm. I followed it up, six years later, with a second volume entitled *Walking Tall*. Many years have passed since then and the old green folder has reappeared. I now have the grandchildren mentioned by David Niven (the eldest now in her teens!) and have recently celebrated 60 years in show business. I thought it was about time, therefore, to update and complete the memoirs, which started back in 1933. I was six years old and needed a haircut...

Chapter One

'John,' I heard my mother call out, 'take that young fella down town and get him a haircut. You'll find sixpence on the mantlepiece.' I hated having to go to the barbers and know that most young lads, in those days, looked upon it much as they would having a tooth out.

Our local barber was aware of this, I'm sure, because he rewarded his young customers with a penny as they left the shop and at the same time, he'd pat their newly groomed heads, praising them for good behaviour and bravery in the face of danger.

My brother John held my overcoat by its lapels while I climbed into it and we headed for the front door.

I was about six years old at the time, and my bigger brothers seemed to find it irritating having to match my walking pace whenever they took me out. So John decided on a plan of action that would make life a little easier.

One of our household possessions at that time was an old pram with very strange looking wheels. They looked just as if they were made from bamboo: quite like those you see on fancy tea-trolleys nowadays. The pram was rolled on to the pavement outside the front door and I was instructed to climb aboard, 'with my back to the engine', as it were; John then leaned forward, took hold of the armrests and, with his left foot resting on the axle, used the other one 'scooter style' to set us off down the road like a couple of guys starting a bobsleigh run.

Pretty soon we were moving along at a cracking pace and, as we headed down the hill towards town, John finally jumped aboard, both his feet now firmly planted on the axle. I can almost feel that wonderful glow of exhilaration as the wind whizzed past my ears, eyes glued to my brother's face, while he encouraged us along by making weird engine noises under his breath: 'Ngaaaaaah...rhummmmm...rhummmmmm...' he whined as our craft careered down Newtown – our speed increasing by the second.

I don't really know what happened next. Maybe we bumped over a manhole, skidded on wet leaves, or my brother's enthusiasm simply reached breaking point but, suddenly, that look of ecstasy that shone from his eyes turned to sheer panic as he lost his foothold. His feet hit the road just behind the pram, causing his head to shoot forward into my stomach. Desperately he tried to hang on – but in vain. I watched the back of his head as it went sliding over my knees, then his chin slowly pulled my socks down to my ankles till, finally, with one last desperate lurch, he was gone. I left him, lying spreadeagled in the middle of the road, as my machine and I sped on, 'driverless'.

You can imagine my situation! I had no earthly way of stopping the thing. I couldn't turn round to see where I was going. In fact, I was so completely petrified that I sat, motionless, except for my eyeballs, which flashed from side to side, first to the left then to the right, exchanging glances with each passer-by. One by one, people stopped in their tracks, slowly turned round on the spot, and stared speechlessly as I disappeared into the distance.

My local knowledge told me that at the bottom of the hill, this particular road was skirted by the wall of our city park. It was a very low wall and I worked out that, from the angle at which my vehicle was moving, the park wall would indeed be my final destination. I didn't bother to shout for help. In fact, by now, I had simply accepted that I was about to reach my final end, at the age of six, as the victim of a 'pram crash'.

And what a pram crash it turned out to be! When at last the front wheels hit the little kerb, the pram simply leaped into the air and, with a sickening crash, collided with the wall. I in turn took off from my seat and, head first, went slithering over the park wall, disappearing down the other side like a snake into a hole. I landed on my head on a cinder-covered pathway just inside and, for a moment, all was still as I lay there – stunned; my poor head tingling from the effects of the cinders.

'Are y'all right, boy?' John said as he stood over me, gently helping me to my feet. I don't know if I answered but I do know that, shortly afterwards, I was seated on a little plank of wood perched across the armrests of the barber's chair (for the benefit of the 'little people') each stroke of the comb and snip of the scissors bringing tears to my eyes. My brother sat on the bench behind me, watching the reflection of my agonies in the mirror. Whenever I dared to take a peek and caught his eye, he would smile a wicked smile, slowly raising a threatening fist as if to say, 'Don't you dare say it hurts or we'll both get into trouble and, what's more, you won't get your penny.'

At the risk of sounding smug, I think I should tell you that I sat through the ordeal without a whimper. I got my reward and I've never told a soul. I think the pram was a write-off though!

When I think about the early part of my life, my first thoughts are of my home. I started life at No.10, Passage Road, in Waterford. Number 10 was one end of a group of four houses or, to be more precise, it was the last quarter of a long, narrow, single-storey building with four front doors, four front windows and one long slated roof with skylights giving a glimmer of light to the attic rooms.

Since our front door led directly on to the pavement, the only garden space was a tiny strip at the back. We also had a little backyard with two outhouses. One was a garden shed, which held the turf for the fire and Dad's gardening tools, the other was a toilet. A tap on the wall outside the back door was our only running water; we never enjoyed the luxury of a kitchen sink or a bathroom.

Dad had built an extension at the rear of the house, which we called the back kitchen: a flat-roofed affair that looked out into the yard and garden. He kept the garden looking like a picture, with a beautiful show of flowers on either side of the narrow path which led to a summerhouse-type building at the bottom. This was known as 'the hut' and was to play a very big part in my childhood.

The house itself had four rooms, two up and two down. Upstairs was really nothing more than an attic with a dividing partition creating two bedrooms: one for girls and one for boys. The stairs were originally a simple set of steps by the wall; these too had been neatly boxed in by my father and a wooden door shut them off from the room below.

The front room, or parlour as it was then called, was where my parents slept for the best part of my young life and the last remaining room was where we really lived. We spent the greater part of our indoor lives in that crowded little place, with its cold stone floor and assorted furniture. The centre piece was a large kitchen table, which the girls took turns to scrub and which my mother never failed to grace with something delicious to eat. By the wall, under the window, was one of those sofas that always looked as if it had an arm missing. Against the opposite wall was our wind-up gramophone on a small table and beside that was an old Singer sewing machine that had to be worked with the feet. It was covered with one of those dome-shaped lids, underneath which you might expect to see a steaming joint of beef. Our selection of family chairs were usually to be found surrounding the open fireplace and on the wall hung our lovely old wooden clock, which chimed its way through the first 20 years of my life.

The short hallway leading to the front door was bare except for a simple octagonal table that usually held a plant pot of some kind. In the corner by the front door, Dad had made a little cabinet – the sole purpose of which was to hide the gas meter.

At a very early age I'd noticed a line of little holes in the old plaster on the gable-end side of the hall; they were tiny craters about an inch in diameter, the origin of which makes quite a romantic anecdote.

Back in the Black and Tan days of the 1918–20s, the citizens of Ireland were subjected to quite rigid nightly curfews compelling them, among other things, to be indoors at a specified time. My father went out one night to lock up before retiring, when he heard a commotion in the street outside. A neighbour had been spotted by snipers concealed behind the wall of the hospital grounds across the road. He was instructed to 'halt' and identify himself but, whatever his response was, he was greeted with a hail of bullets. He dashed to take shelter in our hallway – and left us with this relic. Many were the times I stood there poking my fingers into those little holes, watching as a trickle of white dust sprinkled to the floor like talcum powder.

Everybody knew everybody else in our thickly populated neighbourhood and, if you didn't have plenty of friends, you had only yourself to blame.

The rent man made his rounds at regular intervals, to collect his dues and sign the book. I think our house cost something like a shilling a week. It was an old house and rather cold, as indeed most of those old houses were, but my mother kept it warm with her love and kindness – and I don't think I've known a happier place!

My mother was a most attractive woman, always smiling and happy, and completely unselfish in her devotion to the family. Like most working-class mothers, living under the conditions of the day, she never seemed to worry about herself or what she got from life. It's not difficult to imagine the problems she faced daily, bringing up eight children and coping with all the other chores that running our little home entailed. Come to think of it, I always felt we were quite well-off compared with many of the other families in our neighbourhood and I realise now that the feeling of security stemmed, almost entirely, from my mother's amazing talents for making ends meet. As for her beloved brood of eight, perhaps I should give you a brief introduction to them all.

First there was my brother Ned, whose life was really removed from mine as he was nearing marrying age before I could chat to him about anything other than conkers or cowboys and Indians. He did love sport, though, and took me to lots of games at our local grounds. In later years, when I appeared at concert venues in Dublin, he, together with other members of the family would travel up for a small reunion.

Then came Mary, who was the member of the family I knew least about. She died when I was very young and had been ill for some time previously, so I can't say that I ever had the opportunity of getting to know her.

Next in line, John, who was the extrovert of the family but I've already told you about him. Then Lar, a gentle man who, like Ned, Mary and my other sister, Nancy, had beautiful auburn hair. He too was plagued with illness for a great part of his life and, regretfully, that's how I remember him. He died in 1950.

The fifth arrival in the family, Nellie, was the busy bee of the house – dashing off to work, dashing home again. She loved to spend her spare time singing in church choirs, in amateur musical groups, and so on. As I'm writing this, Nellie is approaching 90 and is the matriarch of a wonderful family, which includes 11 children, 26 grandchildren and 26 great-grandchildren.

Nancy also was involved in all kinds of musical activities and, like Nellie, got tremendous pleasure from the company of her colleagues. She has lived in the United States for most of her life, but has made many visits over the years.

Finally, Una, only a couple of years older than me and the closeness of our ages is reflected in the warmth of our relationship. We were (and are) terrific pals and still spend endless hours just enjoying each other's company.

I am No.8, of course. I was, in fact, christened *Michael* Valentine Doonican – 'Valentine' was added because my birthday is 3 February, not far from St Valentine's Day, and so I was given the added protection of a second saint. However, as our neighbourhood was absolutely overrun with Michaels, Micks, Mickeys and Mikes, I was called Val for convenience and easy identification.

My father died, quite tragically, when I was a boy of 14. In spite of the fact that I didn't spend a great period of my life in his company he, nevertheless, made an enormous impression on me. This, strangely enough, seems to mature with the years – like a good wine.

He was a shortish man with a completely bald head and one of those moustaches that he could comb for special occasions – sharpening both ends with 'spitty' thumbs and forefingers. He had bandy legs and I can almost see him now, coming up the road from work, looking a bit like an old-time cowboy. He carried one of those folded metal rules, which protruded from the leg pocket of his overall – swinging about like a six-gun as he approached.

One of the pleasures I learned to enjoy in his company was walking. He thought nothing of a five- or six-mile walk on a Sunday, my age at that time being on a par with the distance. I loved it. He had a ritual he liked to follow on these occasions.

We'd call at the corner shop where he would buy a pennyworth of sweets. Having placed them in the pocket of his jacket, or overcoat, he would open a book and, with his glasses perched on the end of his nose, walk along the middle of the road by sheer instinct as he read. He was an avid reader, something I didn't inherit from him and one of my regrets.

'Don't walk in the middle of the road,' I remember saying to him, 'you'll get run over by a car.'

'That's where you're wrong, son,' he answered with a smile and still reading, 'It's when you walk on the side of the road that you get run over!'

I've often said, in fun, that when they put white lines on the road anywhere within 10 miles of my home, they simply painted in my father's footsteps.

When I needed nourishment from time to time on our journey, I'd simply help myself to a sweet from his pocket, and then continue my explorations through the fields and woods, keeping in touch with his progress by watching his bowler hat as it bobbed along above the hedges. Sometimes we'd take along slices of bread and butter sprinkled with salt then, resting on the bank of a fresh country stream, we'd pick watercress and make sandwiches. Watercress has never tasted quite the same since!

My father, 'liked his drink', as they say in Ireland. Many's the hour I have spent waiting outside pubs on the road near Knockboy or Grantstown drinking fizzy lemonade which he'd brought out to me. When it was gone I'd pass the time away by either making mud pies in the glass or wandering round to the back of the pub where they had hens, pigs and cattle. It was at times like those that I began to learn the precious accomplishment of how to amuse myself.

One of my favourite Irish stories is the one about a visitor driving along a country road. He got behind an old farm tractor and followed it for a mile or so, desperately trying to find an opportunity to overtake. When, finally, he decided to have a go at getting by, the tractor, without any kind of indication, turned right and went through a gateway. The poor driver of the car swerved to avoid a collision and finished up in the ditch. In a rage, he climbed out of his car and charged up to the old farmer who was closing the gate.

'You fool!' he shouted. 'What the hell do you think you're doing? Turning right like that, you could have killed me!'

The tractor driver looked amazed. 'What do you mean?' he said. 'You should have waited...sure, everybody round here knows that *I'm* goin' to turn in that gate!'

That just about sums up how things were when I was a boy. Everybody knew everybody else and where they lived. One little trick of my father's, that always impressed me, was his ability to walk for several miles, as I described, never taking his eyes off the book, but saying 'hello' to everybody. He knew who would be where, at what time and, above all, he got his greeting right:

'Hello, Mary...is the young lad better now?'

'Mornin', Mick...get the job done in time?'

'How are the asters comin' along, Alice?'

He had an absolute passion for flowers and grew them with enviable success. He did it for the right reasons, too, in my opinion: simply to look at, or to give to people who didn't have a garden.

One of my earliest memories is sitting on the ground in the garden, squeezing the head of an antirrhinum between my thumb and forefinger watching its little pink mouth open and close, and, at the same time, quizzing my father on the names of the various blooms.

'Why do they all have different smells?' I asked, pressing the antirrhinum against my nose.

He gave me a long, serious look. 'The smells come from the sweets that grow in each flower.'

There was no answer to that, so I waited for more. He leaned forward, pointing to a yellowish one, 'Now this is an aster and it will grow a Rainbow Toffee. This one is called a lupin and it's where barley sugar comes from. Wallflowers here, they grow aniseed balls.'

I said nothing but couldn't help looking forward to a good crop.

The lovely thing is, he didn't forget what he had told me and was well aware of how I might await the results.

He was dead right too! I even invited some of my pals to the harvest, which he announced some weeks later. Making sure we were standing well back, so as not to tread on his precious plants, he performed the most impressive sleight of hand, shaking flowers at random and casually handing us the spoils.

You can well imagine the effect it had on us kids. It is not surprising he became known in our street, as 'The Sweet Man'.

My mother assures me that my father 'never laid a hand on any of us' and I quite believe it. Yet he did punish me for any blatant breach of the rules. I remember being in the doghouse, one time, for having a row with my sister and pushing her down some stairs. It was on a Friday and when he came in from work we were having dinner in the usual way when, quite casually, as we all sat round the table chatting, he said, 'What's this I hear about you knocking your sister over today, boy?' I had a strange sinking feeling but knew there was no point in beating about the bush. I owned up. I was looking forward to going to the pictures next day and frankly feared the worst. It came, too!

'When you've finished your meal now, go up to your room and don't come down till Mass on Sunday.'

I did as I was told, without protest.

He came to see me on numerous occasions during my internment and, whenever I came down to the toilet, which as I've said was outside in the yard, he'd smile, have a chat, then off I'd go, back to my cell.

My room, which I shared with my brothers, was very small and, without them, very lonely. Like any attic it came to a point above your head – in this case, where the roof met the wooden partition separating it from the other half. I lay on the bed, looking straight up at the sky through the skylight above me. Pasted to the wall, around my bed, were a few pictures of my favourite film heroes – stolen from my sisters' movie magazines.

The only other furniture in the room, apart from our beds, was a small chest of drawers and a home-made bedside table. On the table, at arm's length, were my simple aids to passing the hours of confinement: drawing-book and pencil (which have continued to be at hand throughout my life), *Beano Annual,* one *Hotspur* comic, two *Champions* and a small cardboard box containing some personal treasures.

From time to time I climbed up to take a look at the outside world, my head peeping through the skylight – now opened as wide as it would go. Across the road, in the grounds of the County Hospital, an old man was digging potatoes, quite unaware of my plight, while on the wind I heard laughing voices as my pals went about their games just round the corner in St Alphonsus Road, a few houses to my right.

When, at last, my term of punishment was over, Dad just said 'Good lad' and the matter was never mentioned again – or forgotten, by the prisoner.

Here's another example of what rules meant to my dad. When I was about seven years old I got my first bout of real sickness. Well, at least it was the first illness for which I was sent to hospital.

All I can remember about the symptoms is the skin beginning to peel off the soles of my feet; not that it's a complete summing up of what it feels like to have scarlet fever, I'm sure. However, there was great excitement and sense of occasion in No.10, as my little suitcase was packed and the sad 'Goodbyes' almost enjoyed by one and all.

My mother had been very worried about me and knew that my going away was the only cure. What I didn't realise was that this particular ailment required the patient to be isolated from the outside world! It was really awful not being able to have visitors for about seven weeks. My family made regular visits to the hospital, however, and waved and talked to me through a large window at the end of the ward. My sister, Una, made faces and ate sweets and I drooled like Pluto the dog. I managed to pass a lot of the time by drawing little pictures and proudly held up my work to the window for my fans to admire during each visiting session.

As I neared the end of my confinement, my father asked me if there was anything I'd like to celebrate my homecoming. Among my sketches was one outlining my idea of the ultimate in trolleys, or scooters, or whatever you call a plank of wood fitted with some old pram wheels and steered by means of a piece of rope used to drag the front axle from side to side. This particular model had such extras as fitted seats, headlamps made from empty tins, number plates and – would you believe – a steering wheel. Without hesitation, my father took the details of my design and, with a kind of grin that I've never seen anybody else use to such effect, gave me the thumbs-up sign.

Two weeks later, with great excitement and relief, I received the news that I was ready to go home. To show how times have changed, I recall the fact that there was no family transport. We couldn't afford to hire any so my journey home, which was only a few blocks anyway, was achieved sitting on my brother John's shoulders, wearing my warm overcoat and a muffler, belonging to my grandmother.

Mother had prepared a wonderful tea with all my favourites, including jam fritters and tarts of every kind. The room glowed with the heat of a generous fire. Later, when all the excitement had died down, everybody was busily chatting and the attention had left yours truly, my father caught my eye and beckoned me towards the hall door. I followed him into the hall, and then turned into the front room. There, in the middle of the floor, was the most exciting present I have ever had.

He had built *my* trolley, complete with not only all my additional suggestions but quite a few of his own inspired ideas, making it look like something by da Vinci. I really was speechless and couldn't wait to test drive it up and down the hall. How I looked forward to getting it outside and showing it off to my friends.

Now, in the midst of the excitement, I well remember my father saying, 'I want you to promise me you won't go on the footpath and possibly hurt somebody.' He was worried that, since the houses had no front gardens, I would go straight from the front door on to the footpath, making it very easy to knock somebody over. I made my promise; to which he added, 'Mind now, if you don't do as I've told you, I'll take it from you!'

We had a ball with that toy for a long, long time until one day, as you've probably guessed, we went belting down the next street – on the footpath – simply because we liked the sound of the flagstones under the wheels. They sounded a bit like the points on the railway track. (I think I should mention that, in those days, cars were so few and far between that it was very safe to go on the road. The occasional oncoming car was so noisy, you heard it long before it presented any danger.) Well, the worst happened: a lady stepped out carrying a shopping bag and immediately tried to jump out of our way. Luckily, we only knocked her back against the wall – leaving her a bit shaken, but unhurt.

I knew that, in a small community like ours, the news would soon get back to my dad. It was next day at lunch when the crunch came. In his usual casual way, without a sign of aggression, he said, 'Are you going to tell me about Mrs Deegan, then?' I knew I was cornered. I looked at him and smiled, told him what had happened and I never saw the trolley again! Some days later I saw the wheels tied together with string hanging up in the garden shed.

I suppose you could say his actions were a bit extreme as it was only a first offence but then, I had the choice of doing right or wrong, and I chose wrong. Throughout my childhood I learned to accept the consequences. He comes to my mind so many times when I fail to follow through my own rules at home. I'm convinced that children look upon it as a sign of weakness and would prefer it if you punished them as you'd threatened.

Up to now, you've probably got the impression that I hero-worshipped my father – this is far from the truth. I knew, at a very early age, that he drank too much; he spent too much of his hard-earned and our badly needed money gambling on the horses; and he smoked non-stop. I can't say he chain-smoked because he smoked an old clay pipe which was brown with age. His tobacco was the plug type which he cut with his penknife and kneaded between the palms of his calloused hands. He also chewed tobacco, just like the old characters in Westerns.

I was always very aware of the tension caused by his drinking and the subsequent shortage of money. I doubt if my mother ever got used to it, or learned to accept him when he showed signs of having had too much. Saturday was usually a bad time. Having finished work at 12.30pm, he'd go for some drinks with the boys. My mother would prepare his lunch and, far too often, it would still be there two or three hours later. On occasions, I would have to go and look for him. I knew which pubs he favoured and would stick my head round the door of each one in turn, shouting, 'Is me dad here?' In those very early years I developed a dislike for pubs that I've never lost. The smell of the beer and the smoke and the sawdust on the floor may have been heaven to the old boys at the bar but, to me, it was ugly and depressing.

My father would leave the pub with me and walk out into the daylight, wiping his moustache with the back of his hand, and carrying under his arm a week's supply of books – which usually numbered about six. He read all night long, from what I could gather.

As my own bedroom lighting was limited to one candlepower, I never went in for reading in bed very much. I'd just lie and count the stars directly above my head – I refer to the ones in the sky, not the film stars I stole from my sisters' movie magazines.

One night during the war I sat bolt upright in bed when I heard what sounded like an approaching aircraft; a rare noise to our ears since Ireland wasn't involved in the war. The others hadn't come upstairs yet so, climbing up on to the end of my bed, I looked out through my observation tower – my eyes twitching in the cold night air. Then I spotted it. The faint flashing lights of what I was now positive was a low flying aircraft, flickered closer. It went thundering over the rooftops, its engines spluttering and obviously in trouble. This much I'd become familiar with from the many war films at our local cinema. Then, in a second, it was gone from my view. I didn't move, just listened as the horrible engine sounds faded into the night. Suddenly, I had my first experience of the sound of silence, absolute silence – and it was loud.

Next morning, news was about town that a German bomber had lost its bearings and gone the wrong way, finishing up in a ploughed field a couple of miles from my home. Naturally, it created enormous interest in Waterford. Most of the local people went on foot, or bicycle, to have a look. With lots of bits and pieces of wreckage about the place, souvenirs were plentiful. I treasured a tiny piece of metal, with a wire attached to one end, for years afterwards. We were informed that the crew were safe and had been sent away – to wherever such people are sent on these occasions.

The pop fan of the family, in the earlier days, was my brother John. He followed all the top singers of the time with great interest; his hero was that young man of song, Bing Crosby. His fanatical enthusiasm nearly drove my father mad for, try as he might, he simply couldn't share John's avid appreciation of the old 'groaner'.

'For God's sake, will ya' shut that fella off,' Dad would groan as John turned the radio up a notch. 'He sounds like a bloody calf, with his moanin'.'

John was my idol as a boy. He really was great fun, teasing me constantly but, like my dad, unstinting with his time. I'd wait patiently at the front door, each evening, once I'd heard the 'knock-off' hooter announcing his homeward journey.

I was painfully thin as a child, a bit taller than most of my playmates, with legs sticking out of my baggy shorts like a couple of 'five irons'. Even in those days, my crooked teeth smiled from beneath my blond fringe.

One of John's party pieces was to encircle my twig-like wrist with his thumb and forefinger then, with one sharp movement and a loud 'Tarrah', he'd slide his right hand up to my armpits and down again – without parting his fingertips. At least, so he claimed whenever he gave one of his frequent demonstrations to all and sundry. My affection for him was a standing joke in the family – and whenever they saw John, they could be sure I wasn't far behind.

One evening I watched him pour a kettle of hot water into the enamel basin on the back-kitchen table, in preparation for a shave. 'Now, stand back,' he warned, 'and don't let me see you fiddlin' with anything, OK?' I moved away, with my hands behind my back and just stood there, staring. He began to soap his whiskers, at the time singing one of Bing's latest hits. 'Love thy neighbour, walk up and say, how be ya'...boo, boo, boo, boo...and get me a clean towel...boo, boo, boo.'

I disappeared and returned, in seconds, carrying a neatly-folded crispy-clean towel still warm from airing in front of the fire. I put it on the table beside him, then, hoping he wouldn't notice, decided to stand my ground. He didn't seem to mind, so I thought it safe to sneak a look at his jar of Brylcreem. Silently, I slid it off the table and began to unscrew its shiny black lid. It worked, and there I was, in a world of my own, my finger testing the lovely creamy white stuff that smelled just like he did.

I was wearing my large shorts at the time, held up by an even larger pair of braces. The next thing I remember was a hand grabbing those braces just between my shoulder blades and lifting me clean into the air. He stood glaring at me like the Incredible Hulk, his voice booming in mock anger, 'Didn't I tell you not to fiddle?' he roared into my face. My trousers got tighter between my legs, till I felt as if I'd slipped off a bicycle saddle on to the crossbar.

Slowly and deliberately he walked towards the back door then, with both hands holding my braces, by now stretched over my head, he allowed me to slide gradually down the door, till the braces reached the huge coat hook.

Looping the elastic over the hook, he dramatically backed away, never taking his eyes off mine. 'Now, I'm going to a dance,' he hissed through his teeth. 'And you will stay right where you are, till I get home at two o'clock in the morning.' He dried his face, slipped on his coat and disappeared, leaving me hanging on the door like an old scarecrow.

In seconds he was back, laughing his head off and bringing the rest of the family to join in the fun. 'God bless us, and save us,' said my mother, coming to my rescue, 'you could do the child an injury.'

I laughed as much as anybody else, despite the discomfort and – thank goodness – it didn't affect my singing voice!

Chapter Two

I had my own special seat by the fire. So close to the fire, in fact, that it was virtually inside the cavity in the wall where our fire burned. My private stool was made from an upturned margarine case and my mother made it more comfortable with the addition of a cushion. I was never happier than when I was tucked away in my corner with a copy of *Beano* or *Dandy,* which I read to the accompaniment of the family's normal activities. We ate, talked, read, played music, listened to the radio, used the sewing machine, did the ironing and many other things, all in that one room. You learned to close your eyes and ears to anything that didn't concern you.

When my mother set the table for meals, Dad's chair was situated in such a way that we sat back-to-back when I was on my stool. I can still smell his oily overalls, mingled with the fumes of his pipe and his beer. Sometimes, if he was eating alone, he would slip his hand behind him and nudge me. When I looked round, I'd come face to face with his dinner fork, bearing a tasty piece of his meat, pointing towards my mouth like the beak of a mother bird feeding its young.

One day, I remember sitting there and noticing a strange smell coming from the table. I took a peep around my father's arm to find him stirring his teacup.

My curiosity got the better of me, so I enquired, 'What's that awful smelly stuff, Dad?' Between swigs, he said, 'Coffee.'

Since I'd never tasted coffee I took his word for it, but couldn't help wondering how it came to be so popular while giving off such a foul smell.

'Wanta drop?' he asked.

'Don't think so,' I mumbled, hoping he wouldn't press the matter.

'Go on,' he said, 'try it. It won't poison you.'

When the cup reached my face the smell was infinitely worse, but I couldn't be a coward. Trying to look nonchalant I took a generous gulp and cannot remember, before or since, tasting anything quite so foul! I suppose I was about 10 years old at the time and it wasn't until 10 years later that I found out the truth about my father's brew.

I was dining with my mother at a Dublin restaurant. When the waitress suggested coffee at the end of the meal, my mother said, 'Yes, please,' and as my usual reaction was to refuse – remembering my father's concoction – I hesitated for a second then, to be sociable, I took my life in my hands and said, 'Yes, coffee for two, please.'

The coffee was poured and, without a great deal of enthusiasm, I took my first sip. My taste buds were ready to revolt because of past experience but, to my astonishment, I found it quite palatable.

'This is not bad, is it?' I remarked to my mother. 'I'm quite surprised...I like it.'

My mother looked up: 'Don't you like coffee, then?' she asked quite innocently.

'Well, I didn't,' I said. 'The last coffee I tasted was some of Dad's.'

'Your dad's?' she queried, in amazement. 'He didn't drink coffee very much but, whenever he did, it was more likely to be half coffee, half rum.'

'Rum?' I choked. 'No wonder it nearly poisoned me!'

She sat back and laughed till her eyes filled with tears. 'You daft fool,' she said, reaching for a hankie. 'If your father was here, he'd die laughin'.'

Sometimes, when my father worked overtime, he'd invite me to go with him. Usually, on those occasions, the 'works' would be closed so, having got the key from the night watchman, he would simply light up his own particular workshop and off we'd go. My first job was to get his little furnace going, in preparation for heating up some bars of iron which he had to forge into different shapes.

Even though I was very young, he would show me how the job was done and then ask me if I'd like to have a go. I'd find myself hammering and shaping pieces of 2 x 1/4 inch flat iron into something resembling the required design. He always let me think that I knew what I was doing and, most importantly, that I was being a great help.

It's easy to feel that this is all rather naive and sentimental, but I believe it's imperative that children feel they are able to make a genuine contribution to helping in the house or other family jobs. We are more inclined, nowadays, to do everything for our children rather than make them feel they can do things for us. I certainly felt very important when I 'helped' and that's something I'm glad I didn't miss; it gave me the confidence to do things on my own later on. Dad never said things like 'You wouldn't understand' or 'I'll tell you when you're older' when I quizzed him. Instead, he gave me the opportunity of deciding, for myself, whether I could understand – or not.

He loved his work and took a great pride in it. As a structural steelworker with a local firm he built things like large farm buildings and hay barns. His workshop had an expansive floor area where he would design each job with wooden templates, marking the floor by means of a stretched piece of string line which he'd rub over with chalk while it was suspended about a half inch from the ground. Then he'd lift the cord and let it spring back against the ground, leaving a long white line as his mark.

I'm sure, by present day standards, that his workshop would seem rather primitive but to me, as a boy, his various machines for cutting half-inch steel plates or sawing huge steel girders were immensely impressive. In fact when I left school, at the age of 18, I finished up working in that same job myself and spent a couple of years toiling over those machines that conjured up such magical memories. But I do know that if my father had been told that I'd gone from school to work there, it would have disappointed him a great deal. Like most fathers, he spent his life doing a job that he felt wouldn't be good enough for his golden-haired boy. Two of my elder brothers, Ned and John, did work there for a long time and I feel, somehow, that my father hoped that I was going to prove the exception.

His ambitions for me were confirmed, to some extent, when we had along talk just before he died – but I'll come to that later.

Like many working men in those days my father was a very talented do-it-yourself enthusiast; he did all our decorating, made a great deal of our furniture, built the outhouses in the garden and, it was automatically accepted, would do 'ordinary' jobs like building cupboards, garden gates etc. Today, people's requirements have changed. To start with, their demands are usually of a much higher standard and, secondly, they can afford to have their jobs done by professionals. Still, I suppose that life nowadays is so demanding that very few people get time enough, away from their work, to do these kinds of jobs.

A good deal of that 'doing-the-thing-yourself' washed-off on all of us – mainly, because he was always willing and happy to show us how things should be done. I mentioned earlier that we never had money for luxury items, and toys most certainly came under that heading. So I tried to emulate my dad by making my own toys; I've still got a little carving of a horse's head that I did when I was about nine years old.

There was a carpentry department in the firm where he worked and models were made for the steel department. So, from time to time, he'd pop in there and collect all the various shaped pieces of waste wood piled up in the sawdust beneath the electric saws. He'd pack them into a large carrier bag and bring them home to me. These old leftovers ranged in shape from circular, oval, half-moon, to square or triangular, and in size from one to six inches. To me, they meant hours of pleasure as I built them into all kinds of fascinating structures.

One evening he brought home a large consignment and, without a moment's hesitation, I emptied the lot on the floor and started on my building activities – oblivious of the fact that my mother would be preparing tea shortly and that this would mean clearing the decks for the table. I was completely absorbed in the designing of something or other, when I heard the 'leaves' going up on the table as my mother started to bring it into the centre of the room.

'Out of the way, love,' she mumbled at me.

'Just a minute, Mum, while I do this,' I answered – hoping she'd go away and knowing she wouldn't.

'Come on,' she said. 'Whatever it is can wait till later.'

I still ignored her and continued with my work. I had about 10 pieces of wood perched on each other when, suddenly, a ball of rolled newspaper came hurtling from the fireside and sent the lot flying! In a rage I looked up, only to see the back of my father's head encircled by a halo of pipe smoke and, over his shoulder, I could see the top of his open book.

'Did you do that, Dad?' I asked furiously.

'Of course,' he said. 'If you won't do as your mother asks you, then there's nothing for it but more violent action.' He said all this with his usual wry grin. Well, I wasn't going to be treated like this so, with a bad case of the sulks, I packed away my playthings and said I didn't want any tea. My mother immediately began to make a fuss about it but my father raised his hand and said, 'Leave him be!' I walked into the garden, very much wanting my tea, not knowing how to put things to rights – especially, when nobody came to fetch me back. Which would definitely have happened had my father not been there!

When tea was over I was still in the garden alone and, finally, heard my father's footsteps approaching.

'OK, son?' he asked.

'Umph,' I answered.

'Will you give me a hand with this rubbish,' he said, 'it really is a mess down here.' Reluctantly, I went to the end of the garden and helped him tidy up and pretty soon I was smiling again – and still hungry. When the job was almost done, he turned to me and said, 'Well, that's better, thank you, boy. I'll finish it off now and you go and have your tea.' I washed my hands under the tap in the yard, and sat down to enjoy my tea.

Later, when I came out and found him, he asked, 'Enjoy that?'

'Great,' I answered.

'Did you tell your mother, it was great?' he went on.

'Nope,' I said.

'I think you should, you know, after all, she got it ready twice!'

I shouted my half-hearted thanks through the back door and went and sat on the doorstep of the hut to talk to him.

'You know, son, you should learn to control that mood of yours; it'll cause you a lot of heartache. If anybody wants to get the better of you, all they have to do is get you a little bit upset and they've got you beaten. I managed to upset you just then – and I don't want to hurt you at all. But, one of these days, you'll find that somebody will really want to hurt you, so you should learn not to put your hurt on show for all to see. Get it out of your system and forget it. Don't sulk!' He was right. It has caused me much heartache and people have upset me too easily.

The ironic thing is, I find myself giving the same advice to my daughters – I hope they learn. It's a valuable piece of information and should be taken seriously. I wonder if you can get rid of these emotional weaknesses, or whether it's an integral part of your make-up and you've got to learn to live with it?

On another occasion I was fighting hard, emotionally, to face up to some disappointment or other and, in my mind, I truly felt that the world had crumbled about me. I was walking along the road with my father, both of us silent, when he finally spoke.

'You're really disappointed, aren't you?'

'Yeah,' I said.

'Is it all that important?' he asked me. 'Think about it!'

At that moment, we were passing a five-bar gate in a country lane where a very old man was standing with his dog. My father nudged me and said, quietly, 'Ya see that fella over there.'

I nodded. 'Well, believe it or not, in spite of the fact that you've never seen him before in your life, he thinks the world revolves around him. You think about that!'

I have done, a lot. He wanted me to know that the easiest thing in the world is to get so wrapped up in yourself, you can forget that other people's lives are just as important to them.

It was about this time that my sister Mary became ill. She had contracted tuberculosis, in a form that was known as 'Galloping Consumption': a type of TB that spreads like wildfire through the lungs, leaving the unfortunate sufferer in the most dreadful physical state.

There was really no way she could be properly accommodated in the upstairs bedroom in this condition, since others had to share with her. It was then that my father decided to move out of the house, and into the hut at the bottom of the garden: the tiny wooden building, barely big enough for his single bed and small table.

Mary, in turn, was moved into the front room where my mother could look after her and from where, with the doors kept ajar, her calls could be heard.

I can't say I recall very much about the period of her confinement. The awful disease was viewed with such horror in those days, that I'm sure my poor mother thought it best if we children stayed away from it as far as possible.

My father's new 'digs', on the other hand, struck me as a great idea, since my young mind linked it with log cabins and bunkhouses, now familiar from visits to the local cinema. Looking back, I dread to think what it was like during the winter weather. I'd sometimes watch him disappear down the garden, one hand holding the flickering oil lamp, the other shielding the glass shade from the night winds. As the door closed behind him and the glow of the lamp flickered at the windows, it never occurred to me how uninviting the chilly bed must have looked – and felt – on those frosty nights.

In today's gadget-filled world, it's hard to imagine the circumstances in the Doonican household. Our one oil lamp provided the only light to read, sew, cook, wash, do your homework and everything else. When someone finally left the room to go to bed, they simply took a candle – in a candlestick or stuck to a saucer.

The day arrived, however, when quite a few people in our neighbourhood acquired electric lights. Pretty soon, the members of our household began to feel deprived, so a delegation must have gone to the master who, after a few discouraging remarks, said he'd think about it. He did think about it and, before long, we were given the news that electricity was on the way.

I'll never forget the excitement when it finally happened. I don't quite remember how many bulbs we had but the night of the great 'switch on' in our living room was on a par with the Blackpool Illuminations. A beautiful 60-watt bulb, hanging from the boarded ceiling, flashed into being and our room was positively snow white with its brilliance! The luxury of being able to do your 'ecker' (a word we used for homework – an abbreviation of exercise) at one end of the room, while your mother was knitting a pair of socks at the other end, was something we never could have anticipated.

One amusing aspect of it all is that, at first, I always waited for my parents to switch on. I felt, somehow, that such a sophisticated acquisition was not for kids. Soon, however, the novelty wore off and all and sundry had a go at it, my mother bought a shade in Woolworths, and our life took on a new chapter!

The next thrill was the wireless. We got one 'on tick' for one shilling a week and I don't think there has ever been such an influence in my life. I adored the radio: the talks, plays, comedy shows, quiz shows, the endless music and, of course, the news. Although, as I mentioned before, Ireland was not in the war, we were so close to it all with the radio in our home.

The nice thing was how the radio became part of the family: we'd sit around in silence and listen to *ITMA*, *Bandwagon*, *In Town Tonight*, *Monday Night at Eight*, *Stand Easy*, *Variety Bandbox* and *Happidrome* as if we were in a theatre audience. The delight of having such a superb service at our fingertips was beyond description and I don't think that any kind of entertainment has made the same impact on me since then. I loved jazz but couldn't afford to buy records, so I would look up the radio shows, many of them not at peak listening times, and often had the radio all to myself.

Around this period, lots of music 'happened' in our home: my brother John played the mandolin quite well, as did my Uncle Larry who lived round the corner. They had many get-togethers when we'd listen to them playing waltzes, marches and pretty duets, written especially for the mandolin. They practised, over months and months, to attain a reasonable standard of playing technique and it all sounded beautiful. John taught me the mandolin and right from the word go I wanted to eventually get a guitar so that I could sing and accompany myself at the same time. My cousins, Paddy and Derry Kavanagh, and my pal Mickey Brennan, with whom I had a lot in common, loved to get together with me when we would do some 'head' (impromptu) arrangements of current songs, then we'd all sing in harmony à la the Mills Brothers or the Sons of the Pioneers.

My great love was going to the film matinees on Saturday afternoons where, for the princely sum of four old pence, we'd get two and a half hours of our heroes in action. From the start, I had a sneaking regard for the singing cowboys – such as Roy Rogers and Gene Autry – and they held a special place in my roll of honour as far as entertainment went. I'd sit in the gods, feet on the wooden bench and bottom perched painfully on the backrest, indifferent to the fact, that two hours of it entailed a most uncomfortable walk home in the late afternoon.

It's quite exciting to remember that I'd listen to Rogers or Autry sing their latest songs, then take home enough of a mental recording to enable me to sing them later on and dictate the harmony to my own harmony group. I'm sure that all this early training could be one of the reasons I found it possible to memorise my weekly television shows when called upon to do them live.

My parents were very careful not to have their domestic tiffs in front of us and usually waited until they were alone. One evening, when I was still very young, I was up in bed huddled up in my blankets and hugging a rolled-up piece of cloth inside which my mother had put a heated flat-iron. This was my hot water bottle, which had been placed by the side of the fire throughout the evening, building up a terrific heat, then at bedtime popped between the blankets so that the heat lasted well into the night.

Anyway, on this particular night, the sound of voices raised in anger carried up into my room, making me pull the blankets from around my face so that I could listen. Lying on my back I could hear more clearly and discovered that the subject of the confrontation was, in fact, myself.

You see, I had no decent shoes to wear to school and my mother was telling my father that she could not afford them from the money she was being given, so she thought my father's conscience should force him to do something about it. Finally, I heard him bring the matter to a close.

'OK, that's enough, woman, leave it at that. You get the boy to meet me tomorrow outside the job and I'll get him some shoes.'

Tomorrow, being Saturday, my father finished work at lunchtime and, on my mother's instructions, I was stationed very firmly by the outside gate, waiting for him. The knock-off whistle went at 12.30pm, sounding a bit like the 'All Clear' signal. Scores of men of all shapes, ages and sizes, descended on the entrance yard and approached the main gates like a crowd of football supporters leaving the ground.

My eyes darted anxiously from man to man, trying to locate the familiar figure of my dad and, just as I was about to think I'd missed him, there he was walking towards me, smiling.

'Are we all set then, boy, eh? Well, let's get those shoes.' He put his hand on my shoulder and off we went, heading for the town centre.

We'd only gone a few hundred yards, when he said: 'Hang on there a minute, son. I won't be long,' and disappeared through the door of one of his favourite pubs. I sat on the kerb outside, worrying that the shops might be closed before he came out. Eventually, he reappeared adjusting his moustache and looking determined to head straight for the shoe shop...it wasn't to be!

His next call was his favourite second-hand bookshop where, as I've mentioned earlier, he would stock up for his week's reading. He fished about among all the grubby-looking publications, picking them up, flicking through them and asking the odd question then, finally, made a choice. It was now nearing 1.30pm and I was no nearer to being shod.

Well, finally, we walked through the doors of one of the town's finest shoe shops. The heavy leathery smell hit my nose like a punch from a boxing glove. That smell, coupled with the darkness of the place and the fact that it was alive with busy shoppers and their families, all smelling of cows, pigs and damp clothes from the light drizzle outside, made this, one of my rare visits to such an establishment, a disappointment.

My father approached the shop assistant. 'Good day to ya',' he said, in a way that suggested the lad should ignore all his other waiting customers and attend to me – and I was half hoping he wouldn't.

I heard my father's voice above the chatter: 'Yes, yes, you give this lad a good pair of shoes and look after him well, I'll be back in time to pay for them.' He then motioned me to a leather-backed chair against the wall and said, 'This man will see to you, boy. I'll be back in a few minutes.' I patiently awaited my turn and it must have been a long wait because, when the man came to attend to my needs, the shop had practically emptied.

'Now then, young fella,' he began, 'what can we do for you?' I must have looked a bit blank because he simply paused for a few seconds and then went on, 'What would you like, boots or shoes?'

I said I really didn't mind but that my mother had told me to get something smart and strong enough to last a long time. 'I see,' he said. 'Brown or black?' 'I don't mind,' I said again.

He went up his little ladder and began to pull down all sorts of boxes. Out came brown shoes, black boots, brown boots, black shoes, ones with tips on the heels, with toe-caps, without toe-caps, ones with a little loop at the back that you put your finger through to pull the thing over the heel.

When I was finally fitted-out with my lovely new footwear, he slapped me on the knee and said, 'Well now, how is that?'

I said it was grand and sat there in my seat, wondering what the hell to do next. Where was my father to pay for them?

I continued to sit on that chair. The shop was completely deserted; every now and then somebody would come in, look at me, look at my shoes, make some enquiry about the price of an article in the window and then leave. The boss and his staff stood behind the counter, the men drinking mugs of tea and the boss himself holding a glass containing something a bit more interesting. I wanted to go to the door to look out for any sign of my father but was afraid that the boss would think I was trying to make a run for it. I felt awful, thinking that all the whispering behind the counter was probably about me. I even thought of taking off my new shoes, quietly slipping out of the shop, and heading for home which was about a mile away. The street outside was still very busy with horses and carts, motor cars, lorries; all their sounds mingling with those of the cattle being herded into carts to be transported back into the country.

At last, I could bear the strain no longer, seeing that the time, by the old clock on the shop wall, was 2.45pm, I stood up and walked painfully towards the door, where I stood gazing at the entrance to the pub across the road. At the same moment, as if by some miracle, the door of the pub opened and out walked three men – the last one was my father. They all started to bid each other those fond farewells that only boozing pals indulge in: slapping each other's shoulders and behaving as if each one was emigrating to a different foreign part and, beyond any doubt, they would never meet again.

My father gave a final flourish of farewells, looked towards the shoe shop and made a beeline in my direction. My feelings of joy turned to horror as he walked, quite casually, into the path of an oncoming car.

There was a screech of brakes – and then, screaming and panic from the onlookers!

Now, I don't know what your reaction would be in such a situation and I don't know why mine was as it turned out to be. I didn't run to my father's side, I didn't stop to find out if he was OK, my only thought was that I couldn't face those men in the shop again when my father looked as though he was in no fit state to pay for the shoes. I simply took a deep breath and ran like hell for a mile to my home. New shoes. Well, I dread to think how my poor feet felt about the whole thing – I'm sure they've never forgiven me. I went through the house like a tornado, to find my mother standing over a big tin bath dipping the sheets she'd washed in blue.

She looked at me, standing there, panting, 'Oh, you've got the shoes, good boy. They look grand.'

I gulped, 'Daddy's been run over by a car – and he might be dead!'

My mother looked up and smiled, 'It would take more than a car to kill your father, boy,' she said, drying her hands on her apron. 'Come on, you just sit down and have your dinner. You must be starving.'

I don't know what I thought at that moment but I do know that father came in about half an hour later, with a plaster on his face. He had paid for the shoes and all was well...he sat down and had his dinner too!

Chapter Three

School for me, on the whole, was good. I suppose I was about average from the IQ point of view but then, we didn't talk about IQ in my youth or, at least, if it was talked about, I didn't notice. I went to the National School that was looked after by the De La Salle Brothers, and a good, hard, healthy schooling it was too. You worked hard or got a clip round the ear and we never questioned the authority of the teachers; when we got out into the playground we called them all sorts of names but, in the classroom, we toed the line.

My education actually began at the Convent School, when I was about four years old. My brother Lar took me on my first day and, very shyly, I sat down in a classroom of little boys and girls, all writing on slates with pieces of chalk. It was in fact a girls' school, but they were kind enough to accept some of the little lads as kindergarten pupils to keep them out of harm's way. I loved it when the nun said it was time to go home; she was a big, red-faced lady who smelled of soap. However, I don't think I was long there before I went to St Declan's National School for boys.

I was fairly well behaved then and never much good at breaking the rules – I always felt it was too much trouble coping with the intrigue. One of my pals rarely did his 'ecker' but would meet me every morning and copy mine word for word. When we got into class the teacher would walk around the room checking up on us. He'd take a look at my workbook, tick off the rights and wrongs, make some appropriate remark then turn to my pal and say, 'I suppose yours is the same.' And pass on to the next desk. I honestly think he'd given that fellow up as a bad job and just hoped he'd win the pools, or something.

I always did well at exams in those early days, usually finishing near the top of my class each year. My favourite subjects were art, music and maths. I played hurling, football (Gaelic, that is), handball, was in the school's gym team and, to use a present day show-business term, was 'middle of the road' at all of them. We had a super school choir at St Declans, though, and won all sorts of acclaim for our harmony singing.

Only once in my whole school life did I 'mitch' (that's the Waterford term for playing truant). Even then, I didn't just not go to school. I went, sat in the classroom and, at the right moment, approached the Brother's table.

He looked up, *'Bhail, a Mhicil, ar mhait leaf dul amach?'* ('Well, Michael' – which is my first name, as I have already said – 'would you like to leave the room?')

I then told him, in Irish, that my mother had to go to work and wanted me to do some things at home.

He trusted me implicitly and said, *'Ta go maith abaile leat anois agus bi annso maidean am aireach.'* ('OK, off with you and be here tomorrow morning.')

I never realised that being a crook could be so easy and I gave him a sad look, which could only be that of a lad whose mother had to go out to work and he has to do all sorts of things at home. I knew that my pal, who hadn't come to school at all, would be waiting in the park across the road, so off I went.

Galloping down the steps to the street, I dashed through the gates and straight into the arms of my mother – who happened to be passing at the time. I realised, from that moment, that I'd never make it in a life of crime.

'Where are you off to?' asked Mother.

'Ah, nowhere...I'm doing something for the Brother,' I stuttered.

'Well, hurry up then and get back to school,' she said and pulled her coat around her as she walked off towards the shops.

I hung around for a bit and then, having given things some thought, slunk back into school. The teacher was pleased things had picked up for the family – and the matter was closed.

Not surprisingly, when later on I went into the secondary school, which was run by the same Order of Brothers and called De La Salle College, and things *did* become a bit difficult at home, my academic standard took a turn for the worse and pretty soon I was way down in the list of runners when exam time came round.

At the Convent School across the road from our house, the nuns used to cater for certain children at lunchtime by giving them a small half-pint bottle of milk and a currant bun with a sugary top. Invariably, when the lunch break was over and the crates of empty milk bottles put away in the school outhouse adjoining the robery (or cloakroom), one or two currant buns also returned with the leftovers. I and my fellow vultures often hung about our old school and 'cased the joint'. If we saw that the bun situation was worth pursuing, we'd have a planning meeting. Sometimes we would slip into the shed and eat them in there – while giving some stick to a packet of five Woodbines – and other times we'd simply nick the buns, take them back to our den and eat them in comfort.

One day we went into the shed, lit our fags and began to eat our buns, when we heard the swish-swishing sound of an approaching nun. The Sisters wore black habits and around their waists they'd have long rosary beads that hung down at one side. They also had a black leather strap hanging side by side with the rosary so, when an angry hand shot to the hip, you never quite knew whether you were going to be belted or prayed for. The swishing movement reached the door of the outhouse and somebody stopped outside. We sat quietly in the corner waving our hands about to disperse the smoke. We heard a key in the door, the lock clicking home and then, to our horror, the swishing skirts slowly fading into the distance – we were locked in!

Well, we sat there and ate the buns, wondering if we'd ever see our families again. Time seemed endless and darkness began to change the whole childish prank into a bit of a nightmare. Much later, we heard the faint sound of a woman's voice coming from the direction of the school and peeping through the window saw a Sister approaching, carrying an empty coal scuttle. With mixed feelings of being caught and rescued at the same time, we stood back against the wall in the dark corner trying to look inconspicuous. The nun opened the door, laid down the coal scuttle on the floor then, in the light of the open doorway, we saw her fingering through the keys as she continued her gentle song. She selected a key and turned on her heel, heading for the door of the adjoining robery. We heard the cloakroom door open, the song went down a notch in volume indicating that she'd gone through the door, and then we made our move. In seconds, we were through the playground and down the street.

A couple of hours later I was sitting at home, when a great commotion outside caused the entire household to rush into the street. Somebody was shouting, 'Call the fire brigade,' and reporting that smoke was coming from the shed next to the cloakroom at the school. No damage was done, however, and the mini-fire was soon extinguished.

I heard somebody say, 'They found cigarette butts in there.'

My father retorted, 'The nuns smoking? A likely story!'

In winter, there was a big coal fire at the top of our classroom at St Declan's, with a long black fire screen around it. Even though the room was still cold at the opposite end the look of the fire was always welcome. It was absolute heaven to stand by it for a minute, especially if you'd just gone through the rigours of visiting the outside toilets. Strangely enough, one of the few unhappy memories of my boyhood was that of feeling cold. I hated the cold when I was a kid and wished for the biggest of fires at all times. Mind you, the old houses were cold and damp and I'm sure they carried the chill of many winters in their plaster walls. I can still hear my mother's repeated warning: 'Go easy on that coal, boy! We haven't got much and it's gone up again!'

Like my wife, I've always felt that I'd rather be warm and hungry than have ample food and be cold.

About a quarter of a mile from our house, at the top of a little country road we christened Looby Lane (a little country lane which was very overgrown with bushes and nettles and used only by people walking their dogs or courting couples), a very large field had been apportioned into several allotments, or 'plots' as we preferred to call them. Dad managed to get one or, should I say, the use of one, and promptly laid it out into neat rows of potatoes, carrots, cabbages, onions, and as many other domestic vegetables as its limited space could accommodate. Most evenings, if the weather was agreeable, he'd wander up there, keeping a close eye on the progress of his crop, weeding a bit here, thinning out a bit there. I loved to go with him and soon learned how to plant the various things and also got to know when they were ready for the kitchen.

When the time came for Dad and me to harvest the potatoes, I was always fascinated by the very smallest of the crop that lay sprinkled about the drills like tiny marbles.

'Pick those up, boy,' my dad would say. 'Put them in a separate bag and hang on to them.'

When we got back home I'd pop my bag of miniature spuds behind the gas stove in the kitchen and forget about them. Then, maybe some nights later when my mother would be gone out to visit a relative or friend, he'd put down his book, wink at me and head for the kitchen. Half an hour later we'd sit by the fireside sharing a plateful of the little floury morsels sprinkled with salt and dipped in butter, thinking about all the people who were silly enough to throw this veritable treat on the compost heap with their weeds. They didn't know what they were missing.

Our bread used to be delivered by a man with a horse and a rather fancy cart with the baker's name on the side – in time, of course, it was brought to us in a van. One of the greatest thrills of my life came when the bread man allowed me to join him on his rounds, carrying a basket from the van to the different front doors.

One great day he said he had to make a special delivery to a place called Dunmore East – a very pretty fishing village some seven or so miles from my home. On the day in question I was overjoyed to find that the local regatta was on there. It was a beautiful day: the harbour filled with boats, bunting strewn over the fishing fleet and people in a happy holiday mood. The bread man went about his deliveries and I sat on the rocks watching the boat races and the greasy-pole competition, while music poured from the loudspeaker perched high on the telegraph poles. It was magical. Too magical, in fact. I was so carried away by the excitement of it all that I forgot to do as I'd promised and ask somebody the time to make sure that I joined my kind delivery man at a prearranged time and place.

Well, we lost each other and there I was, seven miles from home, tired and hungry, with no money and no way of getting back. All excitement gone and feeling miserable and frightened, I began to make my way towards the road leading to town. The cars were few and far between, the pony and traps only concerned with the local passengers, so hope of a lift faded as I walked up the hill from this beautiful little place. By the time I'd walked some two or three miles, I was exhausted and absolutely starving.

I'll never forget reaching the stage when I was forced to go up to a cottage, knock on the door and ask for something to eat and drink. Knowing, only too well, how kind and hospitable my fellow countrymen are, I still can't believe what happened.

A crusty old lady opened the door.

'Ah, please could I have a piece of bread and jam and a cup of water?' I asked. (You can almost hear the 'hearts and flowers' can't you?)

The old lady looked at me for a second or two then, waving the back of her hand towards me, she shouted, 'Be off with ya, ya cheeky little divil, and get home to yer mother!'

She banged the door and I went down the path with my tail between my weary legs and I'm sure that that lady never realised then that she would go down in my book as the most horrible old witch I'd ever met. I got home some hours later and the bread man had told my mother what had happened. My feet are getting better though!

Making my own recreation was almost an obsession with me from an early age but, sadly, boredom seems to be a sort of password among many young people today.

'I'm going to make my own comic book,' I told my dad one evening.

'Good for you, boy,' he said. 'And I hope it sells by the thousand.'

Needless to say, I had my personal supply of copies of *Hotspur, Champion,* not to mention *Beano* and *Dandy,* tucked away under my little fireside stool. I used these as my guide.

First I had to find a name for it and plumped for *The Valiant*, because it sounded like my own name. I created my characters, drew them, made up my little storylines and then set about doing the actual comic strips. I wrote a short adventure story for the centre pages and even threw in a couple of puzzles and games for good measure. The whole thing looked great to me when I'd finished colouring the pictures; although I hadn't dreamed that there would be so much work involved. Proudly I passed it on to my pals, who thought it was quite good. The idea even became infectious and pretty soon there were quite a few home-made comics round the place. At Christmas time I would try to make gifts for my friends and worked hard at making special cards. I still make the cards to this day – on birthdays and other special occasions that are being celebrated by those I love.

Speaking of Christmas reminds me of a rather special festive presentation I was involved in at school when I was about six years old. As it was to be performed in front of our families and friends I found the whole thing very exciting, if a bit nerve-wracking. I became a member of a little orchestra which was to feature home-made instruments of the most weird and wonderful varieties. The 'front-line', or melody section, consisted mainly of comb and paper players – a part of the orchestra I was hoping I could avoid, since I've never been able to stand the way this particular instrument tickled my lips. Thank goodness I was booked into the rhythm section that included the strangest concoction of clanging, banging, scraping and pinging noises you've ever heard.

Another young fellow and myself were to make up the section known as 'The Jamjargonettes'. There we stood, a two-pound jam jar hanging by a string from our left hands, looking for all the world as if we'd lost our tiddlers. In our right hands we held a six-inch nail partly covered with tape in case we stabbed ourselves to death or broke our jam jars during a crescendo! On a given cue we would beat out the time by banging the six-inch nail against the jar, at the same time singing in unison: 'Oh, we are the Emergency Band. Yes, we are the Emergency Band. We can sing. We can dance. We can laugh. We can PRAAAANCE!! We are the Emergency Band. PING! PING! PING!'

As we pinged our way through the first week's rehearsal, little did I know that my first acting role was on the horizon. At one stage the conductor turned to us to say, 'Are we all present?' to which we answered, 'But, of course!' He then called each section in turn and when he said, 'Jamjargonettes?' I had to point the six-inch nail at my chest and say, 'Do you refer to us?' My mother made me a special uniform for the occasion: green silk trousers and a yellow blouse. I practised my pings and my special line so much, that as my family sat there on opening night and I said, 'Do you refer to us?' they actually applauded. It was all a bit too much for me, I think, because I let my six-inch nail fall to the floor. It went down between the floorboards and I had to finish the concert with my finger. Well, it was an 'Emergency Band', after all!

Living within a few miles of the sea, we had the good fortune to be within easy reach of natural beaches that were part and parcel of our very attractive coastline. My favourite was a little place called Woodstown – not the kind of spot you think of as a seaside resort. Indeed, there was no town at all, no hotels and no houses to speak of either, there was simply a very unsophisticated beach stretching for about a couple of miles separated from the road by a raised terrace of sand hills. These were an absolute maze of little humps and hollows which, at weekends, were snapped up by eager families as their private nests for the day. Each little hideaway served as a changing room, dining room, nursery or love nest, depending on the relationship of the occupants.

We spent hundreds of idyllic days at this charming spot, getting there either on foot, bicycle or, on very privileged occasions, by car. My father knew a man who had a car-hire firm and, by some means or other, managed to treat us to that very special day out in a car. The car, on reflection, looked like the ones used by Al Capone or Bonnie and Clyde. But Woodstown became a second home to me and my pals, once I finally managed to acquire my own bicycle – which came about in a strange way.

A couple of miles from my home, at a place called Grantstown, there was an old country house, the grounds of which were used as playing fields for a private school in Waterford. The pupils from the Bishop Foy School came there several afternoons a week to play rugby, hockey or cricket. At the entrance to the premises there was a very small gatehouse in which lived a family named Brennan. Old Mr Brennan was a retired school teacher and my rather vague memory of him is that he looked like George Bernard Shaw and could often be seen, on summer afternoons, sitting on the wall outside the main gate quietly playing a bamboo pipe which he'd fashioned himself. His daughter, affectionately known as Babby, ran a minute confectioner's shop inside the house – one purpose of which was to supply the schoolboys with light refreshments and cigarettes.

My father was very friendly with the Brennan family and always popped in there during his country walks. This pleased me no end as it meant a nice slice of home-made cake and a bottle of lemonade. In return for this special treat, I'd walk 400 yards down the road to the nearby well and fill a big enamel bucket with water for use in the Brennan household. This, as you'll conclude, did not have running water. On other occasions I'd break up a week's supply of kindling for their fire or go out into their back garden and collect a basket of eggs from the hen houses.

When old Mr Brennan died I would, on the instructions of my father, make frequent after-school visits to Grantstown to help them cope with extra chores. It was a labour of love since I enjoyed being in the country and also loved to sit in the long grass and watch the boys playing cricket or hockey; games never played at the National Schools.

You had to keep a sharp watch out at about four o'clock when the boys arrived because they usually came careering down the hill on their bikes and turned sharply through the gate at a dangerous speed. Babby constantly asked them to slow down as she feared the worst would happen if ever their arrival coincided with some local person leaving the shop.

All her pleading was in vain so, in time, the solution was arrived at by the local Guards (Irish Police), who suggested that the gates be kept closed. This forced the boys to dismount at the entrance, wheel their bicycles through the gates, then remount to go to the pavilion. I never knew that this new ruling was to bring me good fortune!

One of the boys came down the hill one day, turned the corner into the entrance – the gate was closed, and he just couldn't stop in time. The result was a very buckled front wheel and a very bruised young man. Some minor first-aid treatment was administered and the wrecked bike left in the garden shed for safe keeping.

After a couple of weeks the same lad arrived on a brand new bicycle and, from then on, I spent many hours gazing enviously at the old rusting model with the damaged wheel lying in the outhouse.

I asked Babby what the chances would be of my acquiring it knowing, in my heart, that if it cost even one pound, it would be out of the question. When she felt that the time was right she popped the question which, luckily for me, came on the same day as her request for his account to be settled. His reaction suggested that he had forgotten the old 'crock' and without hesitation he said, 'Let him pay my bill and he can have it!' He owed three shillings and sixpence.

I chose my moment carefully and put the proposition to my father.

'How much?' he asked.

'Three and six.'

'What kind of a bike is that?'

I assured him that it was beautiful.

'I'll look at it on Sunday,' he said, 'then we'll see.'

The rest of the week just crawled by but, on Sunday, when I proudly opened the shed for my dad and lifted the bike into a standing position, he examined the wheel, then the slightly bent handlebars and with a grunt of amusement said, 'That's a grand little thing. I'll pay for it, and you get it home.'

That afternoon I rolled my newly acquired treasure, on the back wheel only, along the mile or two of road to my home. My family admired it and made me feel thoroughly proud of my first business deal. My dad had me take it to a local shop, where the repairs were done in a couple of days: the handlebars were fixed and a second-hand wheel replaced the damaged one. By the following weekend, after several days of oiling, cleaning, painting and polishing, I was the owner of what was to be one of the most exciting things I've ever had. As I said, from that day on, Woodstown became my second home.

One day, when the tide was full in, I went swimming with the boys and, some couple of hours later as the tide had gone a long way out, we decided to pick some cockles for our families to eat. I had a huge bag of them as I trundled up the beach and then, to my absolute horror, I found my bicycle had gone! I sat down in total dejection, feeling as though my world had come to an end. The lads, whose bikes were OK, offered me a lift home on the crossbar of one of their machines. The evening shadows made the countryside look dull and wintery as we set off for home and, suddenly, I didn't want to go.

'You go on,' I said, 'I'll have another look for my bike. Tell my mother I'm OK.' And, all alone, I headed back to the deserted sand hills.

I walked up and down, hope fading more and more with each trip, when across the dunes I heard my name being called. I ran to the road to find one of my pals approaching, pushing his bike.

'We've found it,' he said. 'It's just thrown in the ditch down the road. Whoever took it just had a ride, then threw it away.'

With a feeling of sheer joy surging up in my throat, I ran through the semi-darkness to the spot where my dear old companion was lying on its side. I felt so happy that, as my father would say, 'I wouldn't call the Queen me Aunt.'

Off we went and before we were halfway home it was pitch dark but we knew the road so well that the darkness didn't bother us as we chatted to each other. We saw a light approaching, it was a Guard.

'Where's your lamps?' he said, and there followed a long story about the cockles and the stolen bicycle.

'What's your name?' the Guard asked.

'Val Doonican,' I said.

'Are you Johnny Doonican's young fella?' he asked me.

'Yes,' I answered.

He put his hand in his pocket and took out a torch. 'Here,' he said, 'take this and be on your way. I'll call and collect it in the morning.'

What a lovely day that was; the cockles, by the way, were delicious!

The most popular seaside spot in the area was undoubtedly Tramore, some six or seven miles from Waterford. We cycled there quite regularly and enjoyed the facilities it proudly offered to the thousands who flocked there throughout the summer. Its magnificent golden beach stretched for miles, from the little town itself to the far off sand hills behind which lay our precious Woodstown. Mind you, to us children Tramore took on the dimensions of a miniature Blackpool. It was the only place in the area which possessed such exotic attractions as a funfair, amusement arcades, dance halls and a long promenade where you could take a stroll and, at the same time, watch the teaming masses enjoying themselves on the sands below.

For me, Tramore's *pièce de résistance* was its unique railway system: a single-line service that ran from a tiny station in Waterford right to the edge of the sea. So convenient that you simply stepped off the train and in a moment or two were settled with your family on the beach. I was indeed saddened when told by my family that the Tramore Railway had closed down and was no more. The magical memories of those little carriages, smelling of burning coal, being trundled along by that big old-fashioned engine, belching out its plumes of black smoke, are still such precious things to me.

'Keep that window shut,' my mother would say. 'You'll get a spark in your eye, then we'll hear all about it!' Our buckets and spades would be stacked on the racks above, while my mother held the carrier bag loaded with sandwiches, drinks and, of course, our swimming things. It was like going to Miami Beach for a month as far as we were concerned and, time after time, I stood face pressed to the window counting the 'tunnels' as we called them. They were merely tiny bridges, facilitating the country roads criss-crossing the line from time to time, but they became our way of determining how much longer we would have to wait before reaching the station and setting off for the sea.

One momentous day the Tramore train didn't stop at the station – it went straight on, through the buffers, through the end of the building and out on to the road leading to the seafront! It was the most wonderful piece of drama, giving us all sorts of thrills, causing all sorts of questions to be asked – not least of them being, 'How the hell do we get home?' Any time I sit and watch films about the old days on the railways of the past, I can't help going back in my thoughts to those beautiful times of the Tramore Train.

Chapter Four

When I was about 13, my father began to do some strange things, to my way of thinking. I'd see him at home at times when he would normally be working then, for some peculiar reason, he would go away to Wales or England or somewhere – I can't recall for how long but, when he came back, he seemed to come in and out of the house all the time dressed in his best blue serge suit and his bowler hat. Then I heard my mother mention that he had sold his precious box of tools; something very odd was going on at home and I didn't know what it was. What I didn't know was that my father was ill.

One day he called me into 'the hut' and confided that he wanted me to do something special for him. 'Now then,' he said, sitting on the edge of his bed, 'there's no need to let your mother know anything about this, OK?' This, I remember, struck me as being very odd, as it had always been quite impossible to keep any secrets in our small and crowded home. Anyway, I agreed and awaited my instructions, which he gave me as follows: 'Now, you know Looby Lane, well, if you walk up there, you'll find the blackberry briars are just coming into blossom. You'll see lots of little pale green buds on each briar. Now, take this jam jar and scissors, cut the briars off about two inches long and bring them back to me, OK? Remember now, mum's-the-word!'

I was puzzled, to put it mildly; keeping the cutting of blackberry briars secret from my mother was quite beyond me. However, I took my James Bond style task and went sneaking through the house, carrying my jam jar, while my mum was too busy to notice. A short while later, I sneaked into the hut and passed over the goods to my father.

I plucked up courage before I left and asked, 'What are they for?' He looked up at me, put his finger to his lips and said, 'Remember, mum's-the-word!'

I then forgot the matter, for the rest of the evening.

As I've mentioned, our only running water was a tap on the wall in our backyard and this was where I had my morning wash before going to school – at least, during the mild weather. When I was going out to wash my face the day after the 'blackberry job', my mother called out to me to empty some rubbish into the dustbin. When I lifted the lid off our rubbish bin, I was greeted with the sight of a bunch of something green and wet lying at the bottom – on closer inspection I found it was the blackberry briars!

The incident was then forgotten as far as I was concerned, so you can imagine my feelings, some 15 years later, while I was touring with a show in Scotland, when I found the answer. Back in my digs one evening, I was flicking through a very old book called *The Home Physician* when suddenly I saw 'Blackberry Briars'. I read on, 'It was widely believed in the country areas of Ireland, many years ago, that if you took the young buds from blackberry briars, boiled them and then drank the water it would cure cancer of the mouth and throat.'

When my father's illness became evident, even to me, I began to feel very sad because, even though very little in the way of real information came my way, I somehow felt that things were very serious. Indeed, it wasn't long before my worst fears were confirmed. He was, as far as I remember, about 64 years old when he left to spend his final days in the hospital, about 10 minutes' walk from our house. The cancer with which he was stricken started on his lip and it was possible to deduce from its location that it was caused, or at least aggravated, by the constant use of his old clay pipe.

I went to visit him every day after school and took him little presents from my mother such as tobacco, matches, newspapers and books. I'd sit on his bed and listen to him chat away about whatever happened to be on his mind. Sadly, as the days passed, his ramblings became more and more incomprehensible. One afternoon, when I was leaving the ward, the sister stopped me and began to ask me what I thought of him and if I liked coming to see him. I said that it upset me to find him in such obvious pain and she told me just how serious his condition was and appeared to be preparing me for the ensuing sadness.

The very next day, he appeared to have improved and talked to me in a perfectly normal and sane manner. When the time was up and I made signs of leaving, he took my hand and said, 'Now listen, boy.'

I slowly sank back on to the side of the bed and looked at him. By this time, the illness had distorted his face and mouth to such an extent that the hospital staff had bandaged his entire face and head, except for his eyes and nose, which were still visible.

He continued, 'You know that I'm going to die, don't you?'

I nodded.

'Well,' he said, 'I think I will be going pretty soon, so I wanted to say something to you.' He paused and then went on, 'Now, you think I'm a great fella, don't you?'

'Yes, I do!' I answered without a second's hesitation.

'Before I go,' he went on, 'I think it's only fair that I should tell you that I'm not! You see, when I'm gone I know that in time people will say to you that your father was no good. Well, nothing would please me more than for you to say, "Yes, I know that, he told me himself."'

That is still the most wonderful thing I've ever known anybody do in my life: he made sure that the deep love I had for him could never be damaged.

It was only a few days after that final visit that my mother was told that my father had died; it came as a crushing blow to her, in spite of the fact that she had known it was only a matter of days. I chose not to go and see him at the hospital mortuary and, indeed, I said that I'd rather not attend the funeral either. When the day of the funeral arrived I explained, rather self-consciously, that I was going down to our local park to play football. All I really wanted to do was to escape from the house and everything that was, in any way, related to our tragic family situation.

I went to the park and took a football with me, but sitting under a tree feeling in no mood to play I looked around at the scene which brought so many memories of times in his company: the bandstand where we spent many evenings listening to our local brass and reed band giving their summer concerts; through the trees I could see 'the job' – the works where my father had spent the greater part of his life. I knew that, before long, at about three o'clock the funeral would come along the road which skirted the park. I was dreading this moment; so much so, that when I finally saw the slow-moving procession of cars and the familiar figures of my brothers, Ned, John and Lar walking in line, I can actually remember standing up and hiding behind the tree. I waited until it had gone by and then, very slowly, made my way home to find my mother sitting by the fire having a cup of tea and being comforted by some of our very kind neighbours.

When my father had that final chat with me at the hospital, he confessed to not being a good husband to my mother and not being a very good father to us – and yet, even today, the deep impression he made on me is lasting evidence that his summing-up was far from accurate. My father gave me the most precious thing a parent can give, in my opinion, and that was his time and attention. I could not ask for any greater compliment than that my own children would remember me with a fraction of the same affection.

My father's passing left an incredible gap in our family life; my sisters Una and Nancy took over the running of the house to give Mum a respite, and somehow life took on a slightly different routine in this new set-up. However, jobs were hard to come by and money was scarce so my mother was forced to go out to work. She went, on certain days of the week, to a nearby house where she helped with various domestic chores. Payment for these services was a pittance but, in our circumstances, acted as a lifeline.

At a prearranged time I'd go to my mother's place of work and stand by the kitchen door till she came to the window and passed the money she'd earned out to me. I'd then hurry home, give it to my sister, who would run to the shops and so assure us of something for dinner. The lady for whom my mother worked was very kind and I can recall her coming into the yard behind the big house, leaving her horse in the care of a groom and then striding to the rear entrance of the house. She'd shout a hearty 'Hello' to me, ask me how I was and invariably offer me an apple. I'd accept gratefully and then go to the orchard nearby and take my pick.

In the 1970s, when I was visiting my mother in Ireland she mentioned that that same lady – who had become a good friend of hers – wanted more than anything to meet me. She was 90 years old, my mother informed me as we went to have lunchtime cocktails at her home by the sea, just outside Waterford. She remembered the apples and said she never failed to visualise me standing by the kitchen door, each time she watched my television shows.

By this time I'd reached secondary school status and daily attended the De La Salle College, a few minutes' walk from the house. Just across the road from De La Salle College, was another educational establishment called Newtown School, whose name came from the road in which it stood. It was better known to us local people as 'The Quaker School', which is precisely what it was; the pupils came from all over the British Isles and the Continent. There was no contact between the two schools because we simply had nothing in common – even our games were different. The lads from the Quaker school played such sports as hockey, cricket and rugby, and we played the national ones like hurling, Gaelic football and handball. But we were always free to go to their sports fields and watch them play their various competitive sports, which we enjoyed very much. At other times we would sit on top of the wall surrounding their playing fields and chant our disrespect for those who dared to be different from us, by singing:

Proddy Proddy Bluebell never said his prayers.
Catch him by the wooden leg and haul him down the stairs.
The stairs gave a crack, Proddy broke his back,
And all the little ducks went 'Quack' 'Quack' 'Quack'.

Proddy, you'll no doubt conclude, was short for Protestant, which to me as a child meant anyone who wasn't a Catholic. Why we should have sung our little ditty to Quakers, I'll never know. The difference between us children was really nothing more than that felt by supporters of two famous football teams. Mind you, that too can get out of hand to an alarming degree. As the De La Salle College was run by the same Brothers who had been responsible for my primary education at St Declan's, my change of schools simply meant going to a different building.

The college was and still is a beautiful looking school, built on top of a hill – it was always an imposing sight to my eyes.

The school clock, which is on a sort of mini-tower on top of the building, could be seen from many vantage points in the area, and became a very familiar landmark. When I see it today, I sometimes get a little shiver in my inside: memories of my final days there. They weren't too happy.

When I first went there, the headmaster – or superior – was a man named Brother Leo; a short, plump, bald-headed fellow with glasses.

For some reason, he was the only teacher I ever had to whom I couldn't relate. Things, as I've said, were not too good at home and, even though I was allowed to buy my books on a weekly instalment basis (paying a mere shilling a week), I was constantly having to say that I just didn't have it. I should add, of course, that there were many other lads in exactly the same position.

Month by month, that morning trek to the classroom became more and more of a chore. Walking down Wilkin Street, which led from Passage Road to the school, I'd watch 'that clock' as it ominously approached our rather odd starting time of 9.10am.

After about a year under Brother Leo's command the students were one day shocked to hear that he was to leave and take up a new post elsewhere. Some weeks later, he was gone.

The man who took his place was so different that he changed my whole attitude to school over those last couple of years. His name was Brother Bruno, a warm friendly man who went straight to the top of the charts as far as the lads were concerned – and stayed there. His reaction to my inability to pay for my books was to loan me some, either from the school library or from his own office.

He also became involved in the Scouts and as, by now, I was a patrol leader, I came in contact with him quite a lot. A great organiser, he had discipline worked out to a fine art. However, I'll tell you more about that later.

Our Latin Master was Brother Patrick, a great character who loved to join us in our sporting and Scouting activities, cycle tours, camping holidays and country walks.

As I was beginning to find my academic life a bit heavy going, I was prone to daydreaming – especially during Latin. One morning my mind was miles away while 'Pakey', as we called him behind his back, rambled on about some paragraph in our text book *De Bello Gallico*. I was awakened from my dreaming by the sound of sniggering and, when I looked up, all eyes were in my direction.

Pakey broke the silence: 'Would you like to repeat what I've just said, Mr Doonican, in your own words of course – I doubt if mine made much impression on you.'

Slowly, I shuffled to my feet and, blushing to my hairline, mumbled, 'Ah, sorry, sir.'

Now Pakey had a funny way of shaking his head from side to side, while softly tut-tutting under his breath. When he finally ran out of shakes and tut-tuts, he gave me a very sad look, and spoke: 'Well, Mr Doonican, what are we going to do with you...tut-tut...shake-shake...I don't know what you intend to do for a living, young man, but one thing I can assure you, mark my words, YOU WILL NOT DO IT VERY WELL.'

I saw him many years later and repeated his words. He did see the funny side of it.

Some time after I'd left school I was working in a band in the west of Ireland.

I went for a walk one day on a lonely country road to get some exercise before going out to work and I saw a man in a black suit and clerical collar, pushing his bicycle, walking towards me. The figure was unmistakable – it was Brother Leo; he'd been recently transferred to the local school nearby.

As we came face to face, I smiled a vague salutation, wondering if he might remember me as one of his old boys. He slowed down as if to pass the time of day and rest his legs but didn't say anything much, he just sized me up.

'Hello, Brother,' I said, knowing he was trying to put a name to the face.

Pointing a finger at me as if to say 'don't think you've got me fooled' he said, 'Kavanagh!'

This wasn't far out as it was my mother's name and the name of my cousins who went to the same school and resembled me in appearance.

Before I could reply, he shook his hand in front of my face.

'No! don't tell me,' he said. 'You're the other one. Doonican.' It was as if he'd won the jackpot.

'That's right,' I said, putting him out of his misery.

Well, we had a chat for a while, me feeling a little ashamed to tell him what I was doing for a living, as I felt sure he wouldn't approve. Some time later I heard the very sad news that he had been killed in a road accident.

Brother Bruno left the De La Salle order shortly afterwards. We missed him a lot in the Scouts, since he taught us everything from cooking to nature study and from first aid to tree felling. And he loved music: he'd organise the singsongs around the fire with the enthusiasm of a young lad, and joined in with everything. We had a pipe band in which I played first the tenor drums, swinging the sticks, with all kinds of well-rehearsed flourishes over my head as we paraded through the streets of my home town; later on, I was moved on to the bass drum, which was my instrument until the end of my Scouting days. Playing the 'big drum' on a windy day can be a very hazardous occupation and one Sunday morning, in particular, proves my point.

We set out on what we called Mass Parade, a journey that took us from our headquarters down a steep hill called Patrick Street, at the bottom of which we took a left turn into Broad Street and headed for the cathedral, near the quayside.

This Sunday was cold, blustery and not very inviting, especially for the members of the troop still wearing short trousers. Walking down Patrick Street wasn't too bad – it was quite a narrow thoroughfare, the buildings on both sides giving us shelter from the elements – but all the boys gritted their teeth against the chill, as we began to round the corner at the bottom, knowing the wind was coming off the river and whipping up Broad Street. I'm not too sure how the gale-force wind did affect their poor knees but I can tell you how it affected me and my big drum. I was hit broadside by the blast of cold howling wind which, contrary to all my well-laid plans, sent me hurtling off at an angle of forty-five degrees – to the right. The rest of the band turned left!

I tried desperately to turn back and follow the boys but the wind repeated its fierce onslaught on the three-foot circular drum skin, which acted like the sail of a small dinghy, dispatching me even further in the wrong direction. Goodness knows where I would have finished up had it not been for the assistance of some passers-by, who grabbed hold of me and kept me from taking off completely. The boys had practically reached the cathedral by the time I rejoined them, ending a little episode that greatly amused both the boys and the many people standing watching along the pavements.

We also had 'Mass Parade', when we went on our camping holidays each summer. The annual fortnight was spent at a beautiful seaside village called Stradbally, some 20 miles or so from Waterford. The campsite was in a field, not more than a few hundred yards from a picturesque cove. The sea made the most lovely background to our little haven, and a river crossed the field just before ending its journey by joining the sea. This river was a perfect place for us lads to do our swimming, washing, fishing or just plain messing about. Across the road from where we spent our days was the entrance to a magnificent estate owned by Lord Waterford, who kindly allowed us not only to camp in his field but also to use his land for our general Scouting activities – like rambling, nature study and tree felling. The latter was strictly supervised by the estate manager.

One of my closest pals in the Scout troop was Mickey Brennan. We both loved music and singing and, right from the start, got together for duets which we performed with great pleasure at campfires and Scout concerts. I used to play the mandolin as our accompaniment – until I got my hands on a guitar.

This great ambition of mine became a reality when a neighbour of ours came back from working in a touring show, proudly carrying a lovely old instrument – the first guitar I'd ever seen in my life, apart from those in the films. This new acquisition, which I had on loan, opened up all sorts of joys to Mickey and me until, pretty soon, we were talked about round town.

You can imagine how thrilled we were one day when somebody contacted us to say that a concert was being organised at the Fisherman's Hall, in Dunmore East (the little village where I watched the regatta, if you remember), and that they would like Mickey and me to appear in it.

The prospect of working on a stage, with the public sitting there watching us, made us feel like hardened pros. So, right away, we set about preparing our contribution. The Fisherman's Hall was the first of many venues we were to play over the coming years.

Each summer there was a two-week fête in Waterford where, apart from all the usual fairground attractions, there were lots of dances, concerts and other live entertainments.

It was at these affairs that Mickey and I seemed to come into our own, finding ourselves being called upon for all kinds of public appearances.

A milestone in my life was reached when the names 'Doonican & Brennan' were suggested for a show in the adjoining town of New Ross. The difference was, on this occasion, that we would be paid for our trouble. Without the slightest worry about losing our 'amateur status', we travelled there with the others in the cast – all of us crammed into the back of a small van, bubbling with excitement. We did the concert and got 10 shillings between the two of us. My first salary as an entertainer!

Chapter Five

I was very unhappy about my mother having to work so hard and I gradually became more and more determined, come what may, to end my schooling and find some sort of job. Jobs were few and far between and, needless to say, the first area of investigation was the place where my father and two brothers, Ned and John, had worked. Ned made some enquiries initially and nothing was forthcoming but he was told that if anything did come along they'd let him know.

The company was called Graves but didn't, as its name might suggest, specialise in making tombstones. It was, in fact, a pretty all-round set-up, with several departments. The works was fronted by showrooms displaying and selling such items as bathroom fittings, tiled fireplaces, decorators' supplies, gardening tools and so on. Next you found the sawmill, with its high-pitched wailing sounds and that lovely smell of fresh sawdust. I loved going in there, passing along the alleyways between rows of neatly piled timbers lying to dry and season in preparation for their eventual sale. The sawyers, who worked in the mill, were a rather glamorous group of people to an impressionable young lad, such as I was; the ones with the odd finger or two missing being the real heroes!

The next building was the ironmongery store, whose alleyways ran between rack upon rack of such things as nuts, bolts, nails, screws, hooks, hinges, doorknobs and hundreds of other delights. I didn't particularly like it, however; it was cold and uninviting compared with the sawmills and had a horrible oily smell. Round the corner was the 'box shop' – a department where machines, manned mainly by young lads, would assemble boxes and crates of all shapes and sizes. There, the finished products would sit in neatly arranged piles waiting to be delivered to local fish merchants, nurserymen, margarine manufacturers, or poultry farmers, whose names would be stamped in gay colours on the sides of their orders.

Next door was the steelworks (where my dad had spent his working life and my brother Ned was now a foreman), and this, in turn, was broken up into several sections, each specialising in different techniques including structural work, agricultural machines, such as farm trailers, wrought-iron gates and so on.

The whole place backed on to the river and had an extensive wharf where deliveries of wood or steel were made – its huge crane hovering above it like some hungry dinosaur. Also suspended over the river was a long row of gents toilets – nothing more than a wooden shed containing a long seat with six or seven holes in it. This area was known appropriately enough among the lads as the 'Rear'.

I was overjoyed when Ned came home one day with the news that there was a vacancy for a young lad in the box shop, and that I was to go and have an interview with one of the bosses some few days later. I was there on time but was not, as I expected, ushered into an office and told to sit down. Instead, I waited in the hallway until a door opened and the man whom I knew to be the boss walked out.

'Follow me,' he said, and moved briskly up the yard towards the box-making department.

I trailed along behind, feeling somewhat cheated that I didn't have to answer any questions, such as 'what's the square root of 121' – or 'what's the capital of Norway'.

The foreman of the box shop met us as we entered. 'Good morning, sir,' he said to the boss, as he rubbed his hands together against the cold.

The boss said something quietly in reply then, waving a hand towards me, said, 'Give this man a hammer, Jack,' and with that he left!

Jack was a nice man to have as a boss on your first job, for he was kind, understanding, and good humoured. He gave me a hammer; an instrument with which I became remarkably adept and I was soon knocking inch nails into boxes with such speed and accuracy that I would have made a worthy interlude on the *Generation Game*.

I was soon able to use the box-making machines, and assist in other jobs, like stencilling the names on the various orders and loading them on to the lorries for delivery. My hours of work were from eight in the morning till five-thirty in the afternoon, except for Saturday, when we finished at 12.30; my wages were 22 shillings and sixpence a week. (In today's currency, one pound, 25 pence!)

My brother Ned who, as I've told you, worked next door to where I was now employed, was very much aware of the lack of any kind of future for me in this firm, and constantly reminded me that I should think of it as temporary and strive for something better. But, how, what and where was anybody's guess.

After about a year of my new career knocking nails into boxes, I was told that there might be a vacancy for me in Ned's department; a move that was to bring me an extra pound per week. The prospect turned into reality some weeks later and I started to learn something about putting iron girders together instead of pieces of timber. My early visits to the workshop with my father had already given me a useful familiarity with the place and its capabilities, so I rapidly got the hang of the simpler jobs. Naturally, Ned was a helpful boss but, as before, he never showed a great deal of enthusiasm for my presence there and was impatient for me to move on to something better.

It was around that time (while I was at Graves) that I met Bruce Clarke. He played piano locally and was also very keen on the guitar. Somebody told him of my love of music, and the guitar in particular, so, happily, he sought me out. He came from England. Bruce's father came to Waterford and was, at that time, managing the biggest iron foundry in the area. Bruce was a 'pattern maker' by trade and was very clever indeed at making things. During the time I worked with him, he built his own guitars and also constructed a caravan in which we eventually travelled with a touring show.

The Clarke family lived in a fine house in Tramore situated on the cliff tops, looking out to sea and it was there that I began to spend a lot of my time when Bruce and I became friends. A couple of evenings a week, guitar in hand, I would board the Tramore train and make that familiar journey to the seaside, the only difference being that now, for the first time in my life, I was learning what it felt like to travel there at night. Most of the time

I would have the train practically to myself, and sitting there in the dimly lit carriage, I often took the opportunity of having my final moments of practice. On arrival, I would walk the three-quarters of a mile or so up the hill to Bruce's home where we'd begin our evening's get-together.

Halfway through our practice his mother would often call us to the kitchen, where she would treat us to tea and delicious cake made from broken biscuits and chocolate. When she discovered how I loved her speciality, she often handed me a special portion, wrapped in paper, to take home.

Our sessions together took us through a whole world of contrasting music with Bruce playing piano and steel guitar. His versatility combined with my singing and playing, allowed us to enter the different worlds of country and western material, pop songs of the time, folk music, Hawaiian numbers and, of course, jazz. Pretty soon our repertoire became quite impressive and the months of devoted practice rapidly extended my musical knowledge and ability.

Of course my partner worked at his 'proper' job during the day, earning his living as a pattern maker, but he never tried to conceal the fact that his heart wasn't in it. It was more than obvious to me and everybody else that music was the most important thing in his life. Each week we'd await the arrival in the post of our copy of *The Melody Maker* keeping up to date on who was doing what, with which band and where. The local music store became a regular haunt and helped to keep us supplied with our needs in guitar and piano music, not to mention gramophone records. It was on one of our many visits there that the lady in charge informed us of a very exciting event which was on the musical horizon.

It appeared that, some three weeks hence, a man would be coming down from Dublin with a mobile recording unit and would be happy to record any local talent that had the courage and financial wherewithal to have a go. We put our names on the list immediately and were assured that, as soon as the appointments were being dished out, the lady would let us know. As far as I remember, we were allowed to record a double-sided record for '30 bob' – or one pound, 50 pence.

With great excitement and determination we made our plans, deciding to launch ourselves into the recording world as instrumentalists. 'Out of

Nowhere', a popular song of the period, was our choice for one side – with Bruce playing piano to my guitar – and we decided to join forces on guitars (Bruce playing steel) in a Hawaiian Medley on the flip side.

After a few weeks of regular rehearsals, we received the anxiously awaited appointment card from the music shop telling us to be there at 10.30am the following Wednesday. Well, glad to say, our efforts were highly praised by the recording engineer; a man we were to meet up with again in later years. Proudly we wrapped up the precious evidence of our many weeks of hard work. Thank goodness Bruce had the money to pay for it – because I didn't!

Over the following months we played the thing a thousand times and, even though we were warned that the heavy-gauge needle in our old-fashioned radiograms would wear the disc out rather quickly, I'm glad to say that last time I saw Bruce, he still had it. With this experience behind us, we decided to try our luck at entering the world of broadcasting. Each week we listened with great interest to the regular talent show *Beginners Please*, which was broadcast on Radio Eireann, our national station. We wondered what our chances would be and, after some initial discussion, Bruce sent a letter to the programme planners putting our names forward as prospective candidates for the show.

In due course we did an audition and were accepted, so, once again, we went into training. Two contrasting items were chosen for our spot: a steel guitar solo featuring Bruce and a song from me to follow. It went very well indeed and, for many years afterwards, I treasured a recording of the occasion: my first broadcast and a milestone in my life.

Slowly I began to collect the odd gramophone record that appealed to me and, where once the household was lulled to the romantic strains of 'Whispering', sung by The Comedy Harmonists, the mood now changed to the more up-tempo rhythms of 'The Quintet of the Hot Club of France' featuring Django Reinhardt on guitar and Stéphane Grappelli on violin. Stéphane later worked several times as a guest on my television shows but as far as I knew, he was completely unaware of the nostalgia his presence created. After all, in his particular case I was one of many millions of admirers who had loved him since childhood, so I never bothered to stress the point.

Many, many times I've expressed how strongly I feel about the whole idea of meeting and working with people you've loved and admired from afar through your lifetime; it's very important to me. When I started out on my efforts to sing songs to guitar accompaniment, I took every possible opportunity to listen to all the people who were, at that time, setting the standards.

One such name was the legendary Burl Ives. I collected his records and books of songs, using his material as the foundation stone of my early repertoire. Pretty soon I was entertaining my family with my own rendition of such songs as 'The Blue-Tailed Fly' and 'Mr Frog Went a Courtin'', always trying to copy the guitar sounds supplied by the expert session-guitarists assisting the 'master' on his recordings.

Some years later, when I was playing in a band in Dublin, I was informed one evening by the manager of the hotel where we worked, that the great man would be appearing there later in the year. When the time finally came round we discovered he didn't want the band on stage so, greatly disappointed, I had to content myself with a glimpse of the back of his head – as I looked through the door of the bandroom – and nothing more. However, in 1971, he flew over from the States to appear on my show and, this time, things were very different.

One evening we sat in the sitting room of my home, together with our wives, and talked at great length of our mutual love of our work.

'You tell me you've got children,' he said.

'Yes, two daughters,' I told him.

'I'd just love to see them,' he went on. 'Are they in bed?'

'Yes, they are,' my wife Lynn said, 'but you're more than welcome to see them, if you'd like to. They won't be asleep yet.'

'I'd sure like that,' he responded, rising from his chair by the fire.

We headed upstairs to the children's bedroom where the girls sat up in surprise to stare at their huge bearded visitor.

They were aged about five and four at the time and said little, just sucked their thumbs through nervous smiles. Burl sat on the bed and chatted to them then, without the slightest encouragement, gently began to sing, 'Fuzzy Wuzzy was a bear – Fuzzy Wuzzy had no hair'. The girls continued to stare in wonderment.

As for me, I stood at the foot of the bed thinking to myself: 'How about that, Burl Ives sitting on the edge of my children's beds singing just for them.' The sad part was that they hadn't the faintest idea who he was!

I've often described the incident as 'The greatest waste of excitement I've ever known'. I felt I should climb into the bed myself.

Burl returned to appear on my show in 1979 and, this time, my daughters were able to appreciate the whole thing much more as we sat in his dressing room at the studios.

My relationship with Bruce Clarke led, quite naturally somehow, to my first professional engagement. It was in the summer of 1947, a job playing and singing in a quartet, led by Bruce himself. The venue was a ballroom at a tiny seaside resort called Courtown Harbour, on the south-east coast of Ireland.

Now that I'd secured my first contract in the world of music, I had some very important details to attend to. You see, I still didn't possess a guitar of my own and a fully fledged professional guitarist-vocalist with no guitar was, to say the least, unsatisfactory. Up to that time a friend of mine, whose parents had a guitar in the attic, with no intention of even dusting it, kindly allowed me to have the loan of it.

Bruce and I saw in the music papers that a man in Dublin, whom we knew to be a guitar teacher and one of the few guitarists of any note in Ireland, had a good quality Gibson guitar for sale. The price was 20 pounds – a sum of money that, to me, at that time, would have built Concorde; I didn't have 20 pence to my name. But the season in prospect was security enough for Bruce to offer to lend me the money. I agreed to pay it back, at the rate of two pounds a week, while we worked together for the summer. So my first problem was solved. I wrote to the man in Dublin, sent a deposit and offered to come up and collect my prize the following week. He agreed and I started to prepare for the trip.

I was 19 years old then and, incredibly, had never been on such a long journey – 100 miles from my home. I got the 20 pounds together, then started to work out how much more cash I would need for the return train journey – this was problem number two. I managed to scrape together half the required sum, knowing that I only had a week to make good the rest. One of my family gave me the tip that a shopkeeper in town drove to Dublin on a certain day each week and that he might possibly be able to come to my rescue.

I appeared in his shop the next morning and asked if I could speak to him. He was very charming and said he'd love to oblige but he'd already promised a lift to somebody else and, besides, would have to stay overnight in Dublin, which would be too expensive for me. I immediately assured him that I would gladly come back on the train, in the early evening, knowing that I had the single fare. He must have been touched by the urgency in my argument, because he scratched his head and said, 'Ah, well, I suppose you could go in the back of the van with the load. Mind you, there are no windows and it's very bumpy. It's up to you.' Without hesitation, I asked what time he would be leaving and then, having arranged to be outside the shop at 8.30am, I rushed home with my heart pounding.

I could never have anticipated the discomfort I suffered on that journey – the twisting and turning on the country roads, as I sat huddled between some wooden crates, was horrific. I was sick twice, and had no way of letting the driver in the front know of my predicament!

Anyway, as I've told you, I was a great radio fan in those days and one of my heroes was Ireland's leading guitarist, Jack Gregory. Knowing that I would be in Dublin for a whole day I had taken the opportunity of writing to him also, asking if I could possibly meet him. I explained that I was trying to learn, on my own, from books, and that a few words of encouragement would go a long way. I had a letter from Jack, telling me to meet him at his place of work at 4pm. (At the time he was featured guitarist with the resident orchestra at one of Dublin's top ballrooms, The Four Provinces.) The day had so much in store for this young man from the country that the misery he suffered in the van was only part payment for the subsequent rewards.

It seemed like a lifetime before the dreadful rumbling stopped, the van squeaked to a standstill and the back door opened to let in my first glimpse of Dublin sunshine. The driver, now aware of my discomposure, sympathised and helped me to my feet. It took my legs quite a while to unfold into their normal position but I soon forgot it all as I walked along the street in search of a bus stop.

The man selling the guitar invited me into his front room, offered me a cup of tea and then produced a magnificent, black, shiny guitar. It really was superb. I sat down and fondled it for a while, hardly believing it was to be mine. While the tea was on its way, I played through my limited repertoire of chords and licks, stopping from time to time to hold my pride and joy up to the light and have another look. I said goodbye at the door and walked away, carrying my new partner lovingly in its black glossy case.

I was on top of the world. I walked for ages and remember passing a park and being tempted to sit on the bench and have another play. I had some fish and chips instead, as I sat on the park bench and watched the time as it approached my afternoon date with my guitar hero.

Dead on time, he was standing at the entrance to the ballroom when I got there. He took me inside, where the lights on the bandstand had been especially turned on. What a very fancy place, I thought, as Jack went to his dressing room and returned carrying a magnificent electric guitar. He plugged it in and just handed it to me. 'Let's see what you can do then,' he said, smiling. 'Go on, don't be nervous.' I was very nervous!

Sitting down, I started to finger the guitar and, as I did so, he opened up the guitar book on the music stand, picked a part at random and said, 'Try that.' Feeling very inadequate, I slowly played my way through it and when I finally looked up for some sort of approval, he simply turned the music over and said, 'Great, try this one.' He then asked me to get my new guitar which, by the way, he knew. 'It is a good one,' he said, 'and I know most of the good ones in town.'

We played together for about an hour. I don't think I can recall any other hour in my musical life which gave me such confidence and inspiration. When he saw me off at the end of our interlude, I was not to know that in a very few years Jack and I would be doing duets on the radio.

At seven o'clock that evening, I boarded the train back to Waterford and thought that I would never get home quickly enough to show my family my treasured instrument. I sat playing till the early hours of the next morning; that guitar and my hands rarely parted company for the next five or six years. Well, I was set for my first job – I managed to borrow an amplifier, until such time as I could buy one of my own, so, for better or for worse, I was a professional.

Five pounds a week was to be my reward according to Bruce, plus my food. With that money I was able to pay the instalments on my first guitar, send two pounds a week to my family and keep a pound for myself. I was in show business; I was loving it and I was never to leave it.

I practised for about six hours every day while I was doing this first season and made up my mind to learn as much as I could, every day, about this great new world of which I'd become a part. When the season was nearing its close, I started to get the feeling that my career was running out too, since there was no sign of any other job on the horizon.

Then, out of the blue, came an engagement that numbers amongst the most peculiar I have ever undertaken. In Ireland, in the mid-to-late forties, the tax on cinema seats was raised to a level that made all the movie-house owners look around for a way of avoiding the evils of the tax laws. One of the escapes came in a form known as cine-variety; what this really meant was that if the film on show at the time was accompanied by live entertainment, the taxes didn't come into operation.

What a blessing this turned out to be for Bruce and me. Working in our little summer venue of Courtown Harbour we were approached by a ballroom and cinema proprietor from a neighbouring town. He wanted to use our talent to help avoid his cinema tax. We asked him about the length of time we were required to be on stage and were absolutely staggered to find that the law required our contribution to be at least as long as the film. Since the feature films were about an hour and forty-five minutes it presented us with the most impossible task.

It's one thing playing for people to dance but it's vastly different when your audience are sitting down just listening. Anyway, jobs were not things to be turned down because you couldn't do them, the answer was to say 'Yes please' and then spend the remainder of the engagement getting yourself out of trouble.

Bruce and I sat down and worked out endless programmes of songs, instrumental duets, etc., that would fill in part of the time at least. This, by the way, was before we'd done variety shows or radio series so we weren't going into the thing with a ready-made library or any such luxury.

But, more power to our elbows, we tackled the thing bravely, only to find that the situation had many hidden problems.

The film began showing in the early afternoon and played three times, which meant that we had to do about six hours of stage work each day – as the variety side came before the film, we would be on the stage at about one-thirty in the afternoon. Now, in a country town the chances of having an audience at that time were non-existent but what we didn't reckon on was that we did get the odd member of the unemployed who, I presume, the boss allowed in for nothing, if only to show them that there were worse things than being out of work.

Some days there were as many as four people in the auditorium: two drunks and a lady doing her knitting, while her little granddaughter tucked her dolly up in a blanket on one of the empty seats.

After a few days the afternoon audience 'dropped off', until nobody came in at all, so Bruce and I would sit on stage and talk. I would then go off for a while and Bruce would practise his scales. After that, we'd reverse the routine, each of us in turn keeping an eye on the door, if an audience came in we'd get together and try to entertain him, or her. The five o'clock show would be a bit more natural and once our final stint was over, we'd sit and watch the film.

I'll always remember our digs in that town. The landlady was an elderly woman who kept her money in her stockings – while she was wearing them. I don't mean she slipped a few neatly folded pound notes into her stocking tops à la Sophia Loren, she simply scrunched them up and pushed them down anywhere she found a space. The overall effect was a pair of legs that looked like a crop of Brussels sprouts.

She served our meals in the front room which had that familiar mouldy smell of damp. On the wall was a picture of an old gentleman, some relation or other, in a large frame; he had a bowler hat, a moustache and a fly-away collar. Like so many of those old faded sepia photos, he wore a look of total astonishment on his face, as though somebody had just kicked his shins as the picture was taken. Day by day we grew to resent that stare in his eyes, which gave the impression that he was hearing our every word.

The landlady must have had an admirer in the sausage trade (he was probably kinky about legs full of money) because we seemed to get them very often. We began to leave quite a few on our plates, so she nagged us about it: 'All the trouble I go to, cooking good food for you lads...' etc. Come to think of it, we were ungrateful pups because she fed us well and charged us very little.

One day, Bruce picked up a leftover sausage and threw it at the picture scoring a direct hit on his bowler. My shot was not so good and would have disappeared over his shoulder. In fact, that's precisely where the 'banger' finished because we just dropped the occasional one down behind the picture. I don't know if she ever decorated the room but, if she did, I'm sure her relative was glad to get the weight off his shoulders.

At the end of this unique engagement, with no work in the book, Bruce and I had little to do but get back to our musical get-togethers in Tramore, while during the daytime he was busy putting the finishing touches to the caravan he'd been building in his front garden.

His job completed, he hitched it up to his old Morris car and took it for its first road test. It was perfect. As we sped along by the deserted promenade, Bruce broke the news that he'd been offered a job with a small touring show, one of those known in the trade as a 'fit-up'. Travelling from one small town, or village, to another, these small companies played the local church hall, cinema, or anywhere else suitable for a performance. More often than not a makeshift stage would have to be erected especially for the occasion, hence the name 'fit-up'.

The company usually consisted of about five or six people, who between them supplied all the required talents for the proposed entertainment.

You might have the boss of the outfit as the comedian, his wife who sang, danced, acted, or played the piano, a son or daughter who did likewise, an accordion player who also did a magical act, and his wife who sang and took part in sketches. Their combined talents gave you, the orchestra, a variety bill for the first half, and the cast of a one-act play for the second part of the evening's presentation.

Bruce was engaged to tour with them for a season of several weeks, playing accordion, piano (if there was one) and any other duties the boss might suggest.

Since the deal did not include me, it meant the end of our musical association, at least for a while. But, a week or so before the opening date, Bruce hinted that since I had nothing better to do, I might like to go along for the ride. I agreed, on condition that I would pay my way as far as possible, sharing food bills and so on. The following week we were on the road heading towards the border with Northern Ireland. The tour was to be just south of the border.

While Bruce did his show at the village hall I'd stay behind, cooking some sort of evening meal on the simple coal stove, the windows steaming up and a plume of black smoke coming from our little chimney. Some kind lady would do our laundry for us, hanging it out on the bushes to dry in the sun while we, at every opportunity, would pop down to the hall and practise our music.

Some evenings I'd wander down, stand at the back of the hall and watch as the boss nipped around between stage appearances to count the takings. Many of the halls were so tiny you wondered how they could possibly make any money.

I did learn one thing though, and that is: don't judge the intelligence of your audience by the size of the hall. As my dear friend Arthur Askey would say, 'Just because there's not many in, you don't have to work half-hearted.'

Chapter Six

Fortunately, the summer of 1948 presented no problem as we were both invited to return to Courtown Harbour for another season. Then Bruce came across an advertisement, in a music paper, offering employment to a 'pianist' and a 'drummer' in one of the more successful provincial bands in Ireland. I had never played drums in my life, except for in the Scouts' band, but my keenness to stay in the music world, and also to continue my association with Bruce, led to my next undertaking.

I applied for the job as drummer with the band (who, luckily had their own drum kit), got a favourable reply and then spent the last few weeks of my summer season practising night, noon and morning in order to equip myself for the awesome task ahead. My knowledge of music made it easy for me to follow the drum parts used in orchestras and bands, but my complete lack of technique made the effort of playing, for any longer than 20 minutes or so, quite exhausting.

However, I joined the band and, good or bad, I stayed with them for six months playing one-night stands seven nights a week, practically without a break. Some quite incredible things were in store for me as a drummer and all very good experience for a young apprentice. The first 'gig' I did with them was a six-hour dance in a place called Dungarven, some 25 or 30 miles from my home. For a start, it took me a painful length of time to assemble the drum kit which they supplied, since it was something I hadn't done before and for which, sadly, I was not prepared. That evening was a nightmare, to say the least.

After one hour of my tense, fumbling efforts, I felt completely demoralised and ashamed, convinced that when the dance ended I'd be sent on my way with an evening's payment and a curt goodbye! By some happy twist of fate the bandleader was unable to be there that evening and left things in the hands of his assistant, Davey, who drove the limousine, chose the evening's programme and was also one of the band's vocalists. Maybe it was because he had so much on his mind that his judgement was dulled, but he certainly treated me well and gave me some badly needed moral support.

The dance began at nine o'clock and by about eleven-thirty my right foot, which was working the bass drum pedal, had become totally paralysed. Try as I may, I could get nothing more than a few nervous twitches from the ankle joint so decided to leave the ground floor portion of my drumming to rest in peace, and manage with my poor aching upper-half. When the evening was finally over and all the gear packed in our trailer, we headed north towards the town where the band was based. After a few fitful hours of rest, I had to go and meet my new boss.

He welcomed me and hoped I wasn't too tired after my ordeal on the previous night and, over some tea, told me my pay would be two pounds a night and that we would be working almost every night of the week.

The travelling was to prove exhausting as indeed were those long six-hour dances but, in my youthful dedication, I still studied music and practised my guitar for hours every day.

The popularity of the band always impressed me and, through it, I learned one of my first vital lessons. When you entertain the public it's no good just having good music or singing, you must also have entertainment value, so people will go home having had a good time. The band itself left a lot to be desired musically, as you'll gather from the quality of my contribution at the time but, overall, it gave great value to the patrons and showed me that my boss had his finger on the commercial pulse.

He knew that I was working hard at music – particularly the guitar – and often tried to persuade me to think more commercially, reminding me that, in those days, the guitar was a bad choice of instrument. (Admittedly, even in the semi-professional world, there were just a handful of people in Ireland who tried to play the guitar.)

Every now and then he would allow me to play a guitar solo with the band but it invariably had the 'novelty' approach associated with more unorthodox instruments such as the zither or the balalaika. Looking back on those days now, it's hard to believe the rarity of the guitar considering the enormity of its popularity today. As the weeks went by I worked hard to improve my efforts on the drums and, though I never achieved any degree of skill, my playing became workmanlike and I didn't feel I was getting money under false pretences. The sadness was that I never really wanted to be a drummer, so I didn't get any pleasure from playing.

The man I was working for at the time was a remarkable character; a heavily built man who played piano and who, when in action always looked to me like a white Fats Waller. He hosted the band with great skill and certainly knew all the tricks of the trade when it came to pleasing the public.

I don't know whether it was because he was getting older or not, but his moods seemed to change dramatically and his behaviour at times was, to a young, inexperienced newcomer like myself, quite alarming.

One of the first things he told me on joining the band was that there were three rules he liked adhered to at all times:

Rule 1. You must not drink any alcohol during working hours.
Rule 2. You must not associate with members of the opposite sex during working hours.
Rule 3. (And how about this!) You must not talk about music while travelling to and from the various jobs.

Needless to say, the third rule was by far the most difficult one to obey, since conversation about music is on the lips of musicians at all times.

During the period I spent with the band, I learned more about the geography of Ireland than I ever did at school. Travelling the length and breadth of the country, week in week out, I began to build up a picture in my mind of the 26 counties of Southern Ireland and the six of Northern Ireland – much more enlightening than that coloured jigsaw we were so familiar with in the classroom. The small towns and villages – up till then, nothing more than names from my exercise book – came to life as we drove through them and have remained in my memory ever since.

One summer's evening we arrived in Longford to play at the CIE

Annual Dance. The initials, CIE, are an abbreviation of the name 'Corus Iompar Eireann' which is the Gaelic name for what is best described as the Irish equivalent of British Transport. But, just a moment, I've realised that I can't tell you the following story without, first, including a supplementary anecdote vital to its maximum effect.

I told you earlier about the bandleader's assistant who looked after the band, drove the limousine, took responsibility for the music and also sang some of the vocals in a typical Irish tenor voice. Well, the boss got the bright idea there was yet another chore Davey could handle for the betterment of our set-up.

We didn't have a string bass in the band and, since many of the touring groups were sporting this vital instrument, the boss decided – in spite of its size and awkwardness in transport – that he'd have one.

I don't know if this came about because he happened across one that was going cheap, or because he really felt it would give our outfit an extra touch of class. Either way, in no time, there it was.

The boss insisted that it came with us on the day it was acquired and promptly instructed Davey to play it in between songs.

'I don't know one note from another,' he said indignantly.

'Who's gonna know whether you do or not?' said the boss. 'You can't really hear them, anyway.'

So Davey became a bass player.

Whenever he suspected that there were any musicians in the hall, he'd make that extra effort and shout to me, 'What key are we in?'

I'd look puzzled and say, 'How the hell do I know, I'm playing the drums.'

To put him out of his misery, I'd look over the boss's shoulder and examine the piano copy. 'E flat,' I'd shout to Davey.

'Where's E flat on the bass?' he'd ask, with a twinkle in his eye.

'Oh, about eight inches up on that second string,' I'd say and then I'd watch Davey grab the appropriate spot and knock hell out of it right through the number. Of course, Davey never even tuned the strings up so he couldn't possibly play a right note anyway – even by accident. For months after that, however, he played the bass every night!

And that enables me to take you back to the CIE dance at Longford. We arrived good and early and set up at the hall which was gaily decorated with bunting, fancy banners and lanterns. Added to those was a long criss-cross of ribbon which zigzagged right down the entire length of the hall, carrying – at intervals of about two feet – a series of cards bearing numbers from one to one hundred. These were to be used as a means of choosing winners of spot prizes (every now and then the bandleader would stop the music and say, 'The couple standing under card number eighty-five,' which usually invited a mad scramble to the bandstand, where the lucky couple would get a packet of cigarettes and a pair of nylon stockings). I had completed the assembling of the drums while all the other fellows were placing chairs, music-stands, microphones, instruments and so on, in their correct positions, ready for action.

It had been arranged, when we'd got everything ready, that we would go to some local lodgings or hotel where we would have something to eat before the six-hour slog began.

A group of the organising committee stationed themselves at a vantage point, quite near the bandstand, in order to watch the famous visiting orchestra go through their daily routine and they seemed most impressed by what they saw. The boss, who was sitting by the bandstand, began to talk to them asking various questions about how many people were coming etc., then, quite without warning, he turned to the bandstand and said, 'Gentlemen, can I have your attention for a minute?'

We felt sure he was going to say, 'Will bacon and egg be OK for the lot of ya?' But no.

He stood there, his hands in his overcoat pockets, then, like an army officer addressing his troops, he began to pace up and down, 'Lads,' he said, 'I feel I must bring this up – much as I hate to do it – I've got to get it off my mind.' Then a pause...'The intonation of the band has been very, very, bad lately. I've been ashamed, at times, that so little care has been taken in tuning-up. So, as from now, it's got to be put right.'

With these words he climbed on to the bandstand, sat at the piano, gave one of the notes a most fearful thump and said, 'Now, everybody, tune-up!' There must have been 10 seconds of shocked silence before a rather awkward fumbling for saxes, trumpets and trombones broke the deathly hush and then followed some weird 'tweeting' of notes. The boss was in full cry now – he kept bashing the poor note on the piano, making it more difficult for the lads by playing the wrong note for normal tuning-up.

'Come on, Bob,' he'd shout to the trumpet. 'You too, Sean – come on, Liam.'

All the boys were madly tuning-up, to his thunderous piano note, as Davey climbed on to the stand carrying a pile of music.

'Davey, will you put that music down and tune-up,' he bellowed.

Davey looked up from his crouching position, 'What's that?' he said.

'Get your bass and tune-up,' the boss insisted.

'Are you coddin' me?' asked Davey, half laughing but, immediately, he knew he'd said the wrong thing with the committee members almost within earshot.

He put the music on to the floor and, with a look of complete terror in his eyes, picked up the bass. Now, to start with, the machines for tightening the strings were rusty, the strings themselves were ancient and, worst of all, Davey wouldn't know the right note even if he heard it.

He grabbed the most convenient machine-head and started to turn it; as he laboured over this operation with his left hand, his right hand gently plucked the string that was giving out a sort of low belching sound. The rest of the band sat down, fascinated. After a whole minute of turning the creaking machine-head, the string had tightened up sufficiently to produce a recognisable note. But the relationship between the note the boss was playing, the note the bass was producing and the note that Davey would eventually settle for, was something that filled us all with expectation.

Davey lost his nerve after a bit and discreetly switched to one of the other machines, which was so stiff that he decided to settle for the devil he knew. The string had now tuned-up so high that you could almost see it getting thinner, and it was beginning to sound like a guitar string. Little friendly whispers began to advise the tuner, 'Don't go any higher, Davey.' 'Tell him you can't turn it any more.' 'The string is going to break.' The boss was beginning to look as though he knew he'd done the wrong thing but was in too deep. All he could do, in front of the committee, was keep on until something happened.

And something certainly did happen.

There was an almighty bang as the tailpiece of the bass could no longer take the strain; the piece of wire which attached the tailpiece to the knob underneath snapped. The action that then took place was similar to that of a catapult: the whole tail section flew into the air like a slingshot, hitting the decorations over the bandstand, snapping the ribbons. The result was incredible. Just like a line of falling dominoes, the zigzag bunting and numbered cards began to fall, first at the top of the hall, where we all sat aghast, then – by degrees – right down to the other end. I shall never forget the sight of the committee members as they stood there, motionless, with the multicoloured decorations strewn over their heads and shoulders. That, as far as I remember, was the end of Davey's career as a bass player.

In some of the more remote areas of Ireland dances of any importance were looked upon as quite an occasion for the entire population. It was fascinating to arrive and find all the seats around the hall taken by children and the very old members of the community. Grannies in their Sunday best, with their pipe-smoking companions, sat there just listening to the band tuning-up and looking forward to a kind of orchestral concert. They'd watch the younger people dance and enjoy themselves until such time as they – and the children – felt it was time for bed. Then home they'd go.

The introduction of the Crystal Ball, and its fairyland effects, made it all rather a dreamlike experience for the non-dancers. As the ballroom lights were lowered and the ball began to revolve, the effect was like hundreds of stars flickering round the room.

Another indelible memory of those nights, back in the 1940s, was the 'smell' of the dance halls. Before the patrons arrived for the evening's recreation, the caretaker would sprinkle a mixture of paraffin oil and candle-grease all around the floor then, by the time the first few dances were over, the whole thing was shining and gleaming like an ice rink. I don't know where the oil and candles disappeared to as the evening passed, but I do know that the smell stayed with me for years.

We arrived one night at a very small country village in the west of Ireland, and I started to cart the gear up through the small village hall, with its familiar smell, and heard the usual echoing sounds of my heavy feet on the slippery floor. Small though the place was, it proudly possessed a shining Crystal Ball and I noticed, on this occasion, that immediately underneath it, in the centre of the floor, stood two large white wooden kitchen chairs!

I tried to guess what they were doing there but I was baffled; they were not tall enough for anybody to have placed them there in an effort to reach the Crystal Ball, neither did they, in any way, match the other chairs around the walls.

When the dance finally got underway I watched with interest to see if, and when, they would be removed by one of the organisers of the function but nobody made any such move.

With each dance the floor got busier and, to all of us on the bandstand, the chairs appeared to be turning into quite a dangerous hazard. Couples in happy abandon went whizzing past them, missing them by inches, and by now the music and singing had become quite secondary as far as we were concerned. The chairs were the stars of the evening.

The first half ended and we made our way to the refreshment room where local ladies served us tea with home-made sandwiches and cakes.

I mentioned the now infamous chairs to the committee members, who just laughed, telling me not to worry about them. I even asked the boss if we should move them, but his reaction was, 'Oh, to hell with them, they've got nothing to do with us. If they want the things moved, let them do it themselves.'

The night was in full swing now and the boss decided it was time everybody really let loose in an Irish dance. A great favourite the 'Walls of Limerick' was announced and all the laughing couples rushed on to the floor, holding hands and shuffling into position. It was only then that the boss felt some action should be taken – fearing that, in the frenzy of the next few minutes, the dancers would find it impossible to avoid the obstacles in the centre of the floor.

'I'll go down and move them to the side of the floor,' I offered, feeling that at last the nagging worry of the chairs would be gone. An announce-ment was made to the dancers to wait for just a minute. I stepped off the stand and started for the middle of the floor; the dancers moving aside to make way for me, at the same time giving a jeering round of applause. I took a chair in each hand and slid them at arm's length to the side of the room, leaving them against the wall. Back on the stand, the time was being stomped out by the boss's heavy foot and the 'Walls of Limerick' were scaled.

Suddenly, amid the happy laughing voices and the dancing feet, there was an almighty crashing sound, screaming voices brought the music to a stop and all eyes turned in the direction of the commotion. The committee members rushed to the middle of the hall, where the dancers stood surrounding a gaping hole in the centre of the floor.

It turned out that, a couple of nights before, some workmen had damaged a few of the floorboards and had not been able to fix them in time, so, what did they do? Like any decent workers they placed a warning sign and, as one of the patrons said, 'If that stupid "eejit" in the band had left the chairs where they were – and minded his own business – nothing would have gone wrong!'

After a six-month stint of one-night stands, coupled with the fact that I was playing an instrument in which I had no interest whatever, I decided I wanted to move on. I still had very little to offer in the way of credentials, as far as a job was concerned, and had to agree with the boss when he tried to discourage me from leaving a steady income while I had nothing else. It was Bruce, once again, who came up with a suggestion: each summer in a little seaside town called Bray, in County Wicklow, a small alfresco entertainment was presented on the minute bandstand on the promenade known locally as 'The Coons'.

An area in front of the stage was railed off and used as an auditorium, where deckchairs were available at a small cost. Passers-by, of course, were free to stand by the rail and watch the show for nothing. For this reason the man who ran the show, a Mr Bolton, together with his wife, took turns in 'bottling' the crowd. (This simply means that between their brief appearances on stage, whether to sing, dance, or take part in sketches, they took a collecting box among those people who dared to stay even long enough to see what was going on.)

That was my next engagement! Between us Bruce and I played guitars, piano, sang duets, did comedy sketches with the comedian, compered and did anything else we were called upon to tackle.

For all that, and twice daily into the bargain, I got six pounds a week. I loved it though because, for the first time, I was doing the kind of thing I enjoyed and was my own boss. We had a lovely summer there and made lots of grand friends. I'm proud to say that, by the middle of the summer, the crowds were getting bigger, we were being asked for requests, and I think I felt the first flutter of excitement at being an 'entertainer'.

One evening I got a message saying we were wanted at the stage entrance (a tiny exit in the side of the little bandstand). Bruce and I went out to find a gentleman who told us his name was Niall Boden.

We were both somewhat flabbergasted, as this chap was one of Irish radio's Terry Wogans of the time. He said how much he'd enjoyed our songs, guitar duets and so on, and wondered if we'd like to add a bass player, of our own choice, to the duo and form a group to do some radio work?

Needless to say we were thrilled and at once found a local player, named Kevin Whelan, who joined us on bass, thus forming the Bruce Clarke Trio.

Niall Boden was doing a 15-minute sponsored programme, twice a week, on Radio Eireann and asked us to do a trial show. The products being advertised were made by a company called Donnelly's, so we became the Donnelly Music Makers and spent our time singing the praises of sausages, ham and black puddings. We did this programme for about six months as far as I remember and, again, were fortunate to get very good public reaction. Being on the radio twice a week kept us in the public ear. Soon we found our services were being sought elsewhere and occasionally we augmented the group with a girl singer.

We taped the Donnelly sponsored programmes in an outside studio in Moore Street, a place best known as an open-air fruit and vegetable market. As you made your way to the Irish Recording Company, tucked away over one of the shops, you were entertained by a chorus of sales pitches all sung in the broadest of Dublin accents: 'Jaffe orangesss, Jaffe orangesss.' 'Nice fresh cauliflowersss, tuppence each.' 'Lovely bananas, five for sixpence.'

Bill Stapleton who owned the Irish Recording Company, was, by a strange twist of fate, that selfsame man who, with his mobile recording unit, had come to Waterford all those years previously, to put us 'on record' for the first time. He was a great friend to us both and not only gave his whole attention to the quality of our radio efforts but also allowed us to use one of his studios as a rehearsal room, when it wasn't otherwise required. To help keep the wolf from the door, Bruce and I started a little music school; he teaching the piano and me taking on young pupils who wanted to make a start on the guitar.

Chapter Seven

I hadn't been on the road very long before I discovered, the hard way, that the world is full of frustrated entertainers.

You just think about it. All you have to do is visit your local pub, social club or dance hall any weekend and, sooner or later, you'll come up against somebody who either wants to get up and sing with the band or play the drums or piano during the interval.

These people can be very insistent, too, especially when their courage has been boosted by a few stiff drinks.

Now, it's a strange thing but I've found from experience that the singers with the greatest tendency to show off are tenors. (I hope that all my friends in high places will know that they are exceptions.) Maybe it's the high notes that make them drunk with power, I don't know, but Ireland was certainly crawling with them in my early days.

I worked with one particular piano player, who had his own wicked method of dealing with these budding Mario Lanzas. Once he'd concluded that there was no way he could get rid of the volunteer vocalist, he'd say, 'All right, what do you want to sing then?'

'How about "Come Back to Sorrento"?' the happy newcomer would say, with 'party piece' written all over his face.

'What key do you sing it in?' our friend Pat would ask.

'Oh! I don't know,' the tenor would admit, and proceed to sing a bit in 'la la la's'.

'Mmm,' Pat would grunt, 'let's say, E minor. That should be OK.'

Once he had all this sorted out, he'd indicate the microphone to the singer and say, 'Right then, here we go, give it everything you've got, old son,' and proceed to play the introduction in G minor, a key that was guaranteed to give the poor man a double hernia before he got halfway through the song.

I was 'filling in' on drums in a band one night, back in the 1940s, when a very 'county' looking gentleman came clambering up on to the stand and headed in my direction. It was break time, so there were just a few of us keeping things going while the rest had a beer.

'I say, old lad,' he said, 'could I have a bash at your drums? I used to play at university you know. Go on, there's a good chap.'

'Sorry,' I answered, 'we're playing for dancing right now and the bandleader wouldn't like it.'

'Oh! to hell with the bandleader,' he shouted impatiently. 'Let's have a bash!'

'Look,' I said, still playing, 'I'll be knocking off for something to eat in a minute, then it's up to you, OK? But do be careful.'

'Oh! you are a sport, old man,' he said, thumping me on the back and breathing beer and whiskey fumes all over me and the drums.

He stood there, swaying from side to side; his hands buried in his pockets, till the set was over and then, eagerly, struggled into my drum seat. 'You know,' he whispered as I was leaving, 'I'm out on the town tonight. My horse won a big race here today and another of mine was placed in the Cambridgeshire, so – I'm in the money. When I've had a bash at your drums...I'll give you a tenner for yourself...how about that, eh? What?' I didn't believe a word and just headed for the tea bar.

When I got back he was finishing his attack on the poor drum kit and I could see, by his expression, that he'd enjoyed every second of it. The band began to set up for the second half.

'Thank you so much, old boy,' he shouted into my face. 'You're a good fellow. Now, I said I'd give you ten pounds and – here it is!' He thrust the 10 pounds at me but no sooner did the thing appear in his hand than it disappeared into the hand of our bandleader, who smiled and said, 'That's kind of you, sir, it will go towards some new arrangements.' And he slipped it into his pocket. 'OK, lads, let's go,' he said, winking at us. 'That'll pay for all the booze tonight – I'm sure Val won't mind.' It was a genuine case of easy come, easy go!

I wondered at the time, with all the money the old gent had and his obvious love of the drums, why on earth he didn't buy a kit of his own. Still, he might have frightened the life out of his thoroughbred horses.

Within a year or so Bruce and I were regulars on radio, in theatres and, of course, in dance bands, becoming more and more established in Dublin, both as partners, and individually. I personally found resident jobs quite a relief at times, since you had all day to 'do your thing' (as they say nowadays), at the same time knowing you had the security of a regular weekly income.

The musicians in Dublin with whom I worked were a terrific crowd of fellows and, even though I will admit to being very much a loner, I did strike up some great friendships.

One of the bandleaders I worked for quite a lot in Dublin was Bob Murphy. Bob was a good musician who played trumpet, led a very successful band but, in the main, was to find his forte as an arranger. We 'gigged' all over the place during the years I was associated with him and a good time was had by all. One job that sticks out in my recollections of his band, was an evening at the Town Hall in Dun Laoghaire, the busy channel ferry terminal outside Dublin.

He had a problem booking all the right guys for the job and, as a last resort, had to fall back on one particular musician reputed to be unreliable because of his taste for the 'bevvy'. 'If we can only keep him out of the bar, we'll be OK,' said Bobby, as we made the journey along the coast road towards the evening's venue.

But one thing he didn't reckon on was that our saxophonist friend might get to a bar before the dance even began at eight o'clock. It was a beautiful evening when we arrived at the Town Hall of this attractive seaside town and we began to set up on stage, chatting to each other and getting up to date with the latest gossip. Eventually, the man of the moment arrived and, as he walked into the hall, I heard Bobby whisper, 'Janey Mac...I don't believe it...he's bevvied already!'

I'd never had the pleasure of meeting the gentleman in question and simply shook hands with him as he prepared his instrument for our tuning-up interlude. From that moment, we all got on with our job and I didn't give him another thought.

One of the things we did in those days was to 'stagger' the band a bit – different groups having their refreshments at different times so assuring the patrons of non-stop dancing music right through the evening. Bobby sent me for an early break while he led a small group of the boys in a kind of 'dixieland' session.

Shortly after I got back, he prepared for another reshuffle; turning to our sax-playing friend he said, 'I'll leave you with Val on guitar and Ronnie on drums. OK? Just do some slow waltzes, we'll be back shortly.' Bobby left the stand and I looked across for some sort of clue as to what was going to happen.

My new partner donned his sax and approached the microphone looking, to my amazement, a bit the worse for wear.

'What'll we play?' I asked, looking up.

'Ah, mmm...slow waltz, isn't it...ah...how about "For You" in three flats?' he suggested.

My electric guitar amplifier turned up, I played a four bars introduction in E flat and off we went. A mike was conveniently placed near me, so I sang a vocal chorus in the middle, 'I will gather stars out of the blue, for you, for you,' and so on. The whole thing was fine and when it ended we acknowledged our applause.

Again I looked up, awaiting my instructions, 'Ah!' he said, looking a bit glassy-eyed, '"Ramona", in G, OK?' I plonked out four bars in G and was just beginning to think what a piece of cake it was when, to my astonishment, he actually played 'For You' again – in E Flat! I did a lightning modulation into his key, looking horrified as, indeed, did the dancers, who were no doubt wondering what was so special about the tune that we should play it again. Rather self-consciously, I sang the song for a second time and longed for it to finish. The applause was, as you can imagine, a bit grudging this time and I hoped we could just get on with things to cover the feeling of embarrassment.

Quite unmoved by it all, however, our featured soloist adjusted his sax-reed, looked across, '"THE ANNIVERSAY WALTZ" IN C!' he shouted. At the end of my four bars introduction I hovered between the two keys, wondering what he would decide to do this time and – you've probably guessed it – he played 'For You' in E Flat. He'd obviously got some kind of mental block and couldn't get the one song out of his head – or his fingers. There was a groan from the dancers who looked up with 'Oh! For God's sake,' written all over their faces, as from the door of the refreshment room came our boss who obviously couldn't believe his ears. This time, when we reached the vocal chorus, I just refused to cooperate, deliberately changed key and sang 'The Anniversary Waltz'. This brought a little relief to the situation and, to round things off, my friend even consented to play a chorus of it to finish.

The band returned to their seats highly amused by the incident and, when Bobby announced a quickstep, I was waiting for some wise guy to suggest 'For You' in E Flat. The guilty party, on the other hand, sat serenely in his chair, apparently oblivious to his crime and probably thinking that he had played three different tunes.

I was in my early twenties by now and quite accustomed to living my life in digs. Since Dublin was only about a hundred miles from Waterford, I made the trip to see my family and friends as often as I could.

It was hard to get used to the change in No.10. It was so quiet with only my mother and brother Lar living there. Ned, Nellie and Una were married and living in their own homes, John was working in London and, as I mentioned earlier, Nancy was in America.

Strangely enough, it was during these visits that I really began to know Lar, having more time to talk to him over meals, or sitting by the fire at nights.

His health had been a constant worry to the family for as long as I could remember, and it was getting steadily worse.

It all began many years earlier when he got a tubercular abscess in his neck glands. It was removed by surgery, only to be followed by another some time later.

Sadly, worse was to follow, and in time the dreaded disease got to his lungs. All kinds of medical steps were taken, culminating in a long period of rest at one of the country's leading convalescent homes.

But it was all in vain and the lung had to be removed. After that, he was never fit or strong enough to take on any kind of heavy work, as the strain would have been too much for his heart. Eventually, he found himself a job doing some light duties at a local market garden and nursery, and seemed very contented.

During one of my visits, sometime around the end of 1949, he asked me if I'd like to go along to a local dance that evening, just to keep him company. I'd never been much of a one for dancing, but agreed to go just for the fun of it. During that evening, I became aware of how many times he had to sit and rest to get his second wind.

He told me the truth on our way home. We were climbing John's Hill which led to our house when he slowed down. 'I'll have to rest for a bit, boy,' he was breathing hard. 'I'm afraid I can't make this hill in one go any more.'

We sat on some stone steps leading to a terrace of houses and talked for a while. 'The doctors tell me the other lung is banjaxed now, and they don't think my heart can take the strain much longer. I could have a real bad haemorrhage at any time.'

There wasn't a lot I could say to help, 'You'll have to rest more, that's all,' I tried.

'Oh, I've accepted the situation now,' he went on. 'I only hope and pray that when it does come I'll be at home, and, please God, in my own bed.'

I hadn't been long back in Dublin when I received a telegram from my brother Ned: LAR PASSED AWAY SUDDENLY THIS MORNING, PLEASE COME HOME.

I was on the next train from Kingsbridge Station in Dublin, wondering what the news would be at home, and how my mother would be coping with it all.

Yes, he did have a haemorrhage, but God heard his prayers all right and waited till he was 'at home, and in his own bed'.

The shock of the whole thing, with the loneliness that followed, proved a great burden on my mother so, in order to give her a change of surroundings, I arranged for her to come to Dublin for a while.

If, by the way, you're beginning by now to come to the conclusion that there was a great dearth of romantic interest in my life, I've got to admit that you're not far wrong. Casual affairs with the opposite sex were never one of my strong points as a lad. That, coupled with the unfriendly hours my work inflicted on me, made my amorous encounters few and far between. I should also add that my enthusiasm for my work at the time was such that, given the choice, I'd probably practise my guitar rather than get involved with someone.

Looking back, I must admit that I missed out on a lot of fun in my early days. But then, who knows, if I'd been a different sort of fellow, I might have married and had three kids before I was 25, made a lot of different decisions as a result – and ended up with no reason for writing this story anyway.

Back in Dublin one morning, one of the members of the sax section turned to me and mouthed 'I'd like a word'. The word was to ask whether I was a member of the Musicians Union. He was the shop steward. My answer, I'm afraid, was in the negative as up to then, nobody had even mentioned such a thing. By the end of our rehearsal, however, I was given the address of the Union in Gardiner Street and took a stroll in that direction. Gardiner Street had seen better days as far as I could see. I walked along, checking the house numbers, keeping an eye out for the brass plate on the wall to show me I had arrived.

A smattering of youngsters played happily on the entrance steps, dolls, prams, scooters and toys of all kinds lay about. One very young girl had decided to take her doll out for a morning constitutional. She was chatting to it, when suddenly, from one of the open windows above came the ear-splitting voice of a real-life Mammy. 'Gwendoleannn!' she screamed in a broad Dublin accent. Poor little Gwendolyn stopped dead in her tracks and looked upwards, petrified. 'Gwendoleann! Will you get up here this minute!' As the little girl started to run, out came a line, which has stayed with me ever since: 'Gwenndoleann! If you're not up here in one minute from now, I'm going to redden your arse the colour of *The Messenger*!'

(For those of you who are not Irish or of my generation, I should explain that *The Messenger* was a regular fixture in my childhood home. My dear mother, like so many of her generation was deeply religious. Indeed, most of her activities outside of the home were linked to the church. While other women's reading matter may have leaned towards *Woman's Own* or the likes, my mum was more partial to *The Messenger* or *The Lourdes Messenger* to use the correct title. As we young ones tied our swimming gear to the crossbars of our bicycles in preparation for a dash to the local seaside resort,

Mum would quietly bring one of our old kitchen chairs out on to the footpath where she would settle with *The Messenger*.

My most vivid memory of this periodical was brought into sharp focus that day in Gardiner Street. It was printed in the brightest red ink you could possibly imagine. Poor little Gwendolyn!

Life for me in the Dublin music world was, by now, a long succession of dance halls, radio shows, rehearsals for various things and, all in all, I was getting all the work I could handle.

However, they say that familiarity breeds all kinds of discontent and in time I was getting that feeling of having done it all before.

Towards the end of 1951, Bruce and I were both working in the resident band at the Olympic Ballroom in Dublin. (Ballrooms were a thriving industry at that time and, looking back, it's hard to believe that so many could find willing patrons night after night.)

One night as we were warming up and the hall was still empty, the manager came walking across the dance floor. 'Val,' he shouted over the tuning-up noises, 'can you pop down to my office for a minute, there's two chaps'd like a word with you.'

The two chaps in question were members of a vocal quartet called the Four Ramblers – an Irish group that was working in England, to which I listened with great interest on a weekly BBC radio show called *Riders of the Range*. Their names were Pat Campbell and Dermot Buckley.

I discovered that a member of the quartet was about to leave, due to illness, and that the purpose of their trip to Dublin was to find a replacement. The qualifications were that he should be able to sing harmony lines, play guitar, do the vocal arrangements and, of course, try not to look ugly. After some initial enquiries, they were given my name by a fellow musician and now, having found me, they were offering me the job.

A change of musical surroundings was just what I needed at the time and, even though the offer contained very little in the way of guaranteed income, I had to say yes.

Within a month or so I'd said my farewells to Bruce, my staunch partner of so many years' standing, been home to receive the blessings of my family and, with one suitcase and a guitar, was boarding the boat for England.

Chapter Eight

The boat train delivered me safely to London and into the hands of one of my new partners, who was there waiting to greet me at Paddington Station. Dermot Buckley, or Dee, as we all grew to call him, took me back to his bedsit for a hearty breakfast of bacon and eggs.

Number 20, Highbury Grange, London, N5, became my world for a while. Dee had a room there as, in fact, did two other members of the group, who lived there with their wives. Our landlord, Ossie, was a great guy, explaining that he sadly didn't have a room for me at the moment, but it was all right with him if I shared with Dee till something came along. He charged me £2 per week.

The boys were, as I've already mentioned, appearing in the BBC radio series *Riders of the Range* written and produced by Charles Chilton, an exceptionally talented man. The programme described life on one ranch in the American West; you could say it was a sort of *Bonanza* idea, tied together with music and songs. That's where we came in – we were the ranch hands, or bunkhouse boys, who happened to sing in the style of the Sons of the Pioneers from the old Roy Rogers, Gene Autry days.

Well, 24 hours after my arrival in London found me, pencil and manuscript in hand, writing the music for our first two or three vocal contributions to the radio show. I remember the feeling of excitement when I first heard the music I had written coming to life, with a group whose vocal style was so familiar to my ear from radio and records. We did the *Riders of the Range* programme for about 13 weeks and I found the new experience very thrilling.

That first three-month period also included my introduction to the British music-hall stage. I learned the Ramblers' established stage act and, glad to say, made a few suggestions of my own which, in time, were incorporated to good effect. We appeared for 'weeks' (one week at a time) at all the major towns and cities all over the British Isles during the next year and, by the time 1952 was over, I was a fully fledged quarter of the quartet.

I made my debut on the British variety scene when it was still in pretty good shape. For as long as I can remember people have propounded the old cliché 'Variety is on the way out', but it certainly wasn't showing any signs of disappearing in those early days. Week in, week out, we would travel somewhere to join the cast of a different show, especially assembled for that one occasion.

Of the dozens of stars who topped those bills, some would fall into the category of older and well-established favourites – names like Jimmy James, Jewell & Warris, Jimmy Wheeler and Max Wall. Then there were the younger stars like Harry Secombe, Max Bygraves, Terry Thomas, Harry Worth, Eric Sykes and so on. But it was undoubtedly the age of the singer. Each Monday, a different name would grace the front of the theatre, as a result of the artist's record and radio popularity. There were scores of them: David Hughes, Alma Cogan, Gary Miller, Lita Roza, Anne Shelton, David Whitfield, Eve Boswell, Jimmy Young, Ruby Murray, The Deep River Boys, The Beverley Sisters, Michael Holliday, Lee Lawrence, Joan Regan, Lester Ferguson and, of course, the visitors of that period: Johnny Ray, Guy Mitchell and Billy Daniels. The list could go on, and on, and on.

Being in the thick of the music-hall world, one of the things I quite naturally wanted to do when I came to London was to visit the London Palladium. This proved much easier than I expected. It was a time of very special variety shows at this great theatre. Such stars as Jimmy Durante, Maurice Chevalier, Judy Garland and Danny Kaye would appear there for a week, their engagement including two matinee performances: one on Wednesday and one on Saturday.

I just couldn't believe my luck when my new partners told me that being a member of an established act, provided you could produce some proof of identity such as your Equity Union card or a visiting card displaying the name of your act, entitled you to free admission on the Wednesday afternoon. So, the weeks when we were in London would find us queueing, with hundreds of other pros, to watch the world's best entertainers in action.

What a treat it was. Time after time I sat there, wondering what it must feel like to stand on that stage starring in your own show. Never, in my wildest dreams, did I think I'd see the day when it would happen for me, not only for the odd week but for a six-month season!

One special area of employment being exploited by London-based agents around that time, involved travelling to Germany to perform in cabaret at the many clubs on American Army and Air Force bases. An offer came our way in the early part of 1953 and, work being a bit thin on the ground at the time, we decided to have a crack at it.

Having sailed by cross-channel ferry to the Hook of Holland, we boarded a Trans-European express that travelled right across Germany; its final destination, as far as I recall, was Vienna.

After sitting up all night, drinking coffee and playing poker while the long snake-like train rumbled its way across the Continent, we finally staggered out on to the platform at Weisbaden in the early hours of the morning.

Weisbaden was to be our headquarters for the duration of that four-week stay. (On other visits that were to follow through the years, we'd find ourselves stationed at locations such as Stuttgart, Munich, Frankfurt or Heidelberg, taking in all the available venues in the respective areas. It was remarkable how such place names as Darmstadt, Mannheim, Karlsruhe and Kaiserslautern became as familiar to us on the passing signposts as were Halifax, Tipperary or Leamington Spa.)

On reporting for duty next day we were surprised and somewhat shocked to discover the unfamiliar system of selecting and distributing the entertainment. Assembling at a large club, with dozens of other acts from Britain and the Continent, we stood around rather self-consciously, wondering what it was all about and what was in store for us.

Entertainment officers from the many bases in the area gathered, with notebooks and pencils at the ready, while each act in turn went on stage and did their bit. At the end of this marathon audition, and when the buyers had made their decisions, they'd go into a huddle with the agent and book their shows for the coming weeks.

Then, depending on what sort of impression you made, the jobs were allocated. Some unfortunate acts got no bookings at all, others one or two. We, proudly, finished up with a very heavy schedule. Ironically, it didn't really matter to us – as we'd been booked on a set weekly salary.

Then started a series of mystery tours of Germany, doing one, two, or even three shows in one night and never before, or since, have I experienced such varied conditions and audience reactions. You could go to a base and do a show at the officers' club in conditions which were on a par with any first-class hotel, then go across to the place of entertainment set out for the enlisted men and be faced with the most horrific contrast.

One weekend we went to do an early evening performance at a place called Bitburg, which was situated just outside Nuremberg. We got there early and took a look around the city and were naturally intrigued to see the home of the famous Nuremberg Trials. It was still daylight when we got to the base and made our way to the NCOs' club; we weren't too surprised to find the room practically deserted as the brilliant sunshine streamed in, reflecting on the cheap-looking chromium tables and chairs.

Now it was the accepted practice that these shows should run for at least 55 minutes, at the end of which time the officer in charge would sign a document stating 'the show was as booked' and all was well. If, for any reason, including being hit by flying beer cans, you didn't do the specified time, 'the man with the money' could possibly refuse to sign the chitty and no dollars would be forthcoming.

We started to set up for the show. On one side of the stage stood a large TV set, about four feet high, worked on a closed-circuit system which supplied the GI viewers with popular American light entertainment. On this occasion, the laughs were being supplied by the, then very topical, *Amos and Andy Show*. As we walked about the place, making our initial investigations, our conversation was interrupted at intervals by shouts of, 'Ho, there, Sapphire!' or 'Holy mackerel, Andy'. We brought our equipment from the car outside and began to cart it round to the back of the stage; I had a guitar in one hand and a very heavy amplifier in the other as I trundled through the swing door.

Looking round, I could see four people there: one fellow in fatigue dress, reading a paper and having a cup of coffee and a hamburger, a couple sitting on stools by the bar and another guy, in cowboy-style clothes, slouched in a chair with his feet stretched across the aisle and resting on an adjoining table.

I slowly approached the latter carrying my crippling baggage and paused, as I faced the barrier made by his outstretched legs. 'Ah, excuse me,' I said apologetically. The Lee Marvin-type character slowly stirred, tipped his hat from off his eyes, looked up and grunted, 'What didya say, man?' I thought my problem was obvious but smiled and went on, 'Sorry to bother you but I'd like to pass, please.'

He looked up at me, giving the impression that he always wanted to play this role that had just come his way, 'You ain't gonna pass here, boy,' he said, just like Lee Marvin would have done. 'Now, why don't you go raht back down there and come up the other sahd, OK?'

He looked at my luggage, 'Are you with the floor show, man?' he enquired. 'Yes, that's right,' I said politely...wanting to add, 'What the hell do you think I am, the milkman?' but, knowing he was 25 per cent of our audience at that moment, I didn't want to antagonise him. Then I added, 'I'd like to get to the stage.'

He looked at me for a long time, smiling through the cigarette smoke that covered his face, 'Well,' he said, 'let me tell you raht now, you ain't gonna make it, chicken, so, why don't you git!'

Now of all the roles I've ever visualised myself playing, I must say, that that of picking a fight with Lee Marvin was the least likely, so, mumbling something under my breath, I lumbered through the tables to the other side of the room.

'Rude bastard,' I hissed.

'Holy mackerel, Andy,' said the TV!

Then came the next problem, or problems; we couldn't find anybody to help us, there were no microphones to be found, no lighting – nothing! Pat, one of my partners, approached the barman, who was leaning on the bar, having a drink and watching the television.

'Pardon me,' he said, 'how do you do a floor show here, or who do you talk to about it?'

'Well, sir,' answered the barman with a welcome smile, 'you've gotta problem. You see, everybody's on manoeuvres right now. So, why don't you talk to Sergeant Gonsky – that's him, with the lady, at the end of the bar.'

'Thank you,' Pat said, grateful that somebody spoke to him, and approached the heavily built man in uniform with 'the lady'.

'Excuse me, Sergeant Gonsky.' He spun round slowly.

'What can I do for you, Mac?' he asked.

Well, Pat told him all the things he could do and explained all the things we couldn't do.

He listened while sipping his rum and coke and, when my partner had finished, he said, 'Oh, well, I guess there's a mike out back somewhere, you won't need lights, there's nobody here – but, I think you'd better do the show just the same, OK?' We couldn't believe it, as we set about the task of looking for the mikes, but we finally got things working sufficiently to make it look as though we were doing the show.

The act before us played the accordion and got the most dreadful reception from the TV viewers, who found him a painful distraction.

When we started, things got worse. The TV programme had now changed to *The Jack Benny Show* and we just couldn't compete. 'Lee Marvin' told us to shut up, then turned the television up to its full volume. Unfortunately, he could still – though barely – hear us, so, calmly, but deliberately, he rose, walked round the back of the stage and – pulled out the mike plug from the socket!

Believe it or not, we battled on, without being audible, until the magic 55 minutes was achieved.

Our job completed, we quickly packed up and hurried from the place, hoping that Sergeant Gonsky had signed our 'release'. The laugh that lives on in my memory was that, as we left and I was struggling through the tables with my bags, a voice from the other side of the room – and I couldn't but appreciate it – said: 'I told you, you wouldn't make it, chicken.'

We certainly did make it on 90 per cent of the shows we undertook on the American bases. In the majority of cases, we were well treated by everybody in charge of the club entertainments, and the servicemen enjoyed the shows and showed their appreciation in no uncertain manner. The whole business of performing for people's pleasure tends to be like most other things in life – you take it as the norm to go on, do the show and everybody's happy. When you get a stinker, you remember it for a long time!

Whenever the pros got together, over a drink in one of the German bars, you'd hear the normal stories of how they 'tore-em-up' at such-and-such a base; 'couldn't get off the stage' at so-and-so; 'did four encores' at this place or that – all this was treated with knowing nods, of the kind extended to anglers who caught one 'that big'. When the stories of horror began, the atmosphere changed and a good laugh was had by all.

We kept hearing about one particular base where the airmen's club had a reputation, second only to that of the concentration camps during the war. It was affectionately known as The Snake Pit for the simple reason that it was downstairs in a kind of cellar and the only entrance and exit was by means of a small staircase at one end of the large room. We finally joined the band of artists faced with the challenge of The Snake Pit and set out with two other acts: a couple of girl dancers and an American, rope-spinning, storyteller. It was a very cold day, I recall, as we arrived at Rhein Maine Air Base where the infamous place was situated.

In spite of our impressions of the place and what we had learned to expect from the stories we'd heard, we couldn't help feeling that it would probably turn out to be just another night's work. As was customary, we got there early and prepared the staging of our acts. (By the way, we worked on all these shows with just piano accompaniment that, by present-day standards, makes one shudder.) We left our clothes and stuff in our dressing room, which we were sharing with the other acts on the bill, and took advantage of the waiting time by having something to eat and drink.

I don't know if you've seen the film *Bad Day at Black Rock* starring Spencer Tracy – if not, forget it but if you have, the next part of my story will certainly ring a bell.

We stood in a line at the self-service canteen and had a look at the board that informed us what was available. I was a bit fed up with hamburgers and French fries, so I decided to try the chilli soup and crackers. I ordered some from a man in a snow-white chef's outfit serving behind the stainless-steel counter, its display cabinet loaded with goodies.

In five or six seconds flat, my bowl of soup with a small packet of crackers was spun on to the counter top.

'Thank you, sir.'

'Coffee?' asked the man in the white suit.

'Oh, yes, please,' I said, fumbling for some money in preparation for the cash desk a few feet ahead.

At that moment a large hand appeared from behind me, holding one of those red plastic tomatoes containing ketchup. As the big fingers gave the soft red ball an almighty squeeze, a resounding squelch heralded a huge dollop of red tomato ketchup into my chilli soup and a voice from over my shoulder said, 'Give it some flavour, man.'

I turned round to find a fellow, who must have been Muhammad Ali's dad, huge in build with a smile from ear to ear.

'That's clever,' I said. 'Do you do it a lot?'

He was enjoying himself, 'No, I don't,' he said, 'but, you know I've enjoyed it so much, I think I'll do it again,' and with these words, my soup received its second squirt of flavouring.

To my great relief I didn't have to do what Spencer Tracy did to Ernest Borgnine in *Bad Day at Blackrock,* and give him a smart karate chop round the neck; I don't think I could have reached his neck, without climbing up on the counter, anyway.

I felt a firm hand on my left arm. On turning round I faced the Master at Arms in his smart blue uniform with a gun slung ominously from his belt, 'Will you follow me, please, sir?' he asked politely, and led me towards my dressing room.

When we were out of earshot of the serving area and its clatter, he spoke again, 'Sorry about that, I'll have some soup and crackers sent to your room. The boys are a bit uptight at the moment, because it's near the time for some of them to go home.' He sat me down in my room and, in no time, a waitress brought me my food 'on the house'.

An hour or so after that incident saw the club filling up with, what looked to me like, extremely young men and their lady friends. We fellows strolled to the bar for a drink, to give the girls a chance to get ready for the show and, by the time we got back, the place was packed.

It was time to go and do our stuff; the patrons were seated and the dance floor was raised into its new position as a cabaret platform – about level with the shoulders of those adjacent to the stage. And, as ever, they were knocking back beer from cans which had two drinking holes pierced in the top – these, to us, were always a hazard and replaced the 'rotten eggs and tomatoes' of the traditional music-hall days.

The technique used to attack any artist who didn't please them, was to put their fingers over the holes in the top of the can, shake it furiously until it was ready to explode and then spin it along the floor in the direction of their victim. It resulted in not being struck by a flying can, but it certainly assured some work for your local dry-cleaners, removing beer stains from your trousers. Over the years we developed great agility at ducking the froth, without missing a note.

The two girls went on first to do their dance spot, also showing great dexterity at avoiding rude, groping hands as they danced by. They came back to the dressing room thoroughly annoyed and depressed by their reception vowing, as we entertainers so often do, that they would 'never go through that again!'

This was not very encouraging for our rope-spinning friend who was on next. Well, he spun his ropes, told his stories and died the most humiliating death. I must give him credit, though, he did his time and 'kindly didn't leave the stage'. (This was something the final act desperately hoped for because any time cut by the first acts, had to be made up at the end – to satisfy the 55-minute rule.)

He staggered back to the room like an injured dog to his kennel, and dropped into a chair. 'Well,' he puffed, 'you're welcome to forty minutes of that bunch, gentlemen,' and slowly began to tidy up his ropes.

We waited for our introduction, heard the piano plonk out our opening music and, like four youngsters taking their first plunge from the high-diving board, walked on – smiling! The noise in the place was deafening. Our first two songs went without any reaction; we knew it would, indeed, be a long 40 minutes that evening. It was about 20 minutes into the act when the first beer can came spinning from the edge of the stage and, ten minutes later, there must have been 16 or 18 of them surrounding our eight beer-splattered legs.

The real trouble came when one GI, feeling dissatisfied with the effect of the ammunition used so far, decided to go for the 'big guns'; he used a can which still contained two-thirds of its capacity and assured himself and us, of a spectacular climax.

He gave it a good shake, struggling to keep his fingers over the sizzling holes in the can – in fact, he had got up such a good head of steam that, as he tried to flick the can in our direction, it slipped – spun off at an angle of 30 degrees – overshot the other side of the stage and caught a fellow GI right on the nose! The old cliché 'all hell broke loose' is about the best description I can find for what followed.

The fellow with the bruised nose threw the beer can directly at the culprit sitting opposite; his reaction was to climb on to the stage, walk across and leap headlong on top of his new-found enemy. Soon their buddies decided to help and before you could say 'Two beers, please', the scene was just like the saloon brawl in a John Wayne film.

We stayed as long as we dared to but finally decided that money wasn't everything and dashed for our room. I can't remember just how long the punch-up lasted but when the military police sorted it out, we were escorted from the club by my good friend the Master at Arms.

It was like heaven, coming out into the cold night air – safe and sound.

From there we headed for the officers' mess to do another show and made some immediate enquiries about having the beer dried from our stage suits. Everybody was utterly charming and offered us something to eat and drink, while our suits were being pressed.

The gentleman in charge of entertainment came and introduced himself as 'Major something or other'.

'I hear you had an unhappy time across at the airmens' club,' he said, smiling.

'Have you ever been over there?' we enquired, thinking it was rather a silly question.

'No,' he said, 'but I hear it can be kinda rough, at times.'

'Kinda rough?' we echoed in astonishment and proceeded to tell him of our night's ordeal. When we finished, we asked, 'Why is it allowed to go on?'

'Well,' he drawled, 'it's like this, I guess. The guys are anxious to get on back home and they're feeling a bit aggressive about it so, we reckon, if they're gonna loose their cool and hit somebody, it's best they hit each other and not the Germans.'

Our 1953 trip to Germany, nevertheless, turned out to be the first of many visits undertaken in the 1950s. We learned to cope with every eventuality and, in time, overcame the fear of the unknown which dogged our early ventures.

Another overseas trip that the group did, around that time, was a month's cabaret at a place called the National Scala in Copenhagen, Denmark. It was a large restaurant, near the Tivoli Gardens, which had a nightly cabaret to the accompaniment of a good-sized orchestra.

We also doubled at the Night Club that was on the roof of the same building – it was much more a place for young people, who danced and had a few drinks.

The group that played up there was quite brilliant; a sextet of very talented Swedes who swapped instruments for different numbers in their repertoire. They also sang well together as a group and their arrangements were very much in the style of the, then, extremely popular Four Freshmen.

One beautiful moment in our association with them happened on our final evening at the club. The leader of the band, Paul by name, introduced us and said how sad they were that we were leaving. We did our act and left the stage to an absolute ovation. When we were about to return to our dressing room, Paul brought us back on stage and asked us to sit in the audience, 'Because,' he explained, 'we have a little surprise for you, as a going-away memento.'

We made our way to a table near the stage, which had been tactfully vacated to accommodate us. The four 'vocal' boys then went off stage, announced 'The Four Ramblers', ran on again and absolutely staggered us – and the audience – by *doing our act!* It was really sensational and the accuracy of their portrayals, of each one of us, was uncanny.

The day we arrived in Copenhagen we went straight to the National Scala and did our rehearsal. The stage manager informed us that we might have difficulty in finding accommodation, since there was some huge convention in the town. As it turned out, the word 'difficult' was a gross understatement and six o'clock that evening found us still searching without success.

Finally the stage manager rang a number and said to two of us, 'I've found you some place – it's not ideal, but it will do until tomorrow, OK?' We readily accepted, collected our cases from the dressing room and set out to find it. Our instructions were to go over the bridge, past the cinema, turn down a small lane on the left, and about 30 yards on we'd find a green door. We were to ring the bell and say, 'National Scala.'

We rang the bell – a voice from a loudspeaker at the side of the door said, 'Hello.'

We said, 'National Scala.'

A buzzer went, the door opened, and a flight of thickly carpeted stairs rose in front of us. We started to climb and were met by a fat lady who gabbled away in Danish and took us down a corridor to the last room, which was tiny, with two beds and a large tiled heating stove, of the circular type, with a chimney that went up through the ceiling in the middle of the room. We left our bags and headed back to do our show at the restaurant. I think we did OK, I can't remember much about the audience or our reception.

When the show was over, we went home – rang the bell – 'Hello' – 'National Scala' – up the stairs – the fat lady again – but now a great clamour of voices from all over the place, there seemed to be one big party going on. We went to bed shattered.

Suddenly, our door opened and the light came on. The fat lady standing in the doorway pointed to me and said, 'Telephone.'

'Me?' I said sleepily. 'Can't be, nobody knows me here.'

She pointed, harder this time, 'You, telephone – National Scala!'

I tumbled out of bed and, in dressing gown and slippers, followed her to her room where she had one of those funny phones on the wall like they had in Humphrey Bogart pictures.

I picked up the salt cellar and bunged it to my ear, 'Hello, Val here,' and I waited for some awful broken English.

Instead, I heard, 'Hello, mate, we can't find any place at all, can you help us?' it was the other two lads in our group.

I then struggled to ask the lady of the house if we could have two more fellows to stay. She smiled and said 'Yes', as if to say, 'If that's what turns you on' – only then did I know where we were staying and why everybody was having such a good time.

I immediately tried to tell her that my pals just wanted digs but she couldn't speak enough English to understand.

'Moment,' she said, putting a finger to her lips – and went away. In a moment she came back with a pretty girl of about 19, wearing a little see-through nightie. 'She speak English, she understand everything,' said the fat lady.

I'll bet she does, I thought as I reeled off our story.

She clarified the situation and I told the boys to come along and, hand in hand with 'baby doll', I walked back down the corridor. We parted, unfortunately, as we reached the first door where somebody was awaiting her return. I went back to bed.

A few minutes later, a knock at our door, and in came two men who proceeded to assemble two more beds in our tiny room. By now, the beds covered the whole room so, strictly speaking, the floor was two foot higher and we were sleeping on it!

Next morning we had four cups of black, evil-tasting coffee and left our 'hotel'. The fat lady said goodbye and no doubt thought we were the strangest customers she'd had in a long time.

The hotel or 'pension', where we finally stayed, was very different from the kind of theatrical accommodation we were accustomed to back home.

It had many rooms, most of them occupied by pros – entertainers that is – of one kind or another, all of the tenants sharing one large kitchen. This was equipped with a row of about eight cookers, each one with an accompanying cupboard containing its supply of pots, pans, dishes and cutlery.

You simply brought your own food, cooked it at your leisure and even had the luxury of a lady who came to help with cleaning up after meals.

The pros came in all shapes and sizes; the most memorable of them indeed, for shape and size, being an African-American double-act called Patterson & Jackson. (I'd seen these two entertainers some time before, when they were appearing at the Prince of Wales Theatre, in London, in a show called *Hellzapoppin*.)

The lift, or elevator, which served our third-floor hotel had a safety notice, which read, 'Maximum Load Three Persons' and, when I tell you

Patterson & Jackson had to travel one at a time, you'll not be surprised to hear they weighed 25 and 26 stones, respectively.

Warren Patterson loved to cook and spent a lot of his time in the kitchen. He was a real jolly soul and tap-danced about the place, in his dressing gown and slippers, while preparing his enormous meals. He proudly informed us one morning that he had worked once as a chef and, to prove it, threatened to cook for us 'the best and most exotic Irish stew we'd ever tasted'. On his instructions, we bought the ingredients for this culinary treat and left them in a carrier bag on the kitchen table.

Next morning the ritual was scheduled to take place, so we all assembled in the kitchen eager to sit and watch an expert at work. Systematically the meat was chopped and the vegetables cleaned and sliced – all in a manner that seemed to prove, beyond any doubt, that this was to be no ordinary Irish stew.

Warren swaggered about, from table to cooker, to the accompaniment of his non-stop scat-singing then, as the special brew finally got under way, he decided to enlighten us on one of the great secrets of cooking.

'You know what this is, man?' he asked, holding up a clove of garlic between his chubby thumb and forefinger. 'Now lots of folks don't like the smell of it, right?'

'Right!' we answered in unison.

'Good,' he nodded, like a schoolmaster acknowledging the success of his pupils. 'You know somethin' else?' he went on. 'Some foods don't like the smell of it either so – what do they do? – they build up a resistance to it. Right?'

'Right!' we chanted once again.

'So! What do we cooks do about it? I'll tell you, man, you must take that food by surprise. See, don't let it know when that garlic is comin', right?'

'Right!' we shouted this time.

He was laughing by now and waving his piece of garlic in our faces, 'Now, here's how it's done.'

And this huge lovable man – the object of his strange demonstration now hidden in his clenched fist – began to jive about the kitchen then out into the hallway and back again, all the time singing some jazz chorus to himself.

Each time he passed the cooker, on which his prize dish was simmering, he simply smiled in the direction of the pot and sang a few special notes to it – as if trying to gain its confidence. On about the fifth circuit, and without any warning, he deftly popped the garlic into the bubbling stewpot.

'Got you, man,' he shouted. Stopping in his tracks and turning to us, he said, 'Now, there ain't no Irish stew in the world can live with that, man.' Then, flopping into an adjacent kitchen chair, he roared with laughter as, indeed, did we: like his clove of garlic he was quite irresistible.

Later we all sat round the kitchen table enjoying a most wonderful meal and agreeing that it was worth waiting for. Mind you, it tasted nothing like Irish stew!

Working abroad is very good experience for any performer in my opinion, since it makes him prepare an act that has international appeal; the kind that will travel. Once you have worked abroad and found out, the hard way, all the things that don't work with a foreign audience, you are forced to expand your material in order to make it acceptable everywhere. This kind of professional 'investment' certainly pays off, by making your act saleable anywhere. How many times have we seen acts that are fantastic in London or Scotland but, when they reverse their location, become a bit of a non-event.

Chapter Nine

We loved going back to Ireland.

The Theatre Royal in Dublin was a truly magnificent theatre to play with its huge auditorium, lots of dressing-room space and boasting a pit orchestra of up to 20 musicians that, by general standards in those days, was quite unique. Alas, like many other fine theatres, it has since been demolished.

We played there many times as you can well imagine, being an Irish act – on one occasion for a long session of several weeks. The show was a very extravagant and spectacular Christmas production which starred several of Ireland's leading entertainers together with some imported acts.

As ever we were employed to take part in all sorts of scenes in the show but, in the main, we concentrated on our own spot. We shared a very large dressing room with three or four other people in the cast and I'll always remember the fun we had together during the run of that particular show.

One of the people who didn't share our room was the star of a very well-established variety act of the period – a lady who went under the name of Karinga. She was a most unusual speciality act, to say the least: accompanied by a couple of male assistants, she'd parade with great pomp on to the stage wearing a long cloak which trailed behind her and, when removed, revealed a tight-fitting, very slinky, leopard-skin outfit which never failed to bring a few whistles from the lads.

She would then perform a series of feats – thrilling! shocking! scaring! – but always entertaining her audience. First she introduced two huge alligators which immediately opened their mouths as if to devour the lady but, with the click of a finger and a few well-chosen words, she somehow hypnotised them on the spot. She then simply carried on with her act leaving the poor things lying there, right through its duration, looking like a couple of broken-down sports cars with their bonnets open!

She handled huge 20-foot snakes, as you and I would the garden hose, then climbed a ladder, 'in her bare feet', the rungs of which were razor-sharp swords. (Their sharpness was naturally demonstrated beforehand by the cutting of pieces of paper, accompanied by the usual theatrical flourish, bringing gasps of approval from the youngsters.)

Finally, Karinga would lie on the stage and a huge slab of stone would be slowly lowered on to her prostrate body then, as she no doubt clenched her teeth in anticipation, her assistants would produce two enormous sledgehammers and proceed to knock hell out of the slab until, eventually, it shattered into pieces round her body.

Slowly, she'd rise, then with a chord from the orchestra, she'd raise her hands on high and run forward to the front of the stage to tumultuous applause. This, she'd acknowledge by making that 'wanting to go to the loo' movement (a sort of semi-curtsy), with her shapely legs – in the style made famous by magician's assistants.

Now, it was customary after our afternoon show to sit in our dressing rooms with our feet up, with possibly a game of poker going on, eating a light snack and having a cup of tea. Other members of the gang would slip through the stage door to the pub just across the road – for slightly stronger refreshments.

On this particular afternoon, I was sitting enjoying a pork pie and a cup of tea when an announcement came over our dressing-room speaker requesting the entire cast to assemble on stage in 15 minutes' time. Pretty soon a great gathering of assorted folk wearing stage make-up, in dressing gowns, hair curlers, some of them finishing their last mouthful of sandwich, littered the huge Theatre Royal stage.

The manager appeared – everybody stared at him in eager anticipation. 'Ladies and gentlemen,' he began, 'if you'll give me your kind attention for just a few moments' – there wasn't a sound anyway – 'I don't want to cause any kind of panic and let me assure you, right away, that there is nothing to worry about but I regret to inform you that one of Miss Karinga's snakes seems to be missing.' There was a shocked silence.

The fellows looked at each other and one or two summed up the feelings of the others with such remarks, as, 'Bloody hell!' The girls, on the other hand, squeaked and pulled their dressing gowns around their legs.

'Now the reptile must be somewhere in the theatre,' the manager went on. 'A thorough search is being made, both front of the house and backstage, so I will ask you to do tonight's show just as you would any other performance and, remember, there is *no* danger; the snake is quite harmless!'

The meeting broke up and everybody made their way slowly back to their rooms looking about them anxiously. I don't think I need to tell you what it was like, eyes were everywhere and there seemed a natural tendency to stand quite still.

'Overture and beginners, please,' came as a kind of icebreaker really, and pretty soon everyone was on stage, waiting for the opening music for our evening performance. Of course, all of us had different ideas as to where the snake might be. Someone suggested it could be in the pit, which, after all, is where they are reputed to be found. This only caused the poor orchestra to play in a half-sitting, half-standing position all evening – ready for take-off.

Ours really is a strange way of life, you know – I swear the 'Pagliacci' thing is absolutely true: as soon as we come in contact with the audience, all else is forgotten. Your private little world can be falling about your ears but you must not let it show when you are on stage; and so it was with the cast of our Christmas show. There was a 20-foot snake somewhere at hand, not having had his tea, and there we were shouting to the innocent members of the public such gems as, 'Oh, yes there is!' to which they predictably replied, 'Oh, no there isn't!' Little did they know.

By the time our solo spot in the show came round things were in full swing and thoughts of our slimey friend were fading, at least temporarily. We sang our first two songs with great success and followed them with a very snappy comedy routine; next came our dramatic and most effective version of the old cowboy classic 'Cool, Clear, Water'.

The lights changed to a moody glow and the monotonous chanting of the word 'water' over and over again filled the theatre with atmosphere. As we poured our hearts into this tragic story of a fellow dying of thirst in the American western desert, I became dismayed when I noticed several people nudging each other and sniggering in the first few rows.

To be honest, on such occasions, the seasoned pro's first reaction is to check if his flies are undone but, alas, the sniggering got worse until, pretty soon, the entire theatre was in hysterics.

We went on singing, 'Keep a movin', Dan – don't ya listen to him, Dan,' at the same time looking at each other for some kind of reassurance, when suddenly, one of our lads whispered aloud, 'Look behind ya!' Gingerly we turned around and there, believe it or not, dangling by his tail from a batten at the top of the back-cloth, his head wandering searchingly, about three feet from the stage, was the snake!

We stood rooted to the spot while the audience continued to fall about laughing, thinking no doubt that it was part of the act. What on earth were we to do?

All at once the hubbub stopped and so did the orchestra as, from the wings, wearing her great cloak, strode Karinga and, in a loud voice reminiscent of Zsa Zsa Gabor, shouted 'Gentlemen! s'cuse me, please, for just one moment.'

We stood, speechless, our backs to the microphone, eyes glued to our new-found partner.

It was to the latter that Karinga turned her attention next; grabbing him by the neck she gave a sharp pull and his long body whiplashed through the air to the stage. She then picked him up and wrapped him twice around her neck, turned his head towards her and looked him straight in the fangs: 'You naughty boy,' she snapped, 'you naughty, naughty boy,' at the same time smacking him on the nose with her spare hand. 'Where have you been? You scare the life out of everybody but, worst of all, you spoil the nice gentlemen's act.'

She waited, as though expecting him to apologise, but he said nothing, so she went on, 'Don't you ever do that again – never!' One last smack on the nose and then she turned to us, 'So sorry, boys – do carry on.' Well, I ask you...you try following that with an impression of the Ink Spots!

It was through the boys that I had my first introduction to golf and, I must say, it's something for which I will be eternally grateful.

Two of the Ramblers, Dee and Pat, were quite keen on a game and for my first try coaxed me to brave the course at Bellisle, just outside Ayr in Scotland. I hired some clubs for half a crown, paid a further few shillings to play and, three hours later, I was hooked. Through the following years we played on a great variety of courses all over the British Isles.

I can't find better words to describe my love for this sport than the ones casually voiced by the great Bing Crosby, with whom I have had the great joy of playing a game. 'You know,' he said, as we strolled down the beautiful 18th fairway at Gleneagles in Scotland, 'if I were to give all I have in the world to golf, I don't think I'd begin to repay it for the pleasure it's given me.' I can't say the quote is accurate but there was no doubt whatever about the sentiment.

Like many other touring acts in those days, we had no cars or any such luxury so we simply travelled to all our theatrical engagements by British Rail, having loaded our personal baggage, our stage props and musical instruments plus, of course, three sets of rather battered old golf clubs, into the fishy-smelling guard's van.

When we played places like Newcastle, Swansea, Glasgow or Clacton-on-Sea, we made enquiries on our arrival as to the whereabouts of the local municipal course – knowing that these courses, which were run by the council, would be much less expensive than the private and more classy ones. We'd find the appropriate bus next morning and off we'd go for our three or four hours of bliss.

They were such happy times that I still can't visit those towns, or indeed hear mention of those same courses, without the memories of my first games flooding back to my mind. Sometimes, the bus would drop us three-quarters of a mile from the golf course and we'd happily walk the rest of the way without flinching.

Dee was a very calm and most reliable member of the group, both socially and musically. (It was he who met me on my arrival in London back in 1951 and, I'm pleased to say, we remained close friends for the rest of his life. 'Uncle Dee' as he was known in our household returned to Ireland in the mid-eighties, where he spent his final years.) His golf, however, was not quite so calm and he looked upon the striking of the ball as quite a vigorous affair.

His greatest asset to me, though, has always been his sense of humour. We were having a game one day, over on the Isle of Man, with dance-band leader, Bob Miller, who led the Millermen on radio for so many years. Bob took his golf quite seriously and, in spite of playing a good game, was never quite satisfied with his efforts.

We'd reached the 11th hole, which was skirted by the airport. Bob was not having too good a game on this occasion and was last to play off the tee. Dee prepared to play his shot, 'Ah, you see, lads, the idea is, emulate the masters,' he said in his impish Barry Fitzgerald style. 'Right now I'm thinking of Ben Hogan,' and with these words, he hit a superb shot down the fairway and smugly walked back to his bag lying on the ground.

'Right,' I said, as I waggled the club behind my ball, 'relax now, Val boy – think of – oh, Perry Como!' My shot went straight down the middle.

It was Bob's turn now and his giant figure towered over the tiny white ball. 'Let me see,' he muttered, 'I'm going to think of Henry Cotton.' He took a magnificent swing at the ball but sent it, slicing away to the right, over the fence into the airport!

Sadly gazing after the little white dot, Dee enquired, 'What happened to ya, Bob. Are ya sure ya weren't thinkin' of "Billy Cotton"?' Bob collapsed into fits of laughter and went to his bag for another ball.

Right from the first day I joined the four boys, I got used to seeing bags of golf clubs lying about the theatre dressing rooms. Like anybody else I was always tempted to slide one of the clubs out of its bag just to see how it felt.

'Don't swing the club indoors,' they used to say. 'You don't realise how long the thing is and you'll end up doing some damage.' Dee said, 'There are more lampshades in Britain broken by golf clubs than by Hitler's bombers.'

I stood in our dressing room at the Empire Theatre, Middlesbrough, back in 1952, a number seven iron in my hand. Slowly and carefully I swung the club back over my shoulder, watching its progress as it went and remembering my partner's advice. It seemed pretty safe to me so, confidently, I took a couple of smooth swings at the spot on the frayed carpet which I'd chosen as my imaginary ball.

'Nothing to it,' I thought to myself moving a little further to the right, just in case, my eyes glancing occasionally at the lampshade. Sad to say, I went a little too far to the right. My backswing reached a very early climax on this occasion, and a horrible sound of splintering wood, accompanied by a strange, distorted musical chord, stopped me in my tracks. My natural reaction was to return the club to its address position, but my efforts to do so only resulted in revealing one of the most horrific sights I can ever remember. There, suspended on the end of my seven iron, looking like a salmon which had just been speared, was my partner's pride and joy – his beautiful handmade guitar which he'd left leaning against the wall. A cold sweat covered my face and, at that moment, I'd have given anything in the world to have been guilty of simply smashing a lampshade.

So, if you're just taking up golf, I can't give you better advice as a beginner than to say, 'Don't swing the club indoors!'

We worked a lot in Scotland throughout the 1950s, doing seasons both long and short and finding that our set act, coupled with local material, helped us no end to cope with the problem of having to change our programme every couple of weeks.

I was fully occupied night, noon and morning during these engagements; not only doing the act, but also taking part in sketches and production scenes and preparing all the music for the following week's programme.

The first half of the show was usually closed by a musical 'scena' of some description, the producers drawing on many different sources, Scottish, Irish, French or American medleys or, maybe, a pot-pourri of melodies from the great musicals.

Once the choice had been made the appropriate costumes would be hired, as required, from a local theatrical costumier, arriving on Monday morning in time for the dress rehearsal.

Everybody made a mad dash to the large 'skips', or baskets (once the principals were suitably rigged out), hoping to get the pick of the bunch and praying for a decent fit. I wasn't too badly off since I was fortunate enough to possess a reasonable set of measurements – something that didn't apply to some of my colleagues. Our bass singer, Dee, for example, was short in stature and invariably found that his sleeves and trouser legs needed hems of several inches before he dared enter the spotlight.

The Merry Widow, we were told, was to be the first-half finale one particular week, so we all set about learning the many melodies that involved our participation.

Our costumes turned out to be pink suits, white shirts and black bow ties so, one at a time, we stood in front of the dressing-room mirror admiring, or ridiculing, our respective appearances, depending on how we had fared in the lucky dip. Sometimes a swapping session took place in the hope of some improvement but it rarely came to the rescue of our problem child, Dee.

Our tenor, a Welsh lad named Frank Davies, drew our attention to his shoes – the squeakiest footwear I've ever known – and it was suggested that he should restrict his movements on stage to those occasions when the music was at its loudest.

Frank, however, was not the kind to be easily subdued so we waited with bated breath on opening night. Halfway through the musical extravaganza, the soprano was to walk forward and offer her rendition of the beautiful melody 'Vehlia'; the four of us, together with other members of the chorus, tastefully scattered about the stage, as if we were enjoying a pleasant evening at the Ball.

The soprano began, 'There once was a Vehlia, the witch of the wood', while we stood, champagne glasses in hand, 'Ooh-ing' and 'Ah-ing' the musical background. At the end of the verse, the music gradually decreased in tempo, culminating in a sort of pregnant pause – as if the whole song was taking a breath.

It was at this point that Frank gently swayed forward on to his toes, then back on his heels, getting the maximum effect from his squeaky shoes. The poor lady soloist flinched, hesitated for a second or two, before sallying forth into the chorus. 'Vehlia, Oh, Vehlia, the witch of the wood,' accompanied, this time, only by a couple of shaky voices, plus lots of sniggering and snorting, as the remainder of the cast tried desperately to contain their laughter.

For the rest of the week this spot in the show was dreaded by one and all – as everybody waited for Frank's sound effects.

The following week we treated the audience to our version of 'Rose Marie'. This time, my partners and I joined the Mounties and what an assortment of Mounties we turned out to be! Dee finished up with a hat that was so big, it needed pages one, two, three and four of the *Daily Telegraph* tucked inside the rim to make it fit.

We spent most of our time in this particular production, marching about the stage and waving our fists threateningly at the audience, as we chanted, 'On through the hail – like a pack of hungry wolves on the trail. We are after you, dead or alive, we are out to get you, dead or alive,' Dee's hat, suspended above his head, looking more like an umbrella and giving the impression it could drop on to his shoulders at any moment, his head disappearing inside.

When the time came for the baritone and soprano to join forces for the familiar 'When I'm calling you-oo-ooo', we discreetly retired to the wings to await our next entrance. We were to march on, in single file, crossing over a ramp at the back of the stage partly camouflaged by cardboard cut-outs of pine trees. On cue, we entered with our usual 'On through the hail' etc., our numbers swelled, this time, by two extra members of the cast in similar Mountie outfits. As we reached the opposite side of the stage we would dash madly round the back, only to enter once again, hopefully, giving the impression of a long stream of redcoats.

It might have worked too, if it hadn't been for Dee's hat...there was no possible way the Royal Canadian Mounted Police could have issued one of those to every 'sixth' recruit!

When we were informed that our next undertaking would be a Dutch scene, we couldn't help wondering what on earth our contribution could be. The only obvious title that came to mind was 'Tulips from Amsterdam' so it was no surprise when the song and its stage presentation went into production. All the dancers stood in line across the footlights, holding in front of them a variety of cut-outs shaped like tulips. These had been treated with luminous paint and at a specified time the stage was thrown into darkness and the ultraviolet lights were switched on. This produced the stunning effect of a long row of multicoloured flowers swaying in time with the music.

At the end of the song the tulips were passed from one girl to the next, gradually disappearing into the wings, where the waiting stagehand would pile them in the corner.

Things were fine until, one night, the stagehand wasn't there. The unfortunate girl at the end of the line stood in complete panic as the tulips, one after the other, were thrust into her arms. 'Will somebody take these bloody things,' she shouted, 'I can't hold on to them.' Finally, the whole lot went crashing to the floor, bringing one tribute to Holland to a most undignified end.

However, once the girls had made their exit, the spotlights, blazed on to the centre of the stage to discover four 'Dutchmen', hands clasped behind their backs, strolling towards the footlights in time for the old song, 'The Jolly Brothers'.

When we reached the microphone we had, believe it or not, to whistle the thing. Now whistling on stage can be a highly dangerous and risky business at the best of times and, what with the collapsing tulips and squeaky boots, the producer, after one or two performances, had second thoughts...and suggested we 'la la' it instead.

Before leaving the subject of production scenes and costumes, I should mention that our greatest problems occurred in 'Scots Week'. You see, this always meant that, a pound to a penny, we'd be wearing kilts. Dressing in this garment is not to be taken lightly in Scotland as, understandably, they're very fussy that you should do the thing properly. However, the kilts arrived in such a variety of shapes and sizes that it was almost impossible to look anything but ridiculous. Poor old Dee ended up one week with a huge kilt tucked up under his arms and secured to his shoulders by a tiny pair of schoolboy's braces! If any true Scotsman in the auditorium had known of such blasphemy, I'm sure we'd all four have been deported.

Chapter Ten

I f entertaining happens to be your chosen way of life, one thing is pretty certain: you are destined to travel – and travel a lot! Your journeys may not take you far afield but, the chances are, they will be varied and frequent. My memories of towns tend to fall into the same pattern as those of golf courses I've visited; the better my 'score' the more pleasant my mental picture of the place is likely to be.

I've got wonderful memories of certain places that may not have the glamour, for example, of San Francisco, Rome or Mexico City. I'm talking of towns like South Shields, Ayr in Scotland or Great Yarmouth, simply because my first visits to those places worked out well and that's how I've continued to remember them. On the other hand, Exeter, which undoubtedly is a lovely place and where I made some great friends, brings a strange chill to my bones.

Way back in the mid-1950s the boys and I did a pantomime there and, for some strange reason, I found it almost impossible to find any decent digs. For the first week or two I just moved from one place to another, only to find myself leaping from 'frying pan to fire' on each occasion.

Since, at that time, I had a small bachelor pad in London and no family in England to spend my Christmas with, I decided to brave the holiday in my digs and be on the spot for our opening matinee on Boxing Day. I told my current landlady of my intentions and assured her I wouldn't be any trouble or impose on the family get-together in any way. 'Please yourself,' she said, 'but I'll be up to my eyes.' Well, I planned to drop a few hints around and maybe be invited to spend Christmas day with somebody in the show.

Alas, as I left the theatre on Christmas Eve, it looked as though I was sentenced to a day in my bedsitter with the gas fire full on and a generous supply of shillings neatly piled on the meter in the corner. Like a good boy, I got up and went to church on Christmas Day and – if you think that was a sacrifice – you only have to think of the alternative: a longer day in my room! I wandered back to my digs along the frosty streets and felt that, as I was on 'full board', I could at least look forward to a hearty nosh in the afternoon. Needless to say there was no telly, or anything like that, so it was down to *Family Favourites* on the radio and a last run through my part for tomorrow's show.

At about one o'clock, there was a gentle tap on my door and the landlady popped her head round the corner, 'Ah, s'cuse me, love – I'll be going out shortly, so would you like something to eat now? I won't be back till early evening.' She just stood there, half in the room and half in the hallway, and awaited my eager, 'Oh, yes, thanks. I'll eat now if that's OK.' The door clicked shut and she pattered off to the kitchen where the rest of the family were making lots of lovely Christmas noises. I cleared my table...and waited.

It seemed an age before the 'yoohoo' outside the door announced the big moment. I rushed to open it, knowing her hands would be occupied with the loaded tray. 'Here you are,' she said proudly, 'I've done you a bit of bacon and egg, a pot of tea and a couple of mince pies. Just leave the tray in the kitchen when you finish. I'll be off out now.'

'Bye,' I said and sat down...to what I think was the longest day of my life!

Next day at the theatre, just as I expected, I was inundated with belated invitations. 'Oh, you should have come to us' or 'We thought you'd be off to London, what a shame'. Yes, it was a shame – I'm better organised these days, mind you!

In recent years I've spent a couple of very happy seasons in the nearby holiday town, Torquay, and, as I've driven along the Exeter bypass on numerous occasions, I've smiled quietly to myself and can practically smell the bacon and egg wafting through my memory.

Considering all the hundreds of wonderful digs we had through the years, it really shows how strange human nature is, when the bad digs are always the ones you remember.

I'll give you a rundown on one or two memorable ones:

There was Liverpool, where the landlady ushered me into a sordid little room with a flag-stoned floor, an old iron bed, a plain wooden table, and in the corner an ancient kitchen sink that was absolutely filthy. On the Monday night, my supper was served in my room and the landlady went off to bed.

An hour or so later, as I lay there trying to sleep, I began to hear all sorts of scratching and scraping sounds coming from the other side of the room. Switching on my bedside lamp, I discovered several families of mice helping themselves to the remains of my meal.

Next morning, I complained to the landlady, and showed her the butter dish. 'Look,' I said, 'you can see the droppings and footprints all over the butter.'

She held the dish closer to her face, her eyes screwing up behind her thick glasses, 'Oh yes,' she whimpered. 'So you can.' Then, picking up a dirty knife, she calmly scraped the butter into a fresh cube and placed it back on the table, disposing of the scrapings on the side of the plate. 'Now then,' she said, as she headed for the door, 'will a bit of bacon be all right for your breakfast?'

Then there was Leeds where I was given what was obviously the children's room, with toys all over the place and Donald Duck wallpaper partly hanging off the wall. Halfway through the night, the bedroom light suddenly went on and I sat bolt upright in bed. Framed in the open door was a huge lady in a voluminous nightdress, sloshed out of her mind.

'Who the hell are you?' she screamed. There wasn't much point in telling her who I was at that stage. 'What are you doing in the children's room, you cheeky begger,' she shouted, as she proceeded to tear the bedclothes off me.

When I did offer some resistance, at the same time trying to explain why I was there, she stormed out of the room crying out, 'Will somebody come in here, there's a man in the children's bed.'

Next thing I heard was a man's voice trying to calm her down. A minute later, a gentle hand switched off my light and slowly closed my door. 'Sorry about that, son,' said the man's voice. 'Sleep well.' I never did discover who the woman was.

There was a parrot in our digs in Newcastle one time, who chatted away happily to all and sundry. His party piece, however, was as follows: every now and then, he'd make a noise for all the world like a man whistling for his dog. Quick as a flash, a big black shaggy dog would come charging through the door and stand in the middle of the room, looking around in amazement, as if to say, 'Did somebody call me?' The parrot, on the other hand, would simply shrug his shoulders, sway gently from one leg to the other, repeating over and over again, 'Silly bugger...silly bugger...'

I never could understand how the dog kept on falling for the gag time and time again. But then, it was theatrical digs, and maybe it was all part of a well-rehearsed double act, especially laid on for the guests.

We had lovely digs in Blackpool on one occasion. The only other guest apart from a Continental acrobat named Bob, and myself, was a charming spinster lady who worked as a teacher at a local school. We saw very little of her since our hours varied so much and we ate at different times.

One of the acts on the bill that week was a musical duo called Woods & Jarrett. Charlie Woods was a slim agile man, who tap-danced and sang. His partner, Bertie Jarrett, was a giant of a man who played piano, sang, and supplied most of the comedy in the act. They were both black, by the way.

One night, during the week, Bertie invited some of us around to his digs to sample his food and drink although I had to decline his kind offer, as I had quite a bit of music to finish for the following morning. However, Bob, the acrobat accepted, saying he'd see me later, and assuring me that he had a key for the front door.

Next morning I sat down to breakfast at the usual time.

'Where's Bob?' said the landlady. 'Is he having a lie-in?'

I said that I doubted it, since he was a very athletic gentleman and liked to get up early.

'I'll give him a shout,' I told her.

Popping my head round the corner of his door, I discovered that his bed had not been slept in.

'He didn't come home,' I reported, as I returned to the dining room.

'Oh yes, he did,' replied the landlady, raising her eyebrows in a knowing kind of way, 'and his steps were very heavy on the stairs too.'

'Well,' I said, getting down to my breakfast, 'he must have gone out again. I hope he didn't disturb the schoolmistress.'

'He couldn't have done that,' assured the cook, putting some fresh toast on the table. 'She went home to see her mother last night.'

Quietly, I left the table and slipped upstairs, heading straight for the schoolteacher's room. There, sleeping like a baby in the spinster's bed, was our Continental friend Bob.

The story unfolded at the theatre that evening. It seems that Bob, who was not used to drinking, had had far too much wine and passed out. Bertie decided to carry him home on his shoulders, had found the key in his pocket, opened the front door, carried him upstairs (hence the heavy footsteps referred to by the landlady), opened the first door he saw, discovered an empty bed, unloaded his passenger on to it, and left.

Can you imagine the situation, had the schoolmistress *not* gone to see her mother? At four in the morning she'd have woken up to find a six-foot-four black man standing in the room with a Continental acrobat on his back – the mind boggles.

Staying in different digs, and sleeping in different beds, can create all kinds of problems for somebody who takes more than a few drinks, as I'm sure people like commercial travellers would agree. You imagine waking up in the middle of the night, slightly the worse for wear. First of all, you can't remember what town you're in, much less remember, as you lie there in the pitch darkness of a strange bedroom, what the geography of the house is, and how to go about finding the bathroom.

This situation was a constant threat to a certain musician I once toured with on one-night stands.

One fateful night, after a heavy drinking session, he woke up, wishing that the bathroom was very close at hand. I was in another of three single beds in the same room, and heard his fumbling efforts as he tried to decide which side of the bed he should emerge from.

After stubbing his toe a few times, and letting out a couple of agonised cries, he seemed to find his goal. I heard the clicking sound of a door opening, and was about to settle back to sleep, when there followed even louder fumbling and moaning noises. It was time to come to his rescue so, climbing out of bed, I headed for the only light switch in the room, which was by the door.

The sight that greeted me when the light came on, caused me to fall on to the nearest bed with roars of laughter. There was our poor friend, in a desperate state of urgency, clambering his way out of the built-in wardrobe with the jacket of somebody's best suit draped over his shoulders.

There's one hair-raising 'town memory' of mine that dates back to February 1953; the town was Bedford. The boys and I were working in a show run by the comedy duo Morris and Cowley and were doing a week at the local theatre there, which was known as The County. Our duties with this travelling company included appearing in the opening and the finale, taking part as required in sketches, cross-overs, or any other production and, of course, doing our act 'proper' to close the first half.

At one point in the show, it was arranged that I made a special entrance as follows:

Harry Morris and Frank Cowley are doing a patter-spot at the microphone, centre stage. On a given cue, I enter from the wings, upstage right, wearing a mackintosh, trilby hat, horn-rimmed spectacles and carrying a suitcase. I walk diagonally down the stage and leave by means of some steps situated in the left-hand corner. I then walk along the front row mumbling the occasional 'Pardon me' as I step over people's feet, continue to walk smartly up the centre gangway and leave the theatre through the front of the house.

Harry and Frank stand and watch this in mock amazement. As I finally disappear through the exit doors, Harry says: 'Who was he?' and Frank replies, 'I forgot to tell you – this is a short cut to the station!' This interruption was one of many that took place during their conversation and, like the old 'I say, I say' routine, was very funny.

Now, as it happened, their double spot was immediately followed by the Four Ramblers singing a song and because of this the timing of my little 'walk-on' was critical. I just had time to run round the front of the theatre, down the alleyway by the side of the building and through the stage door. As I appeared backstage the boys would cue our intro by running on stage, clicking their fingers in tempo. I would then throw off my mackintosh, hat, glasses, don my guitar and rush on to join them, just in time to start the song which was with 'just' four voices with guitar and rhythm accompaniment. If I happened to be a few seconds late, the boys simply repeated the intro once more.

Over a period of several weeks we learned to time the thing to perfection. We did so in Bedford – on Monday, Tuesday, Wednesday, Thursday...but...Friday...tragedy!

On cue I made my entrance, walked downstage to the stalls and out through the front doors into the cold, drizzly, February evening. (Once outside, I'd learned to unbutton my coat and remove my glasses, to save precious seconds when I returned backstage.) As I began to undo my coat, a hand grabbed my arm and a drunken voice shouted, 'Hey, you! Is the show any good, eh?'

'Yes, great show,' I said desperately, trying to pull myself free from his grasp.

'Good is it?' he asked. 'Then why the hell are you coming out?'

'Look,' I shouted, 'I'm in a hurry, let go!'

Instead of releasing my arm, he grabbed my other arm with his free hand. 'In a hurry are you?' Then, looking at the case, he laughed, 'Have you robbed a bank or something?'

By now I knew that my partners would be getting desperate in the wings wondering where I'd got to, 'Let go!' I shouted furiously and swung myself away from him. He went flying as I made a mad dash down the alleyway towards the stage door.

Unfortunately, in my panic, I lost my balance, tripped off the pavement and went sprawling along the cobblestones on my face and hands. Then, as I tried to regain my balance, I twisted my ankle. I lay there for a few seconds in the mud and rain, wondering what on earth I was going to do. Eventually, I staggered through the stage door where my anxiously awaited return was greeted with a voice shouting, 'He's here!' Before I could say a word the three boys were on stage, clicking their fingers like mad, keeping an eye on the wings in anticipation of my appearance.

Little did they know that as they clicked away I was being helped to my dressing room to have my sprained ankle attended to.

When the lads eventually crowded into our room, I looked up. 'Sorry, fellas,' I said, 'you must have been mystified out there, wondering what was happening.'

One of the boys laughed, 'Not half as mystified as the audience,' he chuckled. 'After all, it's not often you see three fellows come on stage, click their fingers for a minute and then – run off again!'

While we were appearing for a week in Sheffield, I bought a new guitar amplifier and, as we didn't possess a car and travelled everywhere by train, I thought it wise to make a soft leather cover, with a reinforced front section to protect the loudspeaker.

Going on the scrounge backstage, I asked the stage manager if he could help. He took me snooping around the prop room and soon found a large display board made from some kind of plywood. 'How about this?' he enquired. 'The leather will cover it up and it's quite strong.'

I was very pleased and went about marking and cutting out a section about 24 inches by 18. The job done, I turned it round to admire the result and there, framed in my handiwork, was a picture of a very beautiful lady.

The caption read 'THE LOVELY LYNNETTE RAE AS ROBINSON CRUSOE'. When I looked at the bit I'd thrown away, it read: 'CAPTAIN AND MATE played by MORECAMBE AND WISE'!

Lynnette Rae was a most successful leading lady, with a great singing voice and two of the shapeliest legs in the business; and it became a standing joke from then on that, each night, I tucked her safely away inside my guitar amplifier.

One Sunday afternoon, a year or so later, we sat quietly in our digs browsing through the Sunday papers and waiting for teatime. A folded newspaper plopped into my lap. 'There's an article in there about your girlfriend in the amplifier,' Dee said, as he got up to stoke the fire.

I thumbed through the pages and found a tragic account of how this popular singing star had suddenly lost her voice while appearing in a famous show of the period, *The Five Past Eight Show*, a regular presentation at The Alhambra Theatre, Glasgow.

She had developed a cancerous nodule on her vocal chords, which meant that for a period of three years she was not allowed to sing a note and, for 12 months of that time, not even allowed to speak. She had to walk about carrying a notepad and pencil as her only means of communication. When, at the end of that time, the medical experts felt that the vocal chords were sufficiently rested and strengthened, the next vital step was taken. The affected area was cauterised after the surgeons had warned the patient that there was no knowing to what extent the voice would be affected, or altered. Luckily for her, the operation was a complete success although, as was feared, the top register of her voice was no longer true.

But there was no stopping the lady. In a short while, and in spite of a greatly reduced salary, she was back on stage using all her past experience and skill as an artist to sell her newly acquired singing voice.

I handed the newspaper back to Dee, and winked my approval: 'You see,' I boasted, 'I don't put just anybody in my amplifier. I know a winner when I see one.'

The fact was, I had never laid eyes on the lady – well, at least, not yet.

Now in my early thirties, I was living in a nice little bachelor pad, in a block of flats on the south-east side of London. One of my partners, Pat, also had an apartment in the same block, where he lived for years with his wife Oona and their children. Quite a bit of the act's rehearsing was done at our respective places, where we would perfect our intended contributions to *Worker's Playtime* or *Midday Music Hall*.

One of the great hazards of being in a vocal group is the difficulty of keeping the fellas together. Unless you are very fortunate, the chances are you will lose a member through either domestic problems or his ambition to make it alone. So many guys in groups find that there is pressure from their wives or girlfriends because of all the travelling involved and, unless the partner is very tolerant, he'll be nagged with the inevitable, 'Oh, you're not going away again' or, 'How long will you be away this time?'

The only thing that makes solo work any different, is that invariably the rewards are greater: you don't have to share the salary, not to mention the fact that you get personal recognition which you don't as one of a group.

During the period I spent as one of the group, I think we had about nine different people as members at various times. Again, when I was the subject of *This is Your Life,* I was faced with them all at once and felt a bit as if I'd been a member of a large male-voice choir.

I stayed with the boys for eight to nine years and enjoyed the work very much. Being with them prepared me for things to come in a way that I never anticipated. Learning to write music freely, reading vocal parts at sight, planning the running order of a stage act, singing harmony with other people, accompanying others on guitar, and, most of all, learning to accept the fact that there are other people involved who may feel very differently about things from you; were all invaluable to me when making my television programmes.

Luckily, I hadn't neglected my solo interests throughout my membership of the Ramblers. Quite early on, in fact just after *Riders of the Range*, Charles Chilton wrote a musical documentary called *The Story of the Texas Cowboy*. It told the story of the West right through its history and, in so doing, explained how the cowboy came into existence. It was illustrated with songs of the West, from round-up songs to rebel songs and from railroad songs to campfire songs. This programme starred Tex Ritter the American cowboy star and he, together with Charles Chilton, did the research in the area of music and songs.

I got a very nice job quite apart from singing and writing for the quartet. Charles told me that Tex knew hundreds of old traditional songs but had no music for them; my job was to go with Charles to Tex's hotel room, discuss the songs then, when Tex found a suitable one, he'd sing it through and I'd write it down as he sang it.

For some strange reason, Tex insisted on calling me 'Cal' and refused to accept the fact that it was wrong. Some nights we worked till all hours and got nowhere; he'd choose a song, sing it, I'd write it down – he'd sing a different version, I'd write that down too – he'd then say, 'I like the older version myself, but I can't think of it right now, so forget that one for the moment.'

This went on for hours and I finished up with a dozen songs, none of which we were going to use. If my face showed any sign of frustration or worry, Tex would smile and say, 'Now, Cal, don't you go gettin' all het up about these derned songs. They're only songs, boy. They'll still be there when we're all dead and gone!'

I must say that I always enjoyed Tex's sense of humour. He was always willing to adopt his 'movie cowboy image' at exactly the right moment and did so – to great effect and to everybody's amusement. Wearing his natty Western-style suit, high-heeled boots and stetson hat, he walked out of the front doors of Broadcasting House in London one afternoon, while I walked behind carrying my guitar case and a bundle of music. We'd just been doing some pre-recording and were heading for BBC's Aeolian Hall, in New Bond Street, for a further planning meeting with Charles, in preparation for the following week.

Tex hailed a passing taxi, which pulled in to pick us up at the kerb. 'Where to, guv?' the driver said, leaning out of his window. 'Can you take us to Aeolian Hall in Bond Street?' asked Tex, as the taxi driver smiled in recognition.

'With pleasure, sir,' he answered.

'Tell me, driver,' requested Tex, almost confidentially, resting his arm on the roof of the cab, 'how much are you going to charge for this service?'

'Oh, about two and six, sir,' replied the surprised driver.

Shaking his head, as though stunned by this outrageous cost, Tex turned to me, 'Sure wish I'd brought my horse, Cal,' he said, smiling all over his face.

That evening, after a long stint of musical research, Tex decided he wanted a late meal. Picking up the phone in his hotel room, he rang the number of his favourite Italian restaurant. 'Hello, Mama,' he shouted, 'this is Tex. Me and my friends want something to eat.' There was a pause. 'What do you mean, closed? Well, you can darn well open up again, 'cause we're on our way.' He put the phone down and picked up his hat.

He got a royal welcome at the restaurant, where a special table had been prepared. I sat fascinated while he and Charles discussed, in great detail, the history of the American West – a subject very dear to both of them.

The proprietress brought the menus and Tex ordered his favourite dish. I just gazed at some of the chef's offerings, as a friend of mine would say, 'like a crow looking into a bottle'.

'Are you having trouble with that menu, boy?' shouted Tex, slapping me on the shoulder.

'I'm trying to find something I've heard of,' I said, laughing.

Before I could say another word, Tex's rich Western drawl rang out across the room, 'Can somebody kindly bring an *Irish menu* for this boy here.'

Good job the place was empty!

Later, as we sipped our coffee, Tex asked me about my name –
Doonican. I told him that, on enquiry, I had discovered I was the only one
in Ireland and I'd traced the name back some 700 years – he was truly
flabbergasted by the idea of anything going back so far. Charles said, 'When
we leave here, Tex, I'll show you something really old.'

We got in the car and Charles drove to London's St Pancras Church.
It was now 3.30 in the morning and we stood at the gates, gazing at the
ancient building surrounded by gravestones and trees.

'That was built about the year 600,' said Charles.

Tex gasped, 'Six hundred?' he whispered quietly. 'God dammit, I never
knew there was anything that old.'

We kept looking.

'You see that old stone seat there, under the trees?' asked Charles. 'Well,
that's where the poet Shelley used to sit and work.'

We waited for Tex's reaction. After a long pause, it came. 'Shelley
eh?...hmmm...well you know somethin', I can quite believe that he
worked among the tombstones...'cause dammit, that guy sure wrote some
mighty dry poetry.'

Charles's next venture that was of interest to us was a musical picture
of the American Civil War. He called this one *The Blue and the Grey*. It
turned out to be of extra special value to me personally, as he kindly
booked me to do three solo numbers with the orchestra. This was, as it
happened, my first solo appearance on British Radio and the first time I
was to hear my own name announced rather than the group.

I used to sing with the guitar quite a lot, just for the fun of it and to keep
my hand in. Thanks to *The Blue and the Grey*, I began to ponder over the
possibility that, maybe, there was a future in it for me.

My own first appearance on the West End stage was a strange one indeed.
It took place back in the mid-1950s, not, incidentally, in front of a regular
theatre audience, but to a completely empty theatre. It took the form of a
rather demoralising audition.

The Four Ramblers were given the chance of putting their talent on the
line, one sunny afternoon, by accepting an audition for the privilege of

appearing in an important summer show. The impresario on that occasion was none other than the ex-bandleader and stalwart of the entertainment world at the time, Jack Hylton. The chosen place of execution was to be the stage of the gigantic London Coliseum.

We arrived, eager and much too early, having rehearsed our party piece for days and nights on end. The selected sample of our wares, by the way, included an array of vocal group impressions, with a strong comedy element; at least, that's what we thought.

At 3.30pm we stood in the wings, as a solitary microphone awaited us, centre stage, in the white circle of the spotlight. A few rows back in the stalls sat the great man, his glasses glinting in the reflected light, his hearing aid placed firmly in position, his hands, in which we had placed our hopes, fiddling with a neatly folded newspaper.

At last we settled ourselves round the microphone. I played the introduction on my guitar. Ahead of us lay our well-rehearsed tribute to the Mills Brothers, the Four Freshmen, the Inkspots, the Four Lads. Early encouragement came from the sight of Mr Hylton tapping his daily newspaper against his knee in time with the music. We looked at each other and winked. Three vocal groups later, however, the winking had stopped, as one of our lads nodded towards the stalls. There sat our would-be employer, his newspaper now open and propped against the seat in front. He was reading. Then as we desperately tried to inject a last bit of enthusiasm into our impression of the famous French harmony group, Les Compagnons de la Chanson, singing 'Little Jimmy Brown', came the unkindest cut of all. Slowly Mr Hylton raised his free hand and removed the hearing aid.

Right through my working years with the Ramblers, I'd learned, more out of necessity than from any kind of musical inspiration, to supply whatever musical backing we needed. For the modest club and cabaret work in London I wrote out accompaniments for piano, organ, bass and drums plus the odd front-line parts for trumpet, sax and so on. Within our own circle of professional friends I gained the misguided, if rather flattering, reputation of being a bit of a whizz kid with the music.

Our business affairs at that time were in the hands of Syd Royce, who in my eyes, at least, was a caricature of the typical agent. He was short, plump, very bald, and spoke with a rich, London-Jewish accent. He organised our working lives from behind a desk in his tiny office in Charing Cross Road.

Syd rang me one day and asked if I could do him a favour. He'd taken under his wing a young comedian/ impressionist, still in his teens, and was anxious to try him out in a few cabaret rooms in town. The young 'hopeful' had 'got his act together' and needed some music. I was offered the sum of eight pounds for the job, and it was arranged that I'd pop along to the office some days later, and see what could be done. A few laughs were in store as I mounted the rickety steps to Syd's tiny place of business above a music store. The young Peter Kaye (not to be confused with the modern comedian of the same name) was already there, bubbling with enthusiasm and sounding more like a fellow just about to open in Las Vegas. He wore a very smart suit, neat white shoes and his *pièce de résistance*, the very latest thing in trilby hats, à la 'Ol Blue Eyes' himself.

I took a seat, my guitar to hand for checking keys, etc., plus a few sheets of music manuscript and a well-sharpened pencil. It was high summer at the time, and in spite of the fact that all the office windows were wide open, it was stifling hot, and dear old Syd mopped his bald pate incessantly.

He couldn't wait for me to see what his young 'find' had in store.

'Go on, son,' he encouraged, 'show him the opening.' Then, turning to me, he said, 'This is sensational.'

'What's the first song?' I enquired, wanting to write something at the top of the page.

'"Mack the Knife",' they both said in unison. Syd turned to the lad: 'Go out on to the landing, son, then you can make a proper entrance.'

Peter buttoned up his jacket, adjusted his precious hat to its most jaunty angle, then, giving the brim a final flick with his fingers, disappeared on to the tiny landing. After a short pause filled with expectancy, he began shouting instructions to me as to what the introduction should be.

'Barrah bah rahbah pow,' he sang, sounding like a one man impression of the entire Nelson Riddle Orchestra playing the intro. The door burst open, and he leaped into the room, clicking his fingers in tempo.

'Oh the shark has...barah bah.' This was accompanied by a few fancy movements. 'Pretty teeth deah...parah pow.'

I sat there, pencil poised, wondering where all those imaginary brass figures were to come from when Nelson Riddle was substituted by a badly played piano and drums. Peter stopped.

'Now, at this point,' he said, 'I take off the hat and send it flying into the wings.' There followed a demonstration.

'Parah...pow,' he repeated, removing the hat and, with a sophisticated flourish, he sent it flying like a 'frisby' across the tiny office. Sadly, in his state of ecstasy, he'd forgotten that all the windows were open. Away went the brand new hat, sailing out over Charing Cross Road, landing like a flying saucer on the roof of a passing trolley bus, never to be seen again.

Peter went on to find great success in television and theatre, and the last time I saw him, the story of his new hat was the highlight of our get together.

Chapter Eleven

As the 1950s neared their end, the time was slowly but surely approaching when I felt I should make some kind of fresh move in my career; I honestly thought that the group had about come to the end of the line. Just then, we were asked to join a concert tour with Anthony Newley. Tony had made a couple of very successful British musical films and, within months, was topping the charts with one hit record after another: songs like 'Do You Mind', 'Personality' and 'Pop Goes The Weasel'.

The tour was a sell-out, opening at the Palace Theatre in Manchester. Travelling up there by train, we took our usual taxi drive to the stage door. Passing the front of the house, all four of us almost yelled in unison: *'Hey, look at the bills!'*

There, across the middle of the colourful posters, we read: 'The Glamorous Singing Star LYNETTE RAE' – the lady in the amp! Inside, I saw her for the first time as she stood on stage taking her rehearsal, wearing a white trouser suit and looking suntanned from a recent tour of the Far East. She really looked worthy of anybody's amplifier.

Our greetings were brief, Mr Newley doing the honours. At that particular moment, in fact, she was much more concerned about some bass parts which were missing from her music. 'I'm sure Val would do them for you,' one of my partners offered.

Within minutes I was scribbling out substitute parts, for which she was grateful, kindly offering to brew us some coffee in her dressing room. We'd made a friend.

Later in the week, Tony announced that the next day was his birthday and a celebration was to take place at a local club which he'd hired for the evening.

As I prepared to leave for the party, Miss Rae appeared through the stage door. 'What's keeping my taxi, Albert?' she asked the doorkeeper.

'Don't know, Miss Rae, I ordered it ages ago,' he answered. 'They must be extra busy tonight.'

I put my window down, 'Would you like a lift, Lynn?' I offered.

I gave her a lift to the party – about the best move I ever made. A couple of years later, we were married.

Funnily enough, it was at that party that another big decision in my life was made. One of the light-hearted items on the agenda was that all the artists in Tony's show had to get on the stage and do some sort of solo performance – their normal stage acts weren't allowed. Singers did impressions, dancers sang, musicians did magic and so on. Since I was a member of a singing group, I was forced to part company with my three partners and try to go it alone.

Frankly, it didn't present too much of a problem for me: I simply got a Spanish guitar, sat on a stool and sang a little Irish folk song – nobody in the company had ever seen me do this before so, it came as quite a surprise to them.

My offering went down very well, not least with Tony Newley, who later spoke to me over a drink, 'Have you ever thought of doing that kind of thing on television and radio?' he said.

'Oh, not really,' I answered. 'Mind you, I used to do it in Ireland years ago so it's nothing new to me.'

'Well,' said Tony, 'I think you've got something there, singing the songs, explaining what they are and so on. I'd give it some thought if I were you, you won't want to stay in the group forever!'

That's what prompted me quite soon afterwards to ask for a BBC audition. Funnily enough, I didn't see Tony again after the season finished, but in 1973 my show followed his into the Prince of Wales Theatre, in London, for a season. When I arrived in my dressing room I found a note on the mirror, 'Hi, Val, who'd have thought you'd be following me into this dressing room. Love to Lynn.'

Tony did come and join me as a special guest on one of my shows in the 1980s. We shared a little medley of his hits from the fifties and sixties. A nostalgic moment indeed.

By the end of the Anthony Newley tour Lynn and I had, as it were, grown accustomed to each other's faces, so we continued to meet quite regularly when we returned to London. She lived with her mother in a flat at Hendon and I soon became a constant visitor. Many's the time I would sleep in some makeshift bed huddled up on the kitchen floor – this was about the warmest spot in the apartment which unfortunately had no heating. We'd go for long walks and talk a lot about our respective lives in this strange profession of ours and, even though at that stage we didn't say too much about the future, I think we both had the feeling that something very permanent was on the horizon for us.

It was about that time that the Ramblers were booked for yet another tour to the American bases in Germany. It was only then, really, that I felt the first pangs of love for Lynn – I just didn't want to go. Needless to say I did go and pretty soon was up to my eyes in the old routine – by now, only too familiar to the four of us.

A week or so later found the act both living and working on an air force base in a place called Hahn. It was a pretty godforsaken spot, especially for us civilians, who did not have our activities planned for us day by day. Time crawled by and, hour after hour, I could be found lying on my bed writing endless letters and cards to Lynn.

One chilly afternoon I went for a long walk around the camp area. I simply wanted to kill time while taking in a sightseeing tour of the place. Making my way through the rows of prefabricated dwellings, which from the air must have looked like a huge Lego set, my mind was busy with my personal problems.

At a time when wedding bells were ringing in my ears, was I wise to leave the act and try it alone in this precarious profession of mine? Both Lynn and I were 'fatherless', so to speak, which meant that no moral or financial support would be forthcoming in that direction. We were both in our thirties by now, so would I be wiser to find myself something more secure for the future?

I stopped at an intersection to allow a gigantic American car to go by, and there facing me on the corner opposite was a tiny Catholic church. I crossed over. The door was 'on the latch' (as they would say at home in Ireland) so I went in to rest for a bit.

As I whispered my way through a quiet prayer, I could hear the sound of a man's voice gently singing the melody of a popular song of the day. It echoed almost secretly through the tiny building and appeared to be coming from nowhere. Curiosity got the better of me so on tip-toe I made my way up towards the altar rails. I could now tell that the singing was coming through the half open door of the little sacristy in the corner. Through the crack in the door I saw, sitting cross-legged on the floor, a man dressed in fatigue trousers, sweat shirt and gym shoes. He was busily doing some repair work on a piece of fishing tackle, while accompanying himself with his vocal refrain.

He sensed my presence and turned his head, 'Hi there, fella,' he greeted me. 'C'mon in.' So saying, he rose and began to pour some coffee. 'I'm Father Delos, the Catholic chaplain here.' And he handed me the coffee.

I introduced myself, explained what I was doing on the base, and he promised to come along and watch the show one evening.

Within 10 minutes or so, we were well into the coffee and he, poor man, was listening to my life story. Like any good father confessor he summed up my problem:

'If this lady is as lovely as you say and you both want to be together, then you don't want to spend your time thinking about your doubts. Don't wait until you have a million dollars before you make your decision.'

But first, let me take you back briefly to the early 1950s in order that I might introduce you to some other very special people in my life.

When I arrived in London to join the Four Ramblers, I was promptly thrown in at the deep end of the music hall. Week after week we trudged about the country going from one provincial theatre to another to appear on various variety bills.

We never achieved any major recognition as a 'Top of the Bill' act over the years, but even though I say it myself, we took a bit of beating when it came to closing the first half of the show. Thank goodness our services were called upon to perform that function with sufficient regularity to keep us all away from the dreaded Labour Exchange. Looking back we closed the first half and, I hope, paved the way for such notables of that period as Jimmy James, Norman Evans and Max Wall, not to mention 'youngsters' like Frankie Howerd and David Whitfield.

It was always considered a real prize to be invited by a promoter to support one of these celebrities for a whole tour. Since it was customary to work each town for an entire week, this kind of offer could keep you going for weeks, or even months. I hadn't been with the Ramblers long before such an offer came along. It involved an extensive tour with a show called *The Radio Party,* starring those two real veterans of the British music hall, Morris and Cowley.

Harry Morris and Frank Cowley (they took their name from the old car Morris Cowley) were brothers, and married to two sisters Edith and Doris. Harry and Edith, or Chubby as she was affectionately known, had a daughter, Peggy, and they travelled everywhere together as a family. Peggy was a singer, but it was in the capacity of company manager, compère, and a 'comedian's labourer' that she worked with *The Radio Party.*

There certainly was a real family atmosphere among the resident cast of this particular company. We travelled as one, all assembling at the local railway station each Sunday morning, where we'd help to load our equipment aboard and head for the next venue. Some weeks our ranks would be augmented by a 'special guest', giving the whole thing a boost at the box office. These guests, I recall, ranged from such seasoned campaigners as Monsewer Eddie Gray, of the Crazy Gang, to a young, or should I say very young, lad named Des O'Connor.

Harry, Chubby and Peggy befriended me since I seemed to be the only one who didn't dash off to the bar between entrances. I'd sit in my dressing room knowing full well that within minutes of the fall of the curtain a gentle tapping on the door would announce that 'tea was brewed'. I'd then retire to Number One and become one of the family.

Yes, we were to become such close friends that on our periodic sojourns back in London, I'd spend at least a couple of evenings a week at their flat in nearby Peckham. This relationship blossomed through the 1950s, and indeed continued long after I'd left the group. In fact when I took my first tentative steps into a solo career, it was Harry who kindly performed the temporary duties of personal manager and professional adviser. He secured auditions, interviews and later broadcasts for me, always offering to come along with me should I need any moral support. His performing days were nearing an end, but in spite of his very demanding commitment as secretary of the Grand Order of Water Rats, he gave me all the time and attention I needed. Peggy was by now (in addition to her own career) my part-time and unpaid assistant, attending to my business affairs.

As anybody who ever tried to get in touch with me during my years on television may know, she ruled the roost, running both my office and fan club for many years. By the way, Morris and Cowley's real family name was Birkenhead.

When I finally decided to leave the Four Ramblers, it was Harry who contacted the then BBC producer, Richard Afton, requesting an audition to appear in one of his many shows. The result of his efforts brought the offer of an interview, which I was delighted to accept.

I was instructed to go along to a church hall in the Shepherd's Bush area where Richard Afton was rehearsing and, on arrival, was told that he would see me as soon as he found a few minutes to spare. I sat and watched the rehearsal for what seemed like hours until, at last, they broke for tea. The cast were sitting around in groups, chatting and having some refreshments, when I received the message that he was ready to see me.

Richard, cigar in hand, as ever, beckoned me to come up to the top of the room. Then, with my foot resting on an old chair and the guitar perched on my knee, I sang one song after another. When I finished he just looked at me, smiled and said, 'Good...very good. I'll give you a TV spot all right,' and before I had time to acknowledge his kind offer, he added, 'As a matter of fact...I'll give you several spots.' And he did!

He was presenting a show called *Beauty Box* at the time – it was a women's magazine show, with beauty and fashion interests. I was to be the musical interlude which was my first experience as a television entertainer. The orchestra on the show was conducted by Alyn Ainsworth and the arranger was Ken Thorne – a man who was to be another of the guardian angels in my life.

There's nothing like a fruitful audition to drive you on to further efforts so, with the taste of success in my mouth, I moved again. I wrote to BBC radio requesting an audition that, to my surprise, was immediately granted and soon I was making my way to Broadcasting House guitar in hand and ready for action. This time I stood in an empty studio, facing a BBC microphone, while the people who were to judge my efforts sat in another studio – neither party had the faintest idea what the other looked like.

I sang a little American folk song, next 'Delaney's Donkey', then 'Scarlet Ribbons'. Again I was passed as fit for radio, and told that, when the right slot came along, they would contact me. Pretty soon a letter arrived, informing me that they had something that might fit the bill and suggesting that I should go and speak to the producer. It appeared that the 'Woman's Hour' programme was off the air for a short summer recess and the BBC were preparing all kinds of alternative ideas to fill the time slot: one of the suggestions was that a selection of solo artists should do 15-minute shows, each one making his, or her, contribution on a specific day.

I sat at home and worked on my 'Wednesday' spots; I finally decided to write short stories that would be linked together with songs. The idea worked well and led to more and more radio including some vocal spots with the Frank Chacksfield Orchestra on Sunday afternoons.

With my new solo career starting to take off, Lynn and I started to make plans. But both of us, strangely enough, had so little time off that we found it extremely difficult to pick a suitable day for our wedding. We decided on Sunday 1 April 1962; as I had a radio show on the Monday morning, no honeymoon was possible for the moment – that would have to wait until we could afford it.

Collecting our joint savings together, we put all we had into buying a house. Neither of us felt that it was important to have a posh wedding and we managed without the fancy cars, flowers, cake, and all that. In fact, Lynn and her mother stayed up most of the night making bridge rolls and things, and we invited only our closest friends.

When they had all gone home we settled into our own house and began our life together. The next day I went to the studio to do my radio show, a married man – of less than 24 hours. Not very romantic, you might think, but we felt that we had what we wanted: each other and a home that we could afford. Lots of fancy cars and cakes and flowers were to come later.

With all the confidence of a newly married man, I did something that took the nerve of Old Nick and, even now, I feel a slight twinge of embarrassment when I think about it. I wrote to the man who, at the time, was Head of Light Music at the BBC asking if I could have an interview (it was a bit like going to see the managing director of a large industry, looking for a job on the assembly line) feeling quite sure that I'd be passed on to a producer. However, to my great surprise and pleasure, the interview was granted.

Mr Baines was seated behind his desk, my letter in front of him, when I came into his office. He told me to take a seat. 'Now then, what can I do for you, Mr Doonican?' he said, looking very friendly. He must have thought me quite naive when I began my story, the sole message of which was that I was looking for work – just like anybody else.

'Well,' I began, I paused for a few seconds, then went on, 'What I really need is a series of radio shows.'

He looked at me for a few seconds, an expression of surprise on his face, no doubt thinking to himself, 'Well, at least the lad's got nerve,' then, picking up my letter, he said, 'According to this, you've been doing some solo work on radio so, let's just say that I'll make some enquiries and then we'll see what we can do.'

He pushed his chair back and stood up, so did I. Having thanked him very much, I left.

A few weeks later, I was somewhat shattered to receive a letter from the BBC offering me an engagement as resident singer on a proposed series of light music shows called *Dreamy Afternoon*. It was to take the form of 13 half-hour shows, consisting of light orchestral items played by Sidney Bright and his music, interspersed with songs from yours truly. Some of my contributions were to be performed with guitar accompaniment, others with the orchestra.

Some of the songs I sang were unusual, to say the least, and needed an explanatory announcement. So, after a week or two, the producer suggested that it might be a good idea if I performed this duty myself.

After a bit of a shaky beginning, I got used to it and, in time, enjoyed it. By the time the series came to an end, my little bits of chat had become quite an acceptable and important part of the show.

This fact became very clear when I received a letter telling me that the show was returning for another series and this time, it was suggested, I should introduce the entire show. I accepted the offer, and the name of the programme was changed to *Your Date with Val*.

So, from singing the odd song, my duties had now been extended to writing and introducing the show, reading out letters and requests and even welcoming the occasional guest. For all that, I received the sum of eight guineas. This was, however, one time when the old adage, 'money isn't everything', applied in no uncertain manner. That series, which was to run for some 120 shows, changed my life. I shall never forget its producer, James Dufour, without whose encouragement and advice I'd never have found the same success on radio.

One little anecdote connected with those shows is, I think, worth relating. Before starting on *Your Date with Val*, I thought it a good idea to write a special signature tune. Having done so, I scored it for three guitars, went to a recording studio, and recorded all three parts – the finished product was most effective.

On the fateful day when it was to 'take to the air', the recorded signature tune was dispatched to the studio. Alas somebody goofed and the vital piece of tape went to the wrong studio, away on the other side of London. 'It might get here on time,' said Jimmy Dufour. 'In the meantime, can you just whistle it through with your guitar, just for timing.' This I did. When transmission time came round, the elusive tape had still not been located. 'Sorry, old lad,' said Jimmy, 'you'll just have to whistle some more.' I did so, on the air, everybody seemed to like it, and that's how it stayed. The tape hasn't arrived yet!

Working on my own was a very comfortable feeling to me. I'm not suggesting there was any strain with the boys, quite the opposite, but there is always the restrictive possibility in a group of having every decision vetoed from four angles. The comfort came from the complete freedom of being your own judge of what to do and how to do it.

★

Slowly, but with great care and forethought, I began to piece my new solo career together. I had my radio show now and hoped I could do it well enough to be asked to continue with it but, I also knew, I'd have to extend my work in other directions, as the radio show paid very poorly.

James Dufour was aware that at the time I had been befriended by one of the country's top arrangers, Ken Thorne, and was having private tuition from him in orchestral arranging. At home I'd sit in my then unfurnished spare room with an old piano doing arranging exercises in the form of orchestral scores of various tunes, each one for different instrumental groups. I'd arrange, for instance, 'Somewhere over the Rainbow' for a small group of strings and rhythm, then do it again for a small jazz group and so on. These scores I would take across to Ken's house in North London.

First we'd have a game of golf together and then, after a light snack, retire to his music studio where he'd go through my work step by step. He explained, however, that the only way I'd learn to know if my arrangements really worked was to hear them played, so my next move was to do something about that.

It was customary in those days that if you sang a song that was on the 'plug list' in a radio or television show the publishers would, in most cases, supply you with a special arrangement. If the score had to be done by a freelance writer, rather than a staff arranger employed by the publisher, then a fee of about eight guineas would be paid for his services. The BBC, on the other hand, had to foot the bill for the lesser-known songs or, at least, the ones that were no longer hot property from the pop charts. Based on this existing situation, it was agreed that both the BBC and most of the publishers would pay the fee direct to me if I did the scores and, incidentally, write out all the orchestral parts as well.

From then on I planned well ahead and did a couple of scores every week, always taking them to Ken who cast his expert eye over them before they were finally committed to orchestral parts.

The whole thing worked like a dream for me and, pretty soon, I was turning out scores quite rapidly – with less and less disastrous results. Ken filled me with confidence and his patience and kindness played a very big part in my early success. He was to arrange and conduct the music for several of my television shows and recordings in later years. The result of my initial arranging efforts changed the fee for my radio show, from eight guineas overall, to 60 pounds or more. The work was very hard and time consuming but then, it's difficult to achieve worthwhile results in any other way.

Incidentally, the reason the programmes were called *Your Date with Val* was that most people were absolutely convinced that nobody would ever remember the name 'Doonican' and so it would best be ignored. Therefore, for two years, I had no surname as far as the radio listeners were concerned. I was either 'that Irish fella who sings on such and such a morning' or 'that Val bloke on the radio'.

Housewives wrote and said, 'What's your proper name?' 'What do you look like?' and so on. I read these letters out over the air and asked them to guess but never made them any the wiser. Their efforts at describing me were great fun – most of them thought I was an old bearded guy like Burl Ives since, as they explained, young singers wouldn't do 'Delaney's Donkey', 'Paddy McGinty's Goat', or old songs like that!

Fortunately, the shows went down great with a lot of people and, pretty soon, I was asked to show myself in cabaret – mainly at functions organised by people who enjoyed the radio programmes. Things were now beginning to happen: I'd learned a lot from the listeners' letters, which I read with great interest and the overall opinion was that I was down to earth, uncomplicated and, as most people put it, 'ordinary'. I hope I still am!

One morning I had a call from an agent whom I knew through the Ramblers and who booked many acts for the US bases in Britain. Most of these places would have floor shows on a couple of nights a week and acts were constantly heading out of London in mini-buses, or cars, to such destinations as Chicksands, Bentwaters, Lakenheath, Mildenhall, Woodbridge and Upper Heyford.

After a short run-through with a pianist at a prearranged meeting place, you'd set off with the prospect of doing one or two shows like the ones I described we did in Germany. Anyway, the agent in question had heard me on the radio and being somewhat surprised that I was no longer with the act said, 'I was wondering if you'd fancy doing one or two spots on your own?'

My previous experiences of US floor shows might lead you to think that I'd turn the offer down flat but, as I knew I had to start somewhere and put a stage act together, I said I'd think about it. 'Now listen,' he said, 'I have a show at Bentwaters on Saturday. It's already fully booked but, if you'd like to have a trial run, I'll give you fifteen quid for two spots.' I hung up, and then sat down with a piece of paper, working out a few things I could do – bit of chat here, an Irish song there – until I had about 16 to 20 minutes ready; enough, I thought, for all emergencies.

He gave me a great welcome on the Saturday and the piano player went through the music that I'd so laboriously written in the meantime. He promised me an extra two quid if I used my own car and took the pianist. 'OK,' I said and headed for Bentwaters – little did I know what was in store for me.

As I entered the NCO club, my heart almost stopped – there, hanging on the wall, was a big orange poster: 'To Nite, 9.30pm, "The Val Doonican Show" starring Ireland's Top Entertainer Specially Flown Over For the Occasion'.

I turned to the piano player, 'Did you know about this?'

'Yeah, sure,' he replied, 'I honestly thought you were a bit low on music but, don't worry, you'll be OK!'

How I got through that show I'll never know. I sang everything – they loved Irish songs, so I did loads of them. Next morning, the agent rang me. 'I'm told you were fantastic last night, son,' he raved. 'Do you want to do some every weekend? From now on, I'll double the money!' Well, I won't tell you what I called him but I took double the money and within a couple of months my act was really beginning to take shape. I've always believed that if you're going to make mistakes and learn by them, you should try to do it where it won't be noticed too much.

I still never quite knew what was in store for me, so I entered all the clubs with great trepidation. One night I went to a club at Mildenhall where almost all the clientele were black. On that occasion, I found myself billed as 'Ireland's Leading Soul Singer'; you can imagine the thrill 'Scarlet Ribbons' gave them – I was lucky to get out alive.

Fate lent me a hand on another occasion though, at Brize Norton, near Oxford. Heavy snow had fallen all day and I had grave doubts about risking the journey at all. My car was a little Austin A40 and I'd agreed as part of the deal to give someone a lift. When I arrived at rehearsal I was told that the 'someone' I was taking would be a quartet of black singers, called The Manhattan Brothers – two of whom were bigger than my car.

With great misgivings I set off in the driving snow through the West End, on to the A40 road to Oxford – my car bursting at the seams. The Manhattan Brothers were enjoying the snow and tried to reassure me, 'Don't worry, man, it'll be fine.' Well, as it happened, the snow got worse and worse and, pretty soon, there was little if any road to be seen at all. Twice I drove straight on to a roundabout, because I couldn't distinguish it from the snowdrifts, but my good friends just got out, lifted the car, like a dinky toy, back on the road again and off we went.

Thanks to those four guys, we got there, did the show and got home. Next day we discovered that we were the only show that made it that night to any of the US bases – and, I'm sure, the only ones who got paid.

I had begun to tackle a few other cabaret jobs by now and was making my way into the northern circuit of clubs. Manchester had an incredible number who booked live entertainment and, because of the kind of act I did, I tried hard to choose carefully.

I went to a club one night that boasted non-stop entertainment culminating in a star act. The whole evening's entertainment was centred round a wrestling ring and the running order was: wrestling bout – act – wrestling bout – act – tag bout – act and so on, for hours. Quite early on I was told to get ready, the wrestling bout ended, the ropes were un-dipped, then in I staggered with my amplifier and guitar. The audience, thank God, took me as an opportunity to refill their pint glasses, and I honestly don't think that anybody at all even knew I was there!

Chapter Twelve

I n between my cabaret and radio shows, I was still able to spend a good deal of time at home, which was marvellous. By then, we were expecting our first baby and naturally I wanted to be with Lynn as much as possible. We turned our spare room into a temporary music studio: I managed to find a second-hand mini piano and attached a draughtsman-style worktop to its front, then, perched on a stool, I'd get on with the job. All day long I'd work on my arrangements for the orchestra, and having completed the scores, change my role to that of copyist and proceed, with pen and ink, to write the separate parts for the members of the orchestra. It really was a chore at times, but once again, it turned out to be of great value in the years that followed.

In July 1963 our first little girl Siobhan was born. When she was only 10 weeks old I was asked to go away to Paris for a month, to entertain the US Forces over there. Lynn and I talked it over and decided that we'd all three go since the weather was so nice. We had a super month, wandering in the parks, round the shops, sitting in Montmartre watching the artists while we ate huge ice creams. We were proper tourists until night time when, once again, I faced the unpredictable audiences.

London wasn't the easiest place for me to find work either. Cabaret and stage work were areas where at least for the moment 'I wasn't very well-in'. One of the rare dates to come my way in 1963 was a week at the Astor Club in Berkeley Square. My salary was to be £90. A fortune, you might think. I thought it a bit too good to be true until I received the full details. I was to do six shows at the Astor, usually at about one o'clock in the morning. I would also do three extra performances at the Columbia Club in Bayswater Road (a house for the exclusive use of officers of the

American forces) and a further three spots at the Douglas House, situated a block further along (a similar establishment for the non-commissioned officers). I agreed to do the 12 shows for the above-mentioned fee. At least I knew I'd have that income coupled with the money from my radio show and arranging: all in all a great week.

What I didn't know, however, was that fate was about to intervene in the form of one of the great tragic events of that decade. Just as my marathon week got underway, the media announced the shattering news of John F. Kennedy's assassination in Dallas, Texas. All entertainment for the American forces was immediately cancelled, and I was informed with much regret that my salary was to be adjusted 'pro rata', as it's described.

I'd like to digress for a moment and relate one of my favourite show-business stories, which the previous incident brings to mind.

In the old days of the music hall a variety show is booked to appear at a certain small provincial theatre. Monday morning rehearsal finds one of the 'turns' down with flu and with no hope of appearing that week. The company manager desperately rings the head office in London and asks for assistance in the form of a replacement. After much to-ing and fro-ing nothing has been achieved and panic begins to take over. The theatre manager, who is a local chap, thinks he might have at least a 'beggars can't be choosers' kind of suggestion.

'There's an old guy who lives here in town who used to tour the Halls years ago,' he tells the relieved company manager. 'He was a magician of the old school, he's in his seventies now, but I'm told he's helped out several times over the years.'

'Really? How did he go?' queries the company manager. 'I mean, can he still do an act?'

'I honestly can't say,' answers the theatre manager. 'It was before my time, but I do know he's stepped in before on a few occasions.'

The old pro is contacted, his dress suit dusted and pressed and his ancient props retrieved from the attic. He is given a six-minute spot in the first half of the bill.

Well, his appearance is a disaster: he forgets his words, he drops his props, and messes up his illusions. After the interval a shattered company manager comes into his dressing room, only to find him quietly packing his little stage basket. The manager forces a smile as the old man turns to greet him.

'Wonderful spot, thank you very much,' the visitor says, having prepared his script carefully. The old man nods his thanks, a knowing look in his eye.

'We're very grateful to you,' the manager continues, 'but believe it or not the show is now running a bit long...so, I feel awful about it, but we don't really need your spot.'

The old man continues his packing. 'That's perfectly all right, sir,' he says softly. 'It's no trouble at all.'

The manager stands there rubbing his hands with embarrassment. 'That's very understanding of you,' he says, relief written all over his face. 'Ah, I don't quite know what to do about money.' He waits.

'Well,' says the old fellow, 'there's twelve shows for the week, and in the past I've always been paid *a twelfth.*'

I managed to get through my six contracted performances at the Astor Club, however, in spite of all the problems that particular room presented. It was almost impossible to achieve any lasting attention through the barrage of conversation, coupled with the sounds of food and drinks being served and consumed. I knew the room of old, of course, since my days with the Four Ramblers. We played the club several times during that period and even though we had each other as moral support it was invariably a daunting experience. I was out there on my own now and felt the full brunt of opposition. One good thing about the Astor, however, was that many important people went there for late-night sustenance. Agents, managers, producers, not to mention well-established entertainers from round the world would sit and watch your efforts at point-blank range. I recall doing our act one night in the 1950s while the great Danny Kaye sat at ringside. I might add that he was very attentive and made us feel good.

There was another memorable occasion when the American comedian Alan King was present, accompanied by a visiting group of singers/musicians, the Trenniers. They were appearing at the London Palladium for a week, and had called in at the Astor after their show. A fascinating incident occurred.

First, I should give you an idea of what the nightly ritual was from the floorshow point of view. After an evening of dancing and dining, things usually got underway with a dance routine featuring the Astor Girls. This would be followed by the first part of the entertainment, such as a stand-up comedian. There would be a little pause, then a second appearance by the girls. By now the room was normally packed with latecomers, the time being around one o'clock in the morning. The top of the bill then filled the final 40 minutes or so of the evening's entertainment, to the accompaniment of the resident band led by Johnny Silver. There were, in fact, two bands which alternated throughout the night, the second one featuring Latin American-style music.

I had still been with the Four Ramblers at the time and as we took our final bows, I remember that the club's resident host would leap on to the stage and take the microphone.

'Thank you, thank you,' he would shout enthusiastically. 'Come on, ladies and gentlemen, let's hear it for the Four Ramblers.' His encouragement would coax every last bit of appreciation out of a sometimes indifferent crowd. 'Weren't they fantastic, ladies and gentlemen? The Four Ramblers, and they will be appearing every night this week.' He would then go on to announce the coming attractions for the next month or so. Before there was time for the room to lapse back into a blur of conversation, he'd continue:

'But the night is still young here at the Astor Club, so we want you to let your hair down and *enjoy yourselves.* Yes, *enjoy yourselves…*'cause *it's later than you think…*' This was the cue for Johnny Silver and the boys to play the musical pick-up for what I can only describe as the longest medley of old chestnuts imaginable: '*Enjoy yourself, it's later than you think…Toot toot, Tootsie, goodbye…I'm Alabamy bound…Nothin' could be finer than to be in Carolina…The stars at night, are big and bright…Maammy…Maammy, the sun shines east…*'

And so it went for some 15 minutes, or at least so it seemed, with everybody dancing, singing and, like the man said, *enjoying themselves.* It really worked, too, and remained a part of the room's 'tradition' for as long as it existed.

Then followed another interlude when everybody who was anybody among the patrons would be introduced in a blaze of spotlights and applause. The celebrities in question would stand up and bow their acknowledgment, wave to one and all, then sit down.

As is the case in many nightspots, if there was the slightest inkling that some extra encouragement might possibly inveigle the said party to come to the stage and say hello, or say a few words, or even sing a few bars of a song, then no effort would be spared. Many well-known entertainers had done so over the years and set a kind of precedent, so who could blame a management for trying?

On the night in question, the old routine went as usual. We did our act, took our applause and retired to our room. The medley of songs came and went and the introductions began. Some 'lesser names' were announced to begin with and then came the 'biggies'.

'Ladies and gentlemen, making a welcome visit to the London Palladium, a very talented group of musicians and singers from the United States...will you meet and greet the fabulous Trenniers.' There was wild applause and cheers as the lads rose for a few brief seconds to accept their welcome to the club.

'And seated right at the same table, we're proud and pleased to introduce one of the world's great comedy talents...Ladies and gentlemen...the fantastic, the fabulous *Mister Alan King*.' Alan King's reception really was something, his popularity in London at that time being one of the talking points among entertainers. He'd appeared for a short season with the great Judy Garland not so long before and made the most amazing impact with the public and press alike.

The applause went on and on while Alan took bow after bow, waving an open hand in appreciation, the customary huge cigar perched between the first and second fingers. He sat down for what he hoped was the last time, turning his attention once again to his guests. The applause continued, reinforced with shouts of 'More' and 'We want Alan'. Mr King tried to ignore it, hoping it would go away, but it didn't. Mein host took what he felt to be the most logical step.

'Would you like to just step up here, Alan, and say a quick "Hello" to the folks?' Alan King declined, waving once again, this time adding a shake of the head as if to say 'Thanks, but no thanks'. The clapping and cheering at last began to fade, when from one of the tables a somewhat disapproving voice shouted, 'Oh come on, mate, stop playing hard to get...tell us a few jokes...it won't cost you anything.'

There was a smattering of self-conscious laughter mixed with a sort of shocked silence, and all eyes were on Mr King. He positively glared at his critic, then slowly but deliberately rose from the table and approached the cabaret floor. Once again the room rang with applause while the atmosphere changed to that of an audience watching a gladiator entering the arena. He bowed to the crowd, shook hands with the host and calmly took the microphone. Now, I can't claim to be able to quote word for word what went on in the next 10 minutes or so, even though I can look back on it as a memorable occasion in my career. The script should read something like this:

(It will help, of course, if you are familiar with Alan King's work and style, that kind of Jacky Mason-ish way of talking, his whole script seeming to consist of complaining about everything. It will also help to know that his assailant in the audience was a short, bald-headed, middle-aged but prosperous-looking man, who sat at a table for two, accompanied by a very young, very busty hostess.)

Alan: 'Good evening, ladies and gentlemen, and thank you very much. I'd like to say that it's good to be here, but I can't, because it's not. It's good to be in London. I enjoy London.

'I'm over here doing some television shows...I've been in the studio all day, rehearsing...I got through at about eight o'clock...went back to my hotel and had a shower. I then picked up my friends the Trenniers at the Palladium and we thought we'd go out and have a quiet meal...Then some joker told us to come here...*(pause).* I've just had the worst meal I have ever eaten...some clown of a waiter has spilled the most expensive whisky in England all down my pants...and now, just to round things off...you've got me working again.'

Interruption: 'Oh come on, you'll make me cry in a minute…tell us a few jokes.'

Alan paused, puffing on his cigar, then thoughtfully gazing at the burning end the way cigar smokers do.

'Do you think we could have a little light on this guy over here for a moment?' he said, slowly approaching his victim. The spotlight operator duly obliged. The two men were face to face for the first time. Alan looked him over, then looked at the young companion. With a wicked smile on his face he moved his gaze around the room, as if inviting everybody to take a look. The crowd were loving it.

'Good evening, sir,' he began. 'Would you mind telling me your name?' The man, looking very annoyed, refused to be drawn.

'Come on now, what's your name? You're not going to tell me, are you? OK, tell you what, I'll have a guess. *(Steps back, places his fingers on his pursed lips in a thoughtful pose and smiles.)* Let's call you Louis for now, all right? Now, tell us, Louis, what do you do for a living?'

(Man stares in silence.)

Alan: 'You're not going to tell me that either, so I'll have to guess again? *(Stands back as before and sizes up his new partner.)* I'd say, Louis, ah, you make ladies' skirts in a little back street somewhere in London, am I right?'

(Man looks more determined than ever to take no part in the encounter, but the expression on his face indicates that he could happily strangle Mr King. At this point Alan King leans on the edge of the table and faces the audience.)

Alan *(waving his cigar like a conductor's baton)*: 'I'd like to give you a hypothetical situation, ladies and gentlemen. I want you to imagine that Louis here has had a really tough day in his little factory in that back street in London. At nine o'clock in the evening he locks up his front door and gets into his car to go home, when up comes Alan King. "Just a minute, Louis," I say. "Before you go home I'd like you to give me fifty ladies' skirts." Now, I wouldn't be a bit surprised if Louis told me where to go. He'd have every right to say, "Why the hell didn't you come during the day when I was open for business?"' *(Pauses and turns to the man.)* 'Isn't that what you'd say, Louis?' *(By now, nobody expects the man to answer, so their eyes go back to Mr King. He then delivers his crushing tag line.)* 'But you haven't heard the worst yet, Louis, not only do I want the fifty ladies' skirts after working hours, *but I want them for nothing!'*

The room erupted to what was the best part of the evening's entertainment as Alan prepared to retire to his table. Then he turned once again to the man and delivered yet another stinging remark.

'I do hope I haven't embarrassed you too much, Louis,' he said apologetically, 'especially in front of your daughter.'

He returned to the cabaret floor, thanked the patrons, and then to everybody's surprise, introduced the Trenniers once again. The boys rose as one and joined him at the microphone. He turned to the pianist and asked for a chord in E flat. Together they closed the proceedings with a marvellous version of the old classic 'Up a Lazy River'.

Some years later I watched him do his full cabaret act at Caesar's Palace in Las Vegas. He was quite superb that evening, but for me the name Alan King will always mean that little interlude at the Astor Club all those years ago.

One of the people who popped in to see my efforts at the Astor that week in 1963 was a well-established agent and manager, Eve Taylor. I didn't know she was there, but a message came through to my dressing room asking if we could have a chat. We met at her office in Regent Street the following week and agreed that we'd sign a working contract for a six-month trial period. Up till then, as I mentioned earlier, I hadn't had a manager.

We decided that if all went well we'd continue our relationship, and if not, then there would be no point in forcing the issue. Eve was to be my business manager for nearly 20 years. She said she would fix me some badly needed dates in London and arrange for some people to come along and watch me work.

The first booking I got was a week at Quaglino's Restaurant in Duke Street. I was to do two shows each evening, the first one in the upstairs dining room, and one much later in the basement nightspot known as the Allegro Room.

There were never many people there for the earlier show. This had little or nothing to do with me, of course, since at the time I wasn't a name and couldn't be expected to attract customers in to dinner at a certain time. I worked to about 15 people on some evenings.

On one of those very quiet nights I was doing my act sitting on a stool, all the tables in front of me being empty except for one solitary lady eating alone. She was very elegantly dressed in a neat blue and white suit. She looked, then ate, then sipped her wine, then looked again, then smiled, then ate again. I sat there and sang, and chatted, and smiled. I think she probably felt a bit sorry for me actually, because she clapped much more than I deserved.

As I sang a gentle little song with the guitar while the resident quartet on the bandstand took a breather, she put down her knife and fork, giving me her full attention. Then I noticed she was pointing in my direction, her eyebrows raised fractionally as though she was surprised. I just sang on. She did it again as if warning me of somebody sneaking up behind me. I gave a sideways glance over my shoulder, but was none the wiser. She did it again, this time with a bit more feeling. Slowly, I felt a warm glow of sweat forming on my forehead. 'Your flies are undone' was written crystal clear in the gesture which she repeated once again. It's amazing, but even though I calmly went on with the song, she knew that I knew. She put her hands down and her face broke into a knowing smile. I sang the final verse of the song on autopilot while I madly worked out my plan of action.

She applauded as I played the finishing chord, and I discreetly slipped off my stool. While I was sitting there doing the song, I had no way of confirming my worst fears, my guitar being between me and the problem. Calmly, I took a bow, acknowledging her approval, and at the same time taking a crafty look. All was painfully true. I turned to the band and walked to my amplifier as though to adjust the controls, then, in a flash (if you'll pardon the expression) all was put right. Returning to the mike I continued as my new-found friend looked, then ate, then sipped her wine, then smiled.

Nowadays, I don't think that the same situation would cause so much embarrassment. We've all become so much more blasé and broad-minded about such things. And yet I doubt if there is a man who would honestly tell you that such an oversight would not make him feel uncomfortable. All I can say is, if it is going to happen to you, try not to be on the stage, sitting on a stool, singing a romantic song. It's the indignity of it all.

The Allegro Room downstairs was completely different, being patronised by a young 'debbie' sort of set. They talked and giggled all the time I was on. Not at my act, I hasten to add – they were just having fun amongst themselves and knocking back lots of 'champers'.

My final performance on the Saturday night was chaotic. A party of some 20 or so teenagers were having a whale of a time celebrating somebody's birthday. Just as I was pouring my heart out in some ballad or another, they chose that precise moment to burst forth in several different keys: 'HAPPY BIIIIRTHDAY DEAR CAROLIIIINE...HAPPY BIRTHDAY TOOOO YOOOU.'

They concluded their vocal tribute to Caroline just as I sang the closing lines of my song. A ripple of applause from the audience mingled with the raucous good wishes for the birthday girl. Having waited for a suitable lull in the proceedings, I began to introduce my next offering.

Suddenly from the furthest corner of the room boomed a loud, husky and instantly recognisable cockney voice.

''Ere, he's bloody good this bloke...wot ya say 'is name was?' The entire room turned to see who was making the row.

'Eh, Val wot?' he continued, oblivious to the attention he was getting. I envied his ability to achieve such silence, and wished at that moment I could be in the audience watching him instead of the other way around. It was one of my favourite comedians, Jimmy Wheeler. When I thought of the countless occasions I had stood in the wings of provincial theatres watching him in action I felt ashamed of my longing to ask him to shut up.

''Ere, quiet, you lot,' he bellowed at the gaping patrons. 'Give the man a chance...now belt up.'

A deathly hush fell on the room and I picked up where I had left off. The remainder of my act was a joy by comparison. Even Caroline's party gave me a hearing. In fact the only interruption I suffered was from dear Jimmy, who continued to shout his approval of my efforts. I was delighted to have a chat with him afterwards: he'd 'had a few', but his genuine concern for a fellow performer was heart warming.

Lynn had been on stage since she was 12 years old when she played Cinderella in pantomime – the first engagement of a long and successful career that was to end when she agreed to be my wife. Everybody knows how difficult it is supposed to be to get the theatre out of your blood; so I wondered, from the start, if Lynn could really manage it.

She swears, to this day, that she has not missed it at all, which seems incredible – but, you know, the answer could be this: our work is always a strain and, no matter how long you've been doing it, you worry to some degree about every single show you do. Some people I've met in my career become physically sick before important performances but, in time, learn to accept it as a fact of life.

If, somewhere along the way, they find that they can give it up the feeling of relief, I'm told, is quite enormous. Lynn admits now that she loves the feeling of security that comes from not 'having' to do it any more.

We had been married for about two years when an old agent friend got in touch with her. He was responsible for booking a certain 'room' in the West End where Lynn had worked over the years and was a great favourite. As it happened, he was wondering if, for old time's sake, she might consent to appear there for a month? We talked it over at great length and finally agreed that it might do her good to get back into harness for a few weeks and see how it felt.

At the time, we were living in a very nice semi-detached house in south-east London with Siobhan, who was now seven months. Together we worked on Lynn's act and I was able to help by writing any new music that was required.

When rehearsal day came around I took her to the club and it was wonderful to see her get such a warm welcome back from everybody there. I was so glad that she'd decided to do it. Our plan was, as I was only working on the occasional evening, that I would take her to work each night, wait outside in the car while she did her stuff and then take her back home again. Her mother was to look after Siobhan. I had lots of music to write for my radio shows, so I made myself a little portable table that clipped on to my steering wheel and, while Lynn was in the club working, I was out in the car doing likewise.

I had a floorshow to do at an American base on the Friday of the first week of Lynn's season, so we arranged a cab for that particular night.

However, it wasn't to be – when Friday came round, I had the most dreadful sore throat. I rang the agent to tell him I couldn't work and, even though he was distressed by my cancelling so late, he could not deny my sincerity when he heard my croaky voice on the phone.

I told Lynn that I could take her to work after all. We sat down and had dinner about 7.30pm, then we put little Siobhan down for the night and Lynn started to get ready.

Later, I sat in my mobile music room outside the restaurant, while Lynn worked as usual. Suddenly, there was a tapping on the car window and I looked up to see the maître d'hôtel beckoning me to open my window.

'Sorry to bother you, Val,' he said apologetically, 'but there's a phone call for you at our reception desk.'

'Phone call for me?' I said, surprised. 'Who is it?'

He hesitated for a second or two, 'Ah, it's your doctor, I think,' he replied, shrugging his shoulders.

Puzzled, I removed my music desk and climbed out of the car.

It was, indeed, our family doctor, 'Hello, Val,' he said, rather quietly, 'this is Aubrey. Ah, I just wanted to ask you to come straight home, when Lynn finishes tonight.'

'Is there something wrong?' I asked.

'Well, little Siobhan's not too good...I'll tell you all about it when you get here,' he replied and hung up.

After the show, Lynn had met some friends inside and wanted me to join them for a drink. I used my sore throat as an excuse for wanting to go straight home but Lynn didn't seem too happy about that, so I had to tell her what Aubrey had said. We were very worried.

We drove down the Old Kent Road towards our home without saying very much and, when we eventually turned into the road where we lived, our hearts missed a beat. There, parked outside our house, we saw a police motorcycle.

As we rushed into the house we were greeted by our dear friend, Aubrey, who stood there with tears in his eyes – we both knew, at that moment, that our little girl was dead.

It was what is commonly known nowadays as a 'cot death' and, as Aubrey told us, there was nothing anybody could do about it; she was dead when Lynn's mother went up to make an hourly check on her.

That was the most shattering moment of both our lives and, at the time, it seemed we would never get over it. But, in many ways, I think we learned something very important and it brought us even closer together.

It happened at a time when things were going exceptionally well for me and we could easily have taken all our good fortune for granted. It was almost as if God had reminded us that we should enjoy the good things of life – but never forget that we only have them on loan! He's been extremely generous with His loans ever since.

The Doonicans in the early 1930s – except for Dad, who wasn't keen on photographs. From top left to right: Ned, John, Nancy, Mom, Nellie, Mary, Lar, me and Una.

Our dear Mom in all her glory!

This is the only photo we have of Dad.

Left: Patrol Leader Doonican around 1940.

Right: Early dance band gigs.

Left: My first proper guitar.

Right: Earning a crust with Bruce Clarke in Bray, Co. Wicklow.

With the members of the Four Ramblers, Peter Roy, Frank Davies and Dermot Buckley, in the 1950s.

On the set of *This is Your Life* with Lynn.

Meeting the Queen Mother with Victor Borge, Terry Wogan and Ken Dodd.

Left: Lynn guesting on one of many BBC music shows.

Right: Lynn starring at the Garrick Theatre in London.

Left: The lady of the amp!

Left: Gone Fishin'!

Right: Siobhan, our first-born child – she is sadly missed.

Left: Time to stop and smell the flowers.

Right: At home with Sarah and Fiona.

Left: Bumper birthday doodle for Fiona – the girls called these 'Doodlicans'!

Right: 'Fore!'

Left: Happy summer seasons with Arthur Askey.

Right: Dave Allen joins the TV show for the 1965 and 1966 series.

Not only Val but also Dud!

'Walk Tall' – Cilla tries for the low notes.

Walking tall.

With the lovely Twiggy.

With Howard Keel – the perfect gent.

Strictly no dancing with Bruce.

Above: Straight down the middle – with Crosby and Tarby.

Right: Tuba duet with Herbie Flowers of the group Sky.

Left: An alpenhorn lesson from Roy Castle.

Right: Magic moments with Mister Perry Como.

Left: 'Farmhouse in Provence'.

Right: 'Wash Day'.

Left: 'The Old Blue Door'.

Right: 'By Ashford Castle'.

Right: 'Pencil Drawing of Dad's Hut'.

Left: 'Morning: The Red Barn'.

Right: 'Afternoon: Irish Homestead'.

Left: 'Evening: On the River'.

Right: Breaking in my new caddy – Max Bygraves!

Left: Lynn with Harry Secombe at the Palladium in about 1960.

Right: Getting to know Australia.

A very happy family day – Fiona's wedding in 1995.

The last remaining Doonicans – Nancy, me, Una and Nellie – in 1995.

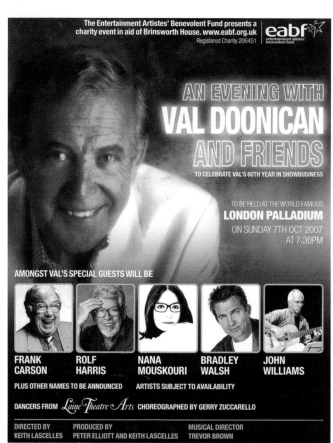

Celebrating 60 years in show business at the London Palladium in 2007.

Duet with Nana Mouskouri at the Palladium.

'Jake the Peg' – Rolf Harris performs one of his best-loved songs at the Palladium.

Rehearsing for the Palladium show with guitarists John Williams and Max Brittain.

Me and my girl.

The Doonican family – (from top left to right) Sarah, Lynn, me, Fiona, Scott and Bethany (photo by Julian Parker).

Chapter Thirteen

I could feel those first waves of success in the air somehow; my phone was constantly ringing with people I hardly knew asking me to take part in this and that: 'Would you like to do a guest spot on the Rolf Harris radio show?' or 'When you're in Manchester in a few weeks' time, how about doing a guest spot with the NDO?'

The BBC Northern Dance Orchestra under its then conductor Alyn Ainsworth was probably the best-known broadcasting band at that time. They had starred in an enormously successful television programme – which they previously did on radio – called *Make Way For Music.* It was a band show in the true sense, featuring wonderful arrangements by such stalwarts as Alan Roper, Pat Nash and members of the orchestra, like Syd Lawrence. The show was introduced in a lovely humorous style by the witty Roger Moffatt who created most of his script at the expense of the band, the conductor, the producer, and of course, the poor vocalists Sheila Buxton and Roberto Cardinalli. Another member of the band who should be mentioned here is flautist Bernard Herrmann. He was to take over the baton from Alyn Ainsworth, and used to be seen on your television screens, in appropriate costume, directing the pit orchestra for the very popular *The Good Old Days.*

They were regular broadcasters doing their own show on radio and working as the resident orchestra on many light entertainment projects put out by the BBC. The ones I took part in were mainly at lunchtime, *Midday Music Hall,* or *Easy Beat.*

Similar shows were going out in London at the Playhouse Theatre on the Embankment, one of the more popular of which was *Parade of the Pops,* featuring the music of Bob Miller and the Millermen. It had much the same formula as the Manchester show with popular singers, male and female, coming along as guests.

And so my date book began to fill up and my bank balance did likewise. I still look back over the years, you know, and ask myself why things happen at a particular time for no particular reason. Now people wanted me to take part in various programmes, doing precisely the same material they had turned down the year before.

I'm sure you'll recall the old *Tonight* shows on BBC back in the 1950s with Cliff Michelmore, Alan Whicker, Fyfe Robertson, Derek Hart and many others. One of the regular features of the nightly transmissions was a closing song, to guitar accompaniment, from people like Cy Grant, Robin Hall and Jimmy McGregor or Noel Harrison. I managed to obtain an audition and sang a cross-section of the little ditties which I was later to feature in my radio shows with great success. At that time, on that day, for some reason, they were not right for the show. Now, some four or five years later I was accepted as a safe bet. It really is a weird and wonderful way to make a living.

In the end, 1964 turned out to be a memorable year for Val Doonican. It all happened, as they say, and in a big way. In fact, so hectic did things become that I find it difficult to look back and put it all in sequence.

A BBC television producer named Travers Thorneloe was given the task of putting together a short series of musical shows that he entitled *Singalong Saturday*. Those two words sum up the shows: they were transmitted on Saturday nights, the musical content was very much in the singalong category, and I was invited to be the host, introducing the items and leading the singing. I was to be joined on the set by the Adams Singers of *Sing Something Simple* fame, plus a small group of musicians. The audience was in vision, and sat in a semicircle of raised seats, in front of my little podium. It was all very new to me, and I loved every minute of it. I included many of my own style of songs, which I chose with great care, endeavouring when possible to have a little chorus where everybody joined in. I can't honestly say whether the whole thing was in any way successful, but I certainly must have made the right impression from the BBC's point of view, because it led to other things.

Also, about that time, a Manchester-based producer named John

Ammonds was doing a series called *Barn Dance,* from the Dickenson Road studios in Manchester. He'd noticed some of my efforts on radio and television and contacted me, suggesting that we should meet and have a chat. On his next visit to London, we met in the basement canteen at Broadcasting House and, over a cup of BBC tea, we discussed the possibility of my doing a guest appearance on *Barn Dance.* My kind of songs, with guitar accompaniment were ideal as far as John was concerned, and he booked me for about six appearances. At that time I had no idea how important my relationship with John would be to my future career.

He was one of the busiest producer/directors in the north, having had much success with such shows as the Harry Worth series and several stints with Michael Holliday. *Barn Dance* was not, as one might immediately assume, a programme of country and western music, but was inspired more by the music of Northumbria. It featured a troupe of country dancers, a traditional dance band specialising in that kind of folk music, and a wide range of guests. The studio at 'Dickie Road', as it was affectionately known, was decked out to look like an old farm building, complete with bales of straw, farm implements and cart wheels, strewn about the place. There was a loft above the main set area, where some of the boys and girls would perch, their legs dangling over the edge. The show was hosted by a local lad, the well-known journalist and broadcaster, Brian Redhead. I shared the solo honours with such people as Roger Whittaker. Needless to say, everybody wore casual clothes in keeping with the setting, the dancing girls sporting pretty summer dresses and the lads wearing check shirts. Lynn looked around the shops and found me some casual things for my wardrobe. Since I tended to look best in those kind of outfits anyway, the 'Doonican Sweater' tag was soon established and became firmly associated with my television personality.

Just about then, the tragic news of the death of singer Michael Holliday shocked the entertainment world. Mike was, I suppose, the first of our home-grown casual entertainers, although from what I gather he found the whole business of performing in public quite a strain. However, he did what he did very well and paved the way for people like myself.

By now, I was also enjoying what I considered to be great success working the clubs up north although, in most cases, it involved 'doubling'.

This means that you were booked to work two different clubs for the same week. You might be appearing at a club in one part of Manchester, Leeds or Newcastle at nine-thirty then, packing your gear into your car, you'd drive to another part of the city, where you would fulfil the other half of your night's work. This was hard graft but, by my standards, the money was very good.

Now one thing I had dearly wanted to do, since about 1960, was to make records. So, armed with some tapes of my radio shows as a kind of audition, I'd attended interviews with several of the bosses of the various companies. All of them listened patiently to me and my tapes but, the answer was always the same, 'We don't think there would be a demand for your style of singing in the present-day market.'

I must say I quite understood how they felt about it and I'm sure, had I been in their position, viewing the material in the charts, I wouldn't have taken the gamble either!

Knowing that my work was being handled full time by Eve Taylor, who had made international stars out of Adam Faith and Sandie Shaw, helped me to concentrate more than ever on the artistic side of things. Eve rang me one day to say she'd had a call from David Jacobs who, aside from his TV and radio work, spent much of his time as a leading light in the running of the charitable group 'SOS'.

David was organising a big charity concert at the De La Ware Pavilion, Bexhill-on-Sea and, to my great pleasure, wanted me to appear on the same bill as people like Vera Lynn, Dickie Henderson, Frankie Vaughan and a host of others. The reason for David's interest was that he had become aware of the popularity of my radio show even though, he admitted, he had no idea what I looked like or – what my performance would be like.

I agreed to do the show and travelled down to Bexhill on the Sunday afternoon to rehearse in preparation for the big evening. My spot in the show came immediately after the opening music and my allocated time was 10 minutes. The audience was lovely and my part of the show went fine. I returned to my dressing room where I had a meal provided by the organisers before journeying home. I couldn't stay for the festivities planned for the late evening because I had an early radio show the next morning.

I was interrupted by a tapping on my door and before I could speak, because my mouth was full, the unexpected visitor popped his head into the room – it was Dickie Henderson.

'Hi there,' he said.

I stood up and shook hands with him.

'You know,' he went on, 'I've just been standing at the back of the theatre watching you, you were great!'

'Thank you very much,' I replied, delighted with myself but not quite sure of what to say – I'd never had a compliment from a star before.

Dickie was in a hurry so, as he left the room he said, 'Quite honestly, I'd never heard of you before but, you've got it – and I'll say this – if you're not a star this time next year, there's no justice in show business.'

Well, what can you say to that? I couldn't make up my mind whether it was a lot of old flannel, or not, while at the same time I told myself that he didn't need to come around to my room if he didn't mean it.

Soon, I was on my way home feeling very satisfied with my night's work. Lynn woke up when I came in and I told her she'd better be prepared for the fact that, very soon, she would be sleeping with a star!

The following week I was booked to do a week's cabaret at the Piccadilly Club in Manchester City Centre and one of the things I had to do, before making the trip, was to have my hair cut. It was my usual practice to have it done at the Barber's Shop in the Piccadilly Hotel in London whenever I was in town and I rang the barber, Jack Lee, and went in on the Wednesday.

While Jack was cutting my hair and we were indulging in the usual hairdresser-customer chit-chat he suddenly changed the subject, 'Oh, by the way,' he said, looking at me in the mirror, 'I had a fan of yours in here yesterday.'

'Really,' I replied. 'Who was it, Marilyn Monroe?'

'No, seriously,' said Jack waving his comb about, 'it was Dickie Henderson – said he was going to tell Val Parnell about you – loved your act on Sunday night.' So, it wasn't the old flannel, he did mean it!

It was at this stage that things began to fall into place. The very next day the man sitting in that barber's chair was Val Parnell – probably the greatest impresario this country had and the man responsible for, among other things, the TV show *Sunday Night at the London Palladium*. As Jack was cutting his hair, he related the story about Dickie and me. Mr Parnell said he hadn't heard of me but showed interest.

As for me, I went off to Manchester at the weekend and booked into my digs for the week. The manager of the club, Jerry Harris, quite staggered me, midweek, by telling me that a gentleman named Alec Fyne was in town and would be popping in for a few minutes. Now, this particular gentleman happened to be Val Parnell's talent Scout and booking manager and, at that time, knew absolutely nothing about the 'barber's shop quartet'. He sat and watched me while he ate and had a drink and, afterwards, sent me his compliments.

Next day, on his return to London, he mentioned me to Val Parnell who, by now, was becoming sufficiently interested to ask where I was working next, in case he decided to come and have a look for himself.

The following week was perfect: I was at The Jack of Clubs, a restaurant owned by a family called Isow, which was situated right in the heart of Soho. I was appearing there, once nightly, at about eleven-fifteen. Somebody up there loved me again that week, for on Monday, Tuesday and Wednesday, the audience were not very interested but – on Thursday, they were wonderful. Mr Parnell chose to have a look at me on the Thursday.

My performance was as good as I could make it and I had nothing whatever to complain about. After I'd finished, I had a message that the great man wanted to speak to me. He was so charming to me and not at all like the impresarios you see in the movies – none of the 'I'm gonna make you a star' bit or anything like that, just a straightforward compliment. 'You were great tonight,' he said smiling, 'very refreshing stuff. I think you'd do well on *Sunday Night at the London Palladium*.'

'What!' I said, sitting bolt upright. 'Are you serious?'

He turned to Alec Fyne who was with him at the table, 'What vacant dates have we got, Alec?' he asked.

After a quick flick through his diary, Alec Fyne suggested the last Sunday in May or the first Sunday in June.

Mr Parnell looked at me, 'What do you say then?'

'Oh!' I said. 'Yes, I can do both those Sundays.' It was meant to be a silly joke from an embarrassed but very excited man. As it turned out – I did both those Sundays.

Arriving at the Palladium on that momentous day, my music under my arm, I wondered whom to approach in the hubbub of such an important occasion.

I needn't have worried, however, as everybody on the staff, from George Cooper the doorman through to the stage manager, looked straight past me, threw their arms up in welcome and shouted, 'Lynn! How lovely to see you. What are you doing here?'

Lynn, who had done a long season there a few years earlier, introduced her husband to all her friends backstage and, before I knew it, I was one of the family. I did my rehearsal – still getting lots of encouragement from my new-found guardian angel, Mr Parnell.

Afterwards, as I sat in my room on the threshold of all sorts of incredible things, my door opened and he came in but didn't sit down. 'Well, I must be off now, Val,' he said. 'I always like to watch the show at home.'

I thanked him for everything he had done and hoped it would come over OK. He offered his hand to me, 'Just be yourself,' he told me, 'and tomorrow, I think you'll be a star.'

Chapter Fourteen

Now, I was being booked for the odd week's cabaret around the country, coupled with a smattering of one-night engagements nearer home, so I thought it was time to treat myself to such niceties as a more expensive stage suit and a better car. My previous models had been an Austin A40 and a Triumph Herald. Now parked outside my door was a gleaming, if second-hand, Mark X Jaguar. I felt a certain glow of pride when I loaded the boot with the tools of my trade, guitar, amplifier, collapsible stool (which I still use today), my personal baggage and, of course, the obligatory plastic suit cover containing my stage wear. A fond farewell to Lynn and I'd be off through the gates of our semi-detatched en route to that week's destination. At least I *looked* more successful.

The entertainment industry, however, never fails to serve up a varied sequence of events guaranteed to keep all its staff in a permanent state of insecurity. Just when you think that maybe you've at last 'got it cracked', as they say, it gives your choke chain a smart pull, just to remind you who is doing the driving.

My racing green Jag sped along the M1 motorway heading for Yorkshire where, for one week, I was to be the 'star' of one particular club's entertainment.

'VAL DOONICAN AND FULL SUPPORTING CAST', I thought as I relished my new-found status. I wondered who he, she or they would be. A few hours later, pulling up outside a somewhat shabby establishment, I found my answer. A handwritten poster on the wall by the entrance boasted 'ALL THIS WEEK…VAN DOONIGAN OF BBC FAME…PLUS…THE LOVELY TANYA'.

Even in those early days I was quite used to people spelling my name with a G, instead of a C, but the VAN was something new. It made me sound like a Dutch clog dancer. All notions of stardom were to fade as that day went on, and I could feel the choke chain tighten. The organist who was to accompany me played badly and cared even less, my dressing room was minute and quite filthy, and my digs were not much better.

'Who is the lovely Tanya?' I asked myself as the landlady cleared the table after a surprisingly tasty dinner. I popped upstairs and had a shave and brush-up before going to face my public.

All was to be revealed, in more ways than one, when I got to the club a little later. The minute dressing room I mentioned also happened to be the only one there, and I was to share its luxury with the lovely Tanya. She was a stripper.

'Hello, chuck,' she greeted me as I entered. There she sat, unadorned and unabashed, gazing at her reflection in the dust-covered mirror as she busied herself decorating the tools of her trade with a pretty arrangement of sequins.

'Oh hello,' I answered, turning to hang my suit on the nearest nail.

'Noisy bloody lot out there,' she warned. 'Mind you, it'll bother you much more than it will me.' As she spoke she rose, stubbed out her cigarette and slipped on a multicoloured housecoat. In no time she was introduced to the waiting males and proceeded to do whatever she did. I decided to change into my mohair suit.

Bless her, she was certainly right about the audience: it was very noisy and bothered me more than it did her. I must say, I developed quite an affection for Tanya as the week went by. She told me she was married and had come out of retirement for a while because they needed some extra money. She was a real 'honest to God' kind of lady and turned out to be the only good thing about that week.

When Saturday night came around it was a bit like Armistice Day or end of term, and I was happy to get away.

'Where are you next week, chuck?' Tanya asked as I packed my things away.

'I'm doing a double,' I told her. 'Chesterfield and Greasbrough.'

'Oh you lucky thing,' she mumbled, pulling on her fur boots for the journey home. 'I've got nothing for weeks...ah well, me old man will be outside...'

'Tarra chuck, have a safe trip.' And she was gone, never to be seen again by yours truly.

The following week turned out much better, even though it meant doing two shows each night with a car journey in between. On Monday, I rehearsed at both rooms, then went back to my digs. My nightly routine would be to do Chesterfield first, then dash over to Greasbrough, which is just outside Rotherham: a distance of about 30 miles.

My ego was fully charged by midweek, the act having gone down quite well at both venues. Thursday night was my best so far at Chesterfield. Elated, I packed my gear into the boot of my car and took the short cut I'd now memorised along the back road towards Rotherham. It was raining as I found a parking space behind the Greasbrough club. I left the car, put my back against the stage door (kept locked from the inside), and gave a couple of hefty knocks with my heel. A dozen or so kicks later I was still there in the drizzling rain. I wondered how long the door would survive this kind of treatment, night after night, week in, week out. Panic began to set in, as I heard the music heralding the final few minutes of the preceding act, a female jazz singer from America.

'I'd better try the front entrance,' I thought and went dashing through the rain to the other side of the building.

The music, the applause and indeed the temperature trebled in volume as I entered the sticky atmosphere of the reception area of the club. The only evidence of my week's engagement I could find there was a black-board, my name written boldly across it in chalk.

A plump man with a red friendly face greeted me.

'Evenin' young man...' he almost shouted, then, showing no sign of recognition, went on: 'Are you a member?'

'No, I'm in the show for the week,' I panted, 'and the stage door is locked.'

'It always is, sir,' he said, laughing and obviously not believing a word I was saying. 'You'll have to knock, and they'll let you in.'

'But I have knocked and nobody can hear me.' Frustration was creeping into my voice by now. 'I'm due on stage in a few minutes, please let me go through the club.'

He was like a brick wall, but still smiling and friendly. 'Sorry, sir, nobody goes through this way but members and ticket holders.'

I thought it was time to play my trump card. 'Look!' I pointed hard to the blackboard. 'That's me, I'm Val Doonican.'

Suddenly the little man stopped smiling. He stared straight into my face, his right index finger pointing up my nose, and his attitude changed to that of a man who had a little power and was about to use it.

'Now listen, son,' he began with a kind of menace in his voice, 'it's like I said, nobody gets past here except members and their guests...and even if you are Val Whateveritis it makes no never mind to me.' He waited as if daring me to argue with him. I had no intention of doing so, having accepted by now that it was a lost cause. His finger still pointing menacingly into my face, he delivered his 'checkmate'. 'I wouldn't give a bugger if you were Johnny "Goon" Tweed.' He sprayed the words at me. 'You'll not pass here.' He turned and walked away.

By this time I was boiling with indignation and frustration. Storming through the doors I almost welcomed the cooling drizzle on my face as I made my way along the sides of the club. In my rage I'd almost forgotten about the show, when the friendly voice of the stage manager brought me back to reality. 'Don't worry, mate, you've plenty of time, and we brought all your gear in from the car.' He was waiting by the back door holding a golf umbrella aloft as he greeted me. Minutes later it was as though nothing had happened. I stood by the side of the stage all ready to go, and sipped a mug of warm tea. My tragic story was related to the cast as we chatted away the final minutes of the interval. Their sympathetic grunts suddenly changed to hysterical laughter when in all innocence I asked, 'By the way, who's Johnny "Goon" Tweed?' In my ignorance of the club circuit I was unaware that he was one of the most successful attractions at that time. '*Sit!*' I thought to myself in anticipation of the tug on my collar.

I'd like to come back briefly to this question of popularity, or fame, or any other name you'd like to call it. It's something I feel we should keep more firmly under control, and so avoid being too bruised by that choke chain.

There are so many steps in that ladder of success, all of them to be relished and appreciated, but very few people, if any, ever get to the very top rung.

In 1975 I was playing golf with the great Bing Crosby, and you won't find many people on a higher level than he managed to reach. It was a magical day. The two of us were putting out on one particular hole at Gleneagles. All around us were those 'she loves me, she loves me not' daisies. It looked for all the world as if there had been a fall of snow. One of the cameramen said, 'More like doing your Christmas show, Val.' Quite spontaneously, Bing and myself quietly sang a few bars of 'White Christmas'. This was a special moment for me – a five-second duet with one of my great heroes. A youngster in the crowd then asked his dad if it would be permissible to ask for my autograph. At the appropriate moment, he approached. I obliged, and as I was about to leave I overheard him whisper to his father, 'Is that man with Val Doonican a star as well?' Laughing, I turned to Bing. 'Boy, will I dine out on that,' I said. 'Well,' said Bing. 'That's the thing about fame. You're only as famous as someone thinks you are.'

We all know that a local personality in Glasgow or Los Angeles can be completely unknown in London or New York. A top-flight entertainer from Britain can go to Spain and be a complete nonentity until he bumps into somebody on holiday from Wigan.

Once, after a concert in Melbourne, I was standing and chatting with some ladies. One of them said, 'I hope you won't mind my telling you this but one of our neighbours has a teenage daughter. She saw me earlier this evening and said, "You're very dolled up. Where are you going?" I told her that we were going to see Val Doonican at the Concert Hall. The young lady looked at us for a moment, then asked "Who's she?"'

The point I'm trying to make is that we are not as important to the outside world as we are sometimes led to believe, so it's best never to assume that the next engagement will be easy, or that at last 'you've arrived'. In my experience at least, I have found that people have much more important things to worry about, and we are simply a little light relief. All of us 'in the media' can get a bit too close to its activities at times. The result being that it becomes self-indulgent, over-commercialised and sadly, on occasions, dishonest.

My radio programme continued to flourish, however, and I spent all my available time collecting, adapting, composing and arranging songs to swell my ever-improving repertoire. My publisher Alan Paramor was constantly on the look out for suitable material for me and took both a personal and professional interest in all my activities. Alan rang me at home one evening:

'I think I've got a great song for you,' he told me. 'There's a young American lad visiting London at the moment and trying to make some inroads as a composer. He's brought in quite a few numbers, one of which is a Mexican-type song. I think you could do it with the guitar. It's called "Carlos Domingues".'

I was due at the BBC Maida Vale studios next morning to do my radio show.

'Tell you what, Alan,' I said, 'I'll come over after the show and have a coffee...you can let me see it.' We agreed on midday.

When I arrived at the office, Alan was all set to sit at the piano and play the song through. By some amazing turn of fate, he had only reached the end of the introduction when there was a tapping at the office door. Alan stopped. 'Come in,' he shouted. His secretary popped her head around the door.

'Sorry to bother you,' she whispered, 'there's a gentleman to see you.' Alan stood up as she ushered in a dark-haired young man wearing a smart 'city' type suit.

'Well, talk about the devil,' Alan laughed, offering his hand to the newcomer. 'We were just playing your song. This is Val Doonican...Val, this is Paul Kane.'

We all three sat down and had coffee. I loved the song, by the way, and did it many times on the radio. I was to record it some time later, when I made my first album. Now, the only reason I have told you this story is that the young man in question was to become one of the great names in the world of popular music. His 'other name' was Paul Simon. I often wonder with the huge success he's had, and the hundreds of songs he's written since, if he'd even remember having written 'Carlos Domingues'.

In fact, John Ammonds released me from one of my *Barn Dance* commitments in order that I might fulfil the Palladium slot, knowing how important it could be to my career, since it had the highest viewing figures of any of the popular shows at that time. During previous weeks he had been discussing with me the possibility of doing a show of my own, so I was pleased in the knowledge that this single television success might swing things in the right direction for me.

Following my second appearance in two weeks, 'all hell broke loose'. Eve's phone was ringing constantly, people suggesting all sorts of things I might like to do. I sat in her office and threw my hands up in a kind of happy confusion.

'What do I accept and what do I refuse?' I asked her, never having had this kind of decision to worry about before.

'I'll tell you what to do,' Eve said quietly, and saying things quietly was not one of Eve's strong points. 'You'll do nothing. You and Lynn should pack a bag and go away for a few days and have a good chat about everything and leave all the hassle to me. The offers will still be there when you get back, so what's needed is time for us all to make the right decisions.'

That turned out to be one of the best pieces of advice I've ever had in my career. We didn't want to go too far from home, because of the other bookings I still had to fulfil. We decided to have a week in Jersey. The weather was quite good so we did as we were told, packed our bags and went.

I'd never been to Jersey before. Neither had Lynn for that matter, so we both looked forward to having a few relaxed days looking around the island. Our horizon looked bright indeed, the prospects for the coming year surpassing anything I might have foreseen only weeks previously. One of the Sunday papers sent a reporter and photographer (with our approval, I might add) to write a feature on our little retreat. They were amazed, but pleased from a story point of view, to discover that we had hired a couple of bicycles and intended to cycle around the countryside, taking in some fresh air and enjoying the scenery. The two lads were really great, getting the whole thing done in as short a time as possible, allowing us to have a bit of time together. They took some good photographs, and brought back what I hope was an interesting article. I've never really considered myself to be what the press call 'good copy'. Over the years, in spite of my considerable success, I've always felt that they found it difficult to make what they wrote about my activities sound all that interesting. In all my years as an entertainer, I've never had any kind of a press agent or publicity representative. I could never imagine what the poor guy would find to talk about.

Anyway, Lynn and I had a lovely week just being away from the usual household routine. We talked endlessly about what the future might hold for us. Deep down inside I had a strange feeling of not wanting to return too quickly, knowing I'd have to make some serious decisions, and having done so, carry out their consequences.

We came home on the Saturday night. Eve rang me on the Sunday asking me to drop into the office on Monday afternoon.

She was a very happy lady indeed, and wore a sort of smug expression, like somebody who knows things that they know you're dying to know. The next hour or so revealed an amazing change in my professional standing. There were offers for television shows of my own, several record contracts at our disposal, a choice of summer season shows, and weeks in cabaret at venues hitherto out of my depth. Eve sat back in her chair and smiled at me, looking pleased for both of us. She summed it up with a phrase that was to become part of my life for years and years.

'Well, love,' she said, 'I'll tell you what I think you should do, and then you can do what you like.' Her tone of voice was reminiscent of my mother saying to me as a child, 'Well, love, you go out without a vest if you want to, but if you get double pneumonia, don't expect me to look after you.' Eve told me what to do, and I did it.

It was decided that firstly, I shouldn't sign any long-term contracts with anybody if I could possibly avoid it, but try from a television point of view to secure one short series of half-hour shows which would enable me to feel my feet. I had little idea at this stage what kind of show I could handle, so making the wrong move, especially over too long a period, could ruin all the good that had been done. Both BBC and ITV had made approaches regarding the prospects of signing me up: this included the suggestion that I might try a stint of hosting *Sunday Night at the London Palladium*. The latter, Eve and I agreed, would be completely out of my reach, since my style was too intimate, and my experience in comparison to Bruce Forsyth and the other compères was negligible.

Secondly, any record contract that we signed should, if possible, be negotiated on a lease-tape basis. This means that we would pay all the expense of having the record made, then having done so present the finished article to whichever record company offered us the best deal. The important element of this kind of contract is that whatever else happens to that tape through its life, it always remains the personal property of the people who made it originally. To this day I possess virtually every song I ever recorded, and nobody can release any recording of mine without first coming to me for the hire of the tapes. Since the number of titles run into hundreds, I owe an enormous debt of gratitude to Eve for her astute guidance at that time.

Eve concluded her good news and rose from her desk. 'Sorry love,' she apologised, 'I have to dash off for an appointment at the BBC. I'll sort everything out and come back to you. I'm seeing Tom Sloan and Bill Cotton in half an hour.'

I came out into Regent Street and waved to Eve as she dashed off in a cab. It's hard to describe my feelings that day. Having worked on the factory floor of show business for such a long time, I now felt as though I'd been offered the job of managing director. It was great to drive home knowing I had such tasty news to pass across the dinner table.

In fact, Eve rang me back later that evening. She rounded my day off with the news that the BBC had agreed to let me do six shows. They were in complete harmony with our feelings that we should start small and get the thing right.

'They'd like you to do six shows from Manchester,' she told me. 'John Ammonds will be producing them, and the NDO will be resident orchestra.' This was exactly what I'd hoped for and I told her so. 'Good,' she said, 'I'll look into the record side tomorrow, so will you go through all the music and demos [these are demonstration records sent by songwriters] and I'll do the same and maybe we'll find something.'

After a few 'thank yous' and mutual congratulations I was just about to hang up when Eve shouted, 'Oh by the way, love,' and what a 'by the way' it turned out to be. 'With all the excitement of today's news I forgot to ask you, how would you like to top the bill at the London Palladium?' There was a pause, and then we both began to laugh. 'I'm serious,' she screamed, still laughing.

'Oh, come on, Evie,' I said. 'If you're serious, why the hell are you fallin' about laughing?'

'Because I can just see your little face, that's why.' Then the serious Evie took over. 'Listen, Val, you know Frankie Vaughan is doing a long season at the Palladium at the moment. Well, in September, he's got to take a night off because he doesn't work on the Jewish feast of Yom Kippur and they want someone to take over for the night.'

The prospect of topping a bill which included such names as Tommy Cooper, Cilla Black, Peter Goodwright and Audrey Jeans was enough to scare the wits out of me, let alone the thought of trying to win over a theatre full of Frankie Vaughan fans.

'You're joking,' I gasped, breaking the silence as Evie waited. 'I'd die on my feet, although I'm sure I should have a go. What do you think?' I knew what was coming, she was 'going to tell me what she thought, and then I was going to do what I liked'. She did just that.

'I honestly don't think you are well known enough to do it, but on the other hand, you're not well known enough for it to do you any harm. I don't think you've got anything to lose.'

That was all the encouragement I needed. 'I'll do it,' I said.

The next week or so saw us wading through dozens of songs with the idea of finding something that might make an interesting single. One of the snags, if I could describe it as such, was the fact that I wasn't known for any particular type of song. I did standards, folk songs, Irish comedy numbers and material which was popular at the time. What sort of thing was I to choose? There was a little country-type song on a demo sent by a publishing friend, Peter Callender, then with Shapiro Bernstein Music, and the title of this little song was 'Walk Tall'. We finally settled for that, and decided to use a thing called 'Only the Heartaches' as a B side. ('Only the Heartaches' was yet another adaptation of the old traditional ballad 'The Streets of Laredo'.)

Arranger Ken Woodman had been doing some writing for another of Eve's artists, Chris Andrews, so it was decided that he and I would get together on the music. I arranged 'Walk Tall' and Ken did 'Heartaches'. As far as I can recall, the entire venture cost a few hundred pounds. I brought the finished product to Eve, and she went into action. After much to-ing and fro-ing she settled for Decca Records, who liked the disc, and my first single was born.

I should add a little footnote to that last paragraph, for the benefit of those who might be familiar with my early recording activities. Another friend from the publishing world, Terry Oates, had, some time previously, offered through his employers, Chappell Music, to put up the money for me to make a record. We made what in those days was called an EP or extended player, a record with two titles on each side. Nothing very much came of that venture, but the record was released and turned out very well.

'Walk Tall' had just been released when my celebrated 'topping of the bill' at the Palladium coincided with preparations for my first television series. Life had become hectic for me and already I was beginning to know what the added responsibility of a degree of success felt like. People were talking about me and naturally more was expected of me than I was used to serving up.

Lynn, who had played dozens of times at the famous theatre herself, came along with Eve to boost my confidence at rehearsals. It was arranged that Tommy Cooper, who was appearing just before the star spot, would introduce me. The stage manager popped his head into my room, or rather Frankie Vaughan's room, and wished me luck. Minutes later, I stood behind those famous curtains waiting for the magic words from Tommy that would begin my ordeal.

'Ladies and gentlemen,' Tommy began, 'as you probably know from the notice in the foyer, Frankie Vaughan will not be appearing tonight.' There was a gasp of disappointment from the packed house, many of whom had obviously not seen the notice. 'However,' Tommy went on, 'we're fortunate to have a young man who is making quite a name for himself' – and so it went on for what felt like forever – 'so let's have a great big welcome tonight for...' There was a sickening pause. Tommy, bless him, obviously had no idea of my name... 'Here he is.' He then mumbled something that sounded like Halm Nillighen – and walked off applauding.

I often look back on that night with feelings of absolute horror. There I was, facing the most important audience of my career, a theatre filled with visitors from all over the world. Not only were they disappointed at not seeing the show they'd paid to see, but they were faced with some fellow who had a name something like Halm Nillighen. Even my mother had never heard of him.

I smiled my way rather impatiently through the opening song, and then tried, with a certain amount of desperation, to explain my presence. I got through that evening somehow, although I don't think of the whole thing as much of a personal triumph. My act, I suppose, was still geared to the kind of club dates I was accustomed to and required quite a bit of adjusting and polishing before I took it into such sophisticated sur-roundings. Anyway, it acted as yet another tug on my professional choke chain, and brought me to heel for a while.

John Ammonds and I had met several times by now to talk over the proposed format for the television series. I was to take over the slot left by the untimely death of Mike Holliday. He and Perry Como were undoubtedly the main influences in the general outline put forward. Like most people interested in entertainment, I was an avid viewer of the long-running Perry Como shows through the fifties and sixties. One important difference, of course, was the fact that I was to have the orchestra in vision and indeed they were to be featured quite heavily in a solo capacity.

My show was, to be perfectly honest, a kind of trial run and the budget was limited, so there was little chance of having any 'star guests' as such. The shows suffered very little as a result, I'm glad to say, and all the work put into making the most of what was at our disposal paid off handsomely.

We went on the air at 7.30pm on Wednesday nights for our six-week run. To put a newcomer on at such a time, competing as it was with the might of *Coronation Street* was, you may think, foolhardy. Whatever the reason may have been for its placing, it suited me just fine. I was able to learn my job of television host without too much responsibility as far as viewing figures were concerned. The outcome was that the show was quite a success in its own modest way, and I was immediately booked for another series.

For one week in that first series my guest was a very attractive young Irish girl who was based in England. It was decided that we would sing something together, and then for her solo spot she would sing a little Irish lullaby. Having heard the song a few times, John Ammonds decided that it might look nice if she were to sing it sitting in a chair by a mock fireplace. A search party from among the scene crew was sent to scour the prop room situated probably somewhere in the bowels of the earth under the old church where we were rehearsing. Eventually, they returned with a black rocking chair, which, having been cleaned and polished, was placed on its mark before the fire.

John now decided that the situation didn't allow for the use of the usual hand mike and asked the sound lads to have a small radio mike concealed down the front of the lady's dress. Once the mike had been secreted, rehearsals continued. Gently, the young mother began to serenade her imaginary baby, only to be accompanied with each rock of the chair by a weird squeaking sound. Since the sound coincided with the movement of the rocking chair, the young lady was asked to move, and the rockers, the cushion, the arms and the headrest were scrutinised for 'squeaks'. The search was in vain, however, so we tried again. The squeak continued loud and clear and rehearsals stopped once more. John was getting a bit impatient by now, as time was running short and there was much to be done. He appeared through the studio door, hotfoot from his control room upstairs. There was great activity around the chair, while further investigations were carried out. At last, to everybody's relief, and to the young lady's slight embarrassment, the source of the problem was discovered. The trouble, it seemed, was the position of the radio mike. Nestling as it was in the comfort of her bosom, it was picking up some extraneous noises from the movement of her bra as she rocked back and forth. The mike was moved slightly one way, then the other, but alas, the squeaky bra continued to dominate the situation. By now, time was at a premium. John ordered the chair to be moved, the young lady to stand by the fireplace, and the song to be performed with feeling, and little movement, in a standing position. Everything was fine, so we broke for tea.

John and I sat in the corner of the canteen with his secretary, Sybil, and assessed the situation. So far, the show seemed to be coming along well.

'T'was a shame about the number in the chair,' John said, sipping his tea. 'It looked really nice in that pool of light, but the sound wasn't quite right, even without the squeaks.' He put his cup down and scratched his head. 'How about trying your ballad sitting in the chair? You could use a boom mike and get away with it.'

I said that I was happy to go along with it if John thought it would work. Fifteen minutes later, we tried it out and the man upstairs was delighted with the result.

'Listen, mate,' he said, making a special visit to the studio, 'that looks really nice, in fact, I think we should finish the show on it.' Everybody looked in amazement. 'Finish a light entertainment show on a quiet ballad, sitting in a rocking chair?' was the general thought. 'I tell you, it's going to look great,' said John, 'take my word for it, I'm right.'

My goodness, how right can you be? Little did any of us know on that evening in the autumn of 1964, what a milestone in my career that old black chair would become. As the trilby hat and the pipe were to Crosby, or as Morecambe was to Wise, the rocking chair and myself have become synonymous. On many occasions, over the 20 or so series I've hosted, I've thought that maybe the time had come to get rid of the chair idea, fearing that people would find it too predictable. In each case the public reaction was such that I retrieved it from the attic, if only for an occasional airing.

In the 1970s, while making an overnight stop at a hotel in Colombo, Sri Lanka, I went into the cocktail bar to pass away some time. A couple of bar stools away was a very handsome middle-aged Indian chap. He smiled politely as he caught my eye, then, almost immediately, he moved one stool along and began to chat.

'Good evening, sir,' he greeted me. 'Are you here on business?' I told him I was just passing through on my way to join my family in the Seychelles for a holiday. 'I get to see a lot of businessmen passing through here,' he informed me. 'I know their faces, you see, and I've seen *your* face before.' I smiled, convinced that he was either giving me a bit of old flannel, or confusing me with somebody else. He read the disbelief in my expression. With his eyes half closed, he pointed a finger at me as if trying to place me exactly. When he spoke, his face broke into a cheeky smile. 'I think by your face, sir, that you are the chairman.' The title was snapped out as if it were the answer to the 64,000-dollar question.

I laughed out loud, thinking, 'The chairman of which company, may I ask? I must talk to them about my salary!'

His face changed now, but the finger still pointed. 'You are the chairman, sir...the chairman...*the chair man*...The man who sits in the chair and sings.' I was flabbergasted. I discovered that he'd just got back from a spell in Singapore, where my shows were transmitted every week. So you see, the chair was just as important to him as I was myself.

I related the story about the origin of the rocking chair to a newspaper reporter in America some years ago. When, eventually, I saw it in print, the headline read: IRISH CROONER FINDS TELEVISION SUCCESS BY NOT WEARING A SQUEAKY BRASSIERE.

I'll never know what words were spoken in high places at the BBC about my initial efforts as a television personality, but news came through from Eve instructing me to go along for an appointment with Tom Sloan (who was Head of Light Entertainment at the time) and his assistant Bill Cotton Jnr.

Sitting in Head Office, complete with glass in hand, I was informed that they were pleased indeed with my work. Such was their enthusiasm that they'd decided to move my next series to London the following year and hoped to make it a much more ambitious affair. They were quick to allay any fears I may have had about losing the now established working relationship I had with John Ammonds. He was, as it happened, in the process of moving to London and would be in charge of things as before.

I'd never really fancied myself as a potential candidate for *Top of the Pops,* but suddenly it was a reality. 'Walk Tall' was now showing in the charts, so Eve had a call from producer Johnnie Stewart asking if I could report to the studio for that week's edition of the show. My run-through was much later than intended due to the late arrival of some American group; the young audience was already filtering into the studio while the camera and lighting men tried to get their house in order.

Perched on a high metal stool, microphone in hand and patiently awaiting my cue to start the song, I glanced downward, coming face to face with two extremely young ladies both chewing bubble gum, a bewildered look on their eyes.

'Oo's he?' one said, nudging a passing stranger. 'Dunno,' he mumbled. Next she tried the floor manager: ''Ere, oo's he?' she repeated, pointing to me over her shoulder as if thumbing a lift.

'That's Val Doonican,' he shouted, then disappeared about his business.

'Wot did 'e say?' she asked her friend.

'Val sumfin', I fink. That's a girl's name.' Then taking one final look at me she sniggered, 'Well, ooever he is...he's not arf old.' Well, I *was* nearly 37.

That was the first of many, many appearances I was to make on this most successful show over the years. We could see that 'Walk Tall' was going to be a huge hit, so I set about preparing my first album. I'd gathered some songs together based on their popularity through the radio show. Strangely enough the final list amounted to 13 titles.

'Do you think thirteen will be unlucky?' I asked Lynn.

'Well, I can't see any of those songs being anything but lucky for you up to now,' Lynn said. 'I'd do them all.' Since the songs were so varied, we decided on the title *13 Lucky Shades of Val Doonican.* They were very lucky shades, too, taking the album right to the top of the charts.

Lynn was expecting our second child during this period, so she was pretty well confined to barracks. Our home in Lee Green had had a certain emptiness about it since the death of our baby girl the previous year and we had spoken often about the possibility of making a move. Strictly from the practical side of my work, I'd always felt that we lived in the wrong part of London. The great majority of the clubs and theatres I was likely to play were in the Midlands, or further north, so I was constantly faced with a trip right through London. We had come to the conclusion that somewhere to the north-west of the city would be the solution.

We drew a circle on the map of the Greater London area, encompassing the start of the M1, the A1, the M4, the M3, London Airport and the BBC Television Centre at Shepherd's Bush. We began our search one morning during the following week. Next day, I had to drive to London again to take part in a broadcast. During rehearsals I sat in the auditorium of the Playhouse Theatre chatting with Keith Fordyce, who hosted the programme each week.

'Lynn and I went house-hunting yesterday,' I said casually, as we watched Kathy Kirby going through her paces on stage.

'Whereabouts are you looking?' Keith asked, sipping his coffee.

'Oh, around Northwood, Pinner and Rickmansworth,' I said. 'I thought it was very nice there, although we didn't see anything we really liked.'

Keith turned to me with a look of disbelief. 'You're looking for a house in Rickmansworth, and I'm trying to sell mine! We're wanting to buy a place nearby that has a small market garden, which is just what we'd like to have.'

Within minutes we'd arranged a viewing some days later. We loved the house the moment we saw it, and decided to have it. As always with house purchasing, the price was a bit more than we intended to pay, but things were looking good for me professionally, so we weren't too worried.

Eve assured us that offers of cabaret and personal appearances were coming in at fees well in advance of any I'd had previously, so we put our house up for sale.

Chapter Fifteen

When the 1965 summer shows were being planned and allocated, my name became worthy of consideration for the first time. I wasn't competing for the 'upmarket' bookings, I might add – in fact, the offer which came my way concerned a theatre listed for demolition: the Palace Theatre on the Isle of Man. Believe it or not, the demolition men went into action during my last week there, covering over the evidence of their depressing task each evening with huge canvas sheets.

Again, the show wasn't a great success. It was still early days as far as my popularity and drawing power were concerned, and the venue couldn't have been described as a going concern. However, it was a good show and I was accompanied in my efforts by a very talented cast. It included singer Jackie Trent, the vocal quartet The Jones Boys, and a very funny young comedian, of whom I'll speak more in a moment.

The eventual move to our new home unfortunately happened to coincide with the opening of my summer show, so Lynn, in spite of her pregnancy, suggested staying at home and supervising matters while I got on with earning the money to pay for it. Each week, weather permitting, I would come to London to record my radio shows and attend to any other business matters, while at the same time popping home to see how things were coming along. Once the painters and decorators moved in, Lynn joined me on the Isle of Man for a well-earned rest.

Prior to the summer season I had done some cabaret work, including a week at one of the most successful nightspots in the north-east, La Dolce Vita in Newcastle. Some old friends whom I'd known since my Rambler days lived in the area and kindly invited me to spend the week with them.

I was delighted to accept since I've never been a great lover of hotel life. I dropped my luggage there in the afternoon and made my way to the club for rehearsals. My supporting act was a name new to me; he had just returned to Britain from Australia where he had been working with some success for a few years. He'd had his own television show there and we talked at great length about the pros and cons of trying to make a career in that particular medium.

Later that evening, I stood in the shadows at the back of the room and watched him go through his paces, and what sure-footed paces they were. He really was a lovely artist to watch, and watch him I did each evening that week with great admiration. We said farewell after the Saturday night show and went our separate ways. I had no doubt in my mind that we were going to see a lot of that gentleman in the future.

One lunchtime, when I returned from a round of golf at Castledown on the Isle of Man, there was a message in my room asking me to ring Bill Cotton at the BBC Television Centre in London. The ensuing conversation was to play a very important part in my career.

'Hello, mate,' Bill said. 'Hope I haven't dragged you away from your golf, but John Ammonds and I have been having a chat about your new series, which, incidentally, will be going out on Thursday nights "live" from the television theatre. I feel that it would be a good idea to have some kind of regular comedy spot.' His idea was that instead of finding a different comedian each week, it would be better to have someone who the viewers could get to know and accept as part of the weekly format. 'Now, I think I know just the lad to fit the bill,' Bill assured me enthusiastically. 'He's had lots of television experience, but he has not been overexposed in this country.' Then to my amazement and great pleasure he mentioned my new-found friend from La Dolce Vita in Newcastle. I agreed without hesitation. That partnership was to last for several years and contribute greatly to the show's popularity. It was inevitable that the man was to go on to great things, as he certainly did. His name was Dave Allen.

Strangely enough the other comedian with whom I shared the summer months was to become another of our stalwarts in the years that followed. I remember sitting with him and his wife in their little apartment, and listening to his disenchantment with his lack of success. He even spoke of giving it all up if things didn't show signs of improving. It was Les Dawson. One thing is certain about this great world of entertainment, you've got to take the good and the bad as they present themselves, otherwise you're in the wrong job.

One of the items in our summer extravaganza was a duet featuring the singer Jackie Trent and myself. Our young producer was evidently a fan of the old Hollywood-type musicals, and suggested this number in the first place. The stage was swathed in white drapes, its sole furnishing being a white grand piano. I stood in the well of the instrument dressed in a white tuxedo and black dress trousers. Jackie, who played the piano very well, sat in a flowing black evening gown. The song chosen for our rather out-of-character offering was the old standard 'So in Love With You Am I'. The producer, who had obviously waited all his life for this opportunity, decided to complete his little moment of self-indulgence by slowly covering the stage with a dry-ice effect, giving the overall impression that Jackie and I were floating in the clouds. Well, I'm sure this sort of thing is fine when it features Fred Astaire and Ginger Rogers, and when the staging is in the hands of Busby Berkeley, but we had no such luck.

Looking back, I'm sure poor Jackie must have hated every minute of it; it wasn't her scene at all. The weather was very hot and humid, so in order to make the whole evening bearable, doors had to be left open, including the scenery doors behind the stage. The fresh air was a godsend to everybody in the building, but alas, it didn't do a lot for our dry-ice effect. As Jackie and I gazed into each other's eyes across the piano, the machine was switched on and the clouds emerging from the wings slowly enveloped our legs, wafting us into our imaginary paradise. However, that gentle evening breeze coming through the back doors sent the sky floating away from beneath our feet and towards our startled audience. Seconds later, as we turned to deliver our romantic message...*Strange dear, but true dear, When I'm close to you dear, The stars fill the sky, So in love with you am I*...we were faced with the astonishing sight of an auditorium covered in a low cloud with hundreds of grinning faces peeping through the top. Jackie was the first to go, bursting into hysterical laughter while I gallantly carried on singing the harmony line to a non-existent melody. Eventually, I too crumbled, the entire thing finishing in complete chaos. The orchestra, which was by now absolutely invisible, bravely stuck to their task of supplying the ghostly accompaniment, little knowing what was happening above the clouds.

I returned from the Isle of Man at the end of that summer of 1965 filled with anticipation of an exciting autumn ahead. There was my television series, now scheduled to be screened at peak viewing time, following the nine o'clock news on Thursday evenings; the pleasure of settling into our new house; but most of all there was the joy of doing so accompanied by our newly born daughter, Sarah Louise. Her arrival just about coincided with my return, so it was indeed a family homecoming.

Our brand new home was beautiful, Lynn's interior decor giving it a warm, homely feeling. She's always had the most amazing talent for interior design and her taste and perception in colour schemes are always impressive. There is little doubt that had she not found her success in the world of the theatre, she could have had a professional career in this field. Our present home in Buckinghamshire is evidence to that, as I'm sure our friends will agree.

Sarah was a lovely child and brought us much happiness in those days as Lynn and I dashed about, coping with our newly found responsibilities. The press were constantly visiting the house to acquire publicity shots of the new arrivals: Sarah's into the world, and mine into the limelight. Plans for the series were now taking place almost daily with John, Dave Allen, the Adams Singers, the Gojos (a quartet of very attractive and talented young dancers who were to be part of the regular line-up of the series – they were the creation of choreographer Jo Cook, and remained with me for many years), set designers, musical arrangers, costume supervisors and anybody else involved. Right from the start I've always been keen to know what's going on, even in those early planning stages. I do believe that if the show has your name on it, and you intend going on the air 'live', then it's wise to know as much as you can about all aspects of it.

Lynn agreed to take the responsibility of finding all the casual wear that, even by now, had become a kind of trade mark of mine. The BBC included the extra money in my fee and then left the choice of clothes to us. The sweaters were a constant source of conversation, and my mail was laden with enquiries as to where such and such a jumper could be acquired. Contrary to popular rumour, incidentally, I was not flooded with knitwear from admiring fans. Virtually every piece of casual wear I used over the years was the result of endless shopping. The myth that little old ladies all over the land were sitting in rocking chairs by their firesides furiously getting next week's wardrobe finished was a figment of the imagination of the popular press. I *was* sent gifts of knitwear from time to time, but strangely enough they were always unsuitable for some reason or another.

The show's format took shape, at least on paper, and included such regular items as a four-minute spot from Dave Allen, a speciality type number from the choir and me, a dance routine from the Gojos and a little 'chat' interlude from me, followed by a song with the guitar. The item with the Adams Singers became very popular indeed, and each week BBC script editor John Law and myself would set some time aside to work on it, John writing the words which I would then set to music. I found John to be a brilliant man with words: his inspiration seemed inexhaustible. Even today, I sometimes read some of our early creations and, though they seem dated and old-fashioned, I marvel at his originality and sense of humour. Sadly, he died in the late 1960s and was a great loss to the scriptwriting world.

Our 13-week series was well received by the public and the critics alike, and established me as part of the television scene from then on. Dave's impact was inevitable and his fast growing band of followers eagerly awaited his weekly interlude. As I previously mentioned, his spot in the show was a mere four minutes, but it proved to be sufficient time for him to win over the audience. There were weeks I remember when that entire allocation of time was devoted to telling one simple joke, a technique he developed with great skill as we could see from his work for many years to follow.

Choosing a follow-up to 'Walk Tall' was a difficult task. I often think that your second single can be more important than the first since you have so much to lose. The first release is invariably 'in the lap of the gods', whatever your standing in the business, but the follow-up will decide whether you can really establish your position as a recording success. The temptation, of course, is to find a similar kind of song to your original. After much heart-searching, Eve and I felt we should risk something completely different. The same publishers who had sent 'Walk Tall' came up with a ballad called 'The Special Years', written by an American lady named Martha Sharpe. This was released in the autumn of 1965 and immediately entered the charts. With the help of the popularity of the television series it was soon in the top three.

My inclusion in that year's edition of BBC's *Christmas Night with the Stars* ended a memorable year for the Doonican household. Life being what it is, however, I wasn't going to be allowed to have ideas above my station. As I've said before, show business has that happy knack of bringing you back down to earth. On my way to the studio to rehearse my contribution to the Christmas celebrations I paused to pop into a tobacconist's shop on the A40 (I was an avid pipe-smoker in those days.)

'Good morning,' I said, rubbing my hands together, the weather outside being somewhere around zero. 'Could I have a two-ounce tin of Balkan Sobranie pipe tobacco, please.'

The gentleman behind the counter looked up from his morning paper.

'Certainly, sir,' his voice tailed off as he caught my eye, he looked for a second or so and then shook his head. 'Sorry, mate,' he said apologetically, 'I know it's rude to stare, but you're an absolute dead ringer for that Val Doonican bloke on the telly.'

It was my turn to smile now. 'Yeah, I know,' I answered. 'Lots of people have told me that lately.'

He reached on to a shelf behind him and produced my tin of tobacco. Still sniggering to himself he then said, 'What a pity the wife isn't here this morning, we could have had one over on her.'

I slipped the tin into my pocket. 'Why do you say that?' I asked him.

'Well,' he said, 'she'll never miss that bloke, she thinks he's marvellous.' Then, shaking his head in disbelief, he added, 'I can't stand the bugger myself.' As we both had a laugh at Val Doonican's expense he said with a glint in his eye, 'Mind you, I wouldn't mind having a bit of his money these days.'

I stretched out my hand. 'Well, there's a quid of it for a start.' I laughed this time as he handed me some change. I said cheerio, wished him a Happy Christmas and left. As I sat in my car preparing to pull out into the passing traffic I looked back to see a puzzled face gazing out between the chocolate boxes in the window. The joke at this stage was on both of us.

My next summer show was to be at probably the best-known resort for seaside entertainment, Blackpool. It boasted in those days some six or seven major venues, all of which presented seasonal productions featuring big-name entertainers. My professional home for the summer months, where I shared honours with comedian Charlie Chester, was to be the Queen's Theatre, previously known as Feldman's, and a place long associated with one of the great names in show business in the north, Jimmy Brennan. For as long as I could remember, his reputation and that of this grand old theatre went hand in hand. Stories about Jimmy were part of backstage gossip right up to the time of his death. Here's one of my favourites, which as the years go by and one witnesses the ups and downs of entertaining, seems like a little lesson in common sense.

The tale goes that on one occasion, Jimmy's summer show was doing disappointingly at the box office. Night after night he'd come in to find the theatre only partly filled. He'd make regular visits to the star's dressing room to cheer the poor fellow up. However, it was the star on this occasion who seemed to find an endless stream of explanations for the unsatisfactory attendances.

'We should use a bit more advertising, you know,' he told his boss. 'I've met several people in the last week or so who were surprised to see me. "Gosh, are you in town this year?" they asked me. "We haven't seen any posters about."' The following day his excuse was, 'I'm told the roads are flooded outside the town after that terrible rain,' and so it went on night after night.

As the weeks went by and things were not improving, Jimmy wondered if his star attraction was ever going to run out of excuses. Wandering into the back of the stalls one evening he found the place less than half full. He could take it no longer.

Walking into number one dressing room, he raised his hands in a gesture of despair, at the same time silencing any attempts from the star to go through his routine.

'I know, I know,' Jimmy said with tragedy in his voice. 'I've heard all about it, it's that bloody Catholic procession in Bristol.'

The poor chap sitting there had no idea, I'm sure, that what he was saying each evening had become so predictable, and indeed so ridiculous. We all fall into the trap of forgetting that the other guy has probably heard it all before. Members of the public, on the other hand, say things to us all the time that are no less predictable, not realising that we've heard them hundreds of times.

My dear old friend, the late Arthur Askey, who trod the boards while I was at nursery school, made me aware of it when we first did a season together. 'Watch this fella now,' he'd say as he saw some chap approaching, knowing by the look on his face that he was going to stop and make some remark. 'He's either going to say "Get up off your knees then, Arthur" or "You're even smaller than I thought you were."' He was invariably right.

If, by the way, you'd like to avoid some of the most obvious clichés, let me offer you a few tips. For instance, when people are standing around while a personality is signing autographs, try not to fall into the trap of saying, 'Have you got writer's cramp yet?'

Don't hand him a cheque book and ask him to 'sign here'. You'll probably be about the third one to do it that morning.

If someone says to the personality, 'You must get fed up doing this,' don't be tempted to chip in with, 'It's when people don't ask him he'll have to worry.'

Watch out also for what is probably the greatest chestnut of all, a phrase which I have heard everywhere from the smallest village in Ireland right across the world to Sydney, Australia. 'If you go well in this town you'll go well anywhere. They're very hard to please, you know.'

My most common one is when people see me at a golf club or in a bar or restaurant and say to their friends in a loud voice, 'Oh, look who it is, Sandra! It's Des O'Connor (or Terry Wogan, or Max Bygraves).'

Sadly, Jimmy Brennan's career had ended prior to my initiation into the Blackpool galaxy of summer stars. His passing heralded the gradual decline of the Queen's Theatre, which was soon to disappear altogether from the already diminishing list of British theatres. My competition was formidable, to put it mildly, other names occupying a place of honour outside the opposing establishments including Ken Dodd, Des O'Connor, Kenneth McKellar, Adam Faith, Arthur Haynes, the Bachelors, Eddie Calvert, Arthur Askey and many others far better known than myself. Whatever the merits or otherwise of the season, I had a great time. Lynn and I, together with our young daughter, rented a nice bungalow and settled there for four months. Strangely enough the thing I best remember is the wonderful companionship I enjoyed with all my fellow 'pros' on the golf course at St Anne's Old Links. Day in, day out we'd gather there to compete in the most amazing succession of contests concocted over a drink at the bar:

THE OPERA HOUSE. THE QUEENS. THE NORTH PIER *versus* THE CIRCUS. THE ABC. THE SOUTH PIER

THE ENGLISH *versus* THE REST OF THE WORLD

THE COMEDIANS *versus* THE SINGERS

Visiting artists who happened to play golf would be roped in for these occasions: Donald Peers, Ted Ray, and many more. The hospitality extended to us by that particular golf club and its members is something we will always remember with gratitude. It's a relationship that still flourishes to this day. Such was the fervour with which some of these sporting events were approached that I recall one morning when the comedian Arthur Haynes arrived having painted his woods, one red, one white and one blue, leaving us foreigners in no doubt as to the quality of his British patriotism. He was quite amazed to find the Rest of the World unwilling to follow suit.

By the end of the season, I'd been booked in advance to go to Great Yarmouth the following year, accompanied by Arthur Askey.

My 1966 television series seemed to hit the jackpot and to round things off my latest single 'Elusive Butterfly' was taking me again to that enviable position in the upper reaches of the Top Twenty.

In fact, 'Elusive Butterfly' was one of those milestones that caused a certain degree of mixed feelings as far as I was concerned. It was written by a young American named Bob Lind, who recorded it over there. I'm not sure of the story of its success in the States, but can remember how enthusiastic everybody appeared to be about my recording it for the British market. I agreed to do what is known in the trade as a 'cover version'; in other words, a similar recording to be released here at home. What I honestly didn't think would happen was that Bob Lind would come over here and promote his original version in this country. The upshot was that we both finished up on *Top of the Pops* singing almost identical versions of the same song, and standing at No.4 and No.5 in the charts. It's something I didn't enjoy, since, after all, he wrote the song and created its popularity, and I never set out to compete against him. When I met him at the television studios he was polite and friendly, although I'm sure he must have felt a certain resentment at having to share his moment of glory with someone else. On the other hand, of course, you could argue that as composer of the song he had the achievement of being in the best sellers twice at one time.

Roughing it in the clubs can be hard and sometimes even demoralising work, and most entertainers naturally look forward to the prospect of being elevated to performing in the more exclusive and prestigious rooms. From time to time I'd read with envy that so-and-so was appearing for a month at the Talk of the Town, or that such-and-such an artist was doing a month's engagement at the Savoy in London. You never know if these bookings will come your way, when other budding artists will envy you as they sit in some noisy little dressing room flicking through *The Stage*. Since I am one of the people who eventually saw the other side of the coin, it's interesting to be able to write some home truths about the reality of the situation.

I'm sure that many of my colleagues will agree that the Savoy can be either a pleasure, or one of the most difficult and unrewarding engagements an artist could undertake. I went there at a time when I assumed my television popularity was reaching a kind of peak, in the mid-to-late sixties. I was to appear each evening, Monday to Saturday, for a month. I booked six of the singers from my show, together with my own group of musicians under the supervision of my musical director. I also invited the Gojos to do the season for good measure. Our programme and its staging were carefully planned and, after a week's preparation in a private rehearsal room, we spent all of the opening day hard at rehearsals.

'How long did you intend to do?' the resident manager asked me. Being accustomed to cabaret engagements I had assumed that I'd be called on to do at least 45 minutes or so.

'Well, I was planning on about three-quarters of an hour. What would you advise?' I said, noticing a slight look of surprise on his face.

'Knowing this room as I do,' he said, looking quite serious, 'I'd say that's a bit long.' He had that 'I'm only telling you this for your own good' tone in his voice. But like the man said, 'he knew the room', so I wasn't going to argue with that, at least until I saw how things went on the opening night. He looked through the running order on his desk. 'I'd settle for thirty minutes, top whack, if I were you.' He put the papers down. 'Come on,' he said, 'I'll show you where you're dressing.'

There was some coffee in my room so we sat down and made the necessary adjustments to my programme. He seemed much happier but I was none the wiser about how it was all going to turn out.

I still had the feeling that half an hour was a bit on the short side, but at the same time I knew that I was best guided by the man who worked in the room 52 weeks a year. Running through my mind all the time were the words of comedian Dickie Henderson, who had worked there many times and to whom I had spoken about a week previously.

'Oh, you're doing a month at the Savoy, are you?' he said. 'Have you been there before?'

I told him it was my first time. 'I believe it can be very tough,' I said, hoping he would assure me otherwise, or at least throw some light on the situation.

'Well, let me put it this way,' croaked Dickie, in that much-impersonated voice of his, 'it's different...you'll never really know what kind of reception you're gonna get from one night to another.' I suggested that this was nothing new in cabaret. 'Yeah, but this place is something else,' Dickie went on. 'There'll be nights when you'll probably wonder what you're doing in the business, but then the next evening you'll come off stage wondering if you're still in the same room. One thing is certain, it'll keep you on your toes, and that's not a bad thing.'

I felt very nervous on the Monday night, and frankly, I thought the audience was a bit on the cool side. Tuesday evening things were much better and we all got quite a reception. Wednesday night was just incredible. The young compère thanked the resident dancing girls for their opening routine, chatted for a few minutes while my group got set up, then with great pomp and ceremony announced me, *the star of the show*. I could hardly believe what followed. I can honestly say it was the only occasion in my career, either before or since, when I walked out on to the stage to a great musical fanfare, and not one single person in the entire room clapped, or indeed showed any interest whatever.

The band swung into bright, happy, opening music while I strode from one side of the raised cabaret stage to the other, going through the motions of acknowledging the welcoming applause, which on this occasion wasn't there. It was the strangest experience, everybody simply getting on with their eating and drinking, here and there the odd face turning in my direction in a kind of vague awareness of my being there. Our 30-minute stint ended on that evening to a rather lukewarm round of applause. Every night from then on I was to stand in the wings awaiting my entrance with bated breath.

My dressing room was one of the first-floor bedrooms, minus the bed, and each evening I'd be there an hour before show time. I wore some specially designed casual wear, in keeping with my television 'uniform' of the time; the band, singers and dancers were wearing appropriate matching colours. About five or ten minutes before zero hour we'd all congregate in the downstairs corridor adjacent to the backstage entrance, sharing our last-minute enthusiasm, or lack of it. As I've said earlier, when you've done as much national television as I'd done by then, you could fall into the trap of assuming that most people would know who you were, at least, and that perhaps you're in that category sometimes referred to as 'household names'.

One evening during our second week we assembled as usual in the backstage passage awaiting a cue to stand by for action, when I noticed a small middle-aged couple in elegant evening wear coming down the corridor in our direction, obviously heading for the dining room. When finally they came into earshot I overheard the following:

LADY: Oh God, Henry, don't tell me there's a show going on during dinner, I always find it so irritating.

GENT: Yes, I'm afraid so, darling.

LADY: Oh, I don't think I could bear it, couldn't we go and eat somewhere else? You know what happened last time, we left.

GENT: Come on darling, it may not be too bad, in fact, I think it's that chap you sometimes watch on the television.

LADY: Which chap is that? You know I don't like television.

GENT: That chap who sits in the chair, and sings rather quaint little Irish songs.

LADY: Really? Can't place him, but I like him, do I?

GENT: Yes, darling, but I promise, if it's too dreadful we can leave and eat later.

LADY: Oh, very well then.

They disappeared into the dining room leaving the gang and I lost for words. One of them summed up the situation in a nutshell: 'I hope we don't get many of "her" in tonight.' I often wonder if they stayed the course, as I didn't have many quaint numbers in my programme that evening.

I was to make two return visits to the Savoy as a performer in the following years. There were evenings, of course, when roles were reversed and I sat among the patrons enjoying a meal, while watching fellow performers go through the hoop. I couldn't help feeling on those occasions that the majority of the guests would have been just as happy to forego the distractions of the stage show and simply get on with dinner, plus the odd knees-up on the dance floor, between courses.

My mother was holidaying with us during the final week of one of my engagements there, so Lynn thought she'd take her along one evening to watch me work. Mom was about 80 at the time and didn't like to be out too late, so this was one of her rare opportunities to see me in a cabaret setting, the show commencing at about nine o'clock.

Like many elderly people, she always insisted that the band was far too loud, and would have been much happier had my entire performance been accompanied by Mary O'Hara on her harp. Knowing that Lynn had secured a ringside table I advised our guitarist, who was standing very close to their table, 'Take it easy tonight, my mother will be right next to your amplifier.'

Everything seemed to be going fine, although I did spot her once or twice as she discreetly placed a hand over her ear. With a certain relief I embarked on a Irish folk song. Bright in tempo but very gentle, it was performed at a virtual whisper to my own guitar accompaniment. I'd completely forgotten, however, that it ended very quietly followed by a short, sharp chord from the band. Mother sipped her Chablis, proudly watching her young lad of 40 years, his lyrics awaking all kinds of nostalgic memories in them both. The final stanza tailed away in volume, culminating in a surprise punchline. A short pause followed, while the whole thing sunk in, then came the loud, shock chord from the lads. Mom was just about to put her glass down and applaud when the musical explosion occurred. To tell you that her reaction was dramatic would indeed be an understatement. She literally flung her glass of wine into the air as she leaped from her seat.

'Jesus, Mary and Joseph,' she shouted, 'what was that?'

Still coughing and spluttering on the sip of wine she'd been about to swallow, she picked up her little evening bag, and sloshing the guitar player across the shins she said, 'What do you think you're doing, for God's sake, frightnin' the life out of people?' Well, I did warn him.

Any time I glanced towards their table for the remainder of the evening Lynn was wiping the tears from her eyes. In fact she still laughs about it today.

The idea of presenting cabaret in the main dining room was to end some time later. Who knows, maybe Henry bought the place after seeing my act and put a stop to the whole affair for the sake of his wife's digestion.

Chapter Sixteen

Back in 1966–7, when my television shows had reached such an unexpected level of public acceptance, John Ammonds was keen to broaden our horizons as far as guests were concerned. We were by now, incidentally, winning a viewing audience of some eighteen and a half million, and when you consider the relatively small number of sets there were in Britain at the time, it must have been thought impressive. I was hardly aware of it myself since I was quite new to the television game and hadn't yet become too aware of the 'ratings battle'.

Whether the ratings turn out good or bad, frankly there's not a lot you can do about it except to change things completely. However, this is a kind of panic measure, in my opinion, and you might be better examining your own personal standing in the popularity stakes.

'How about some classical guitar playing next week?' John Ammonds said to me one morning during a rehearsal break. "Twould be a lovely change, you know, and anyway the guitar is so popular it would go over very well.' I was delighted with the idea myself and told John so. 'I wonder if we could get John Williams to come along and have a chat about the prospects of a guest spot.' John then asked me to carry on with matters in hand while he went and made a few phone calls.

Next day he reported that he'd been in touch with John Williams and that he seemed very keen on the idea.

'I wonder if you could do something together,' my producer said, thinking of the entertainment value. 'If we find the right idea, and it's just for fun, then I don't see any reason why it shouldn't work.'

'Let's have a think about it,' I said, 'and maybe by the time John comes in we'll have something to suggest to him.'

One of the numbers in the Top Twenty at that time was a single by the Seekers, called 'Morningtown Ride'. 'If you could play the tune,' our musical director Ken Thorne suggested, 'then maybe I could write some nice classical style variations for John, then add a string quartet if it feels right. Leave it to me, I'll write something out.'

John Williams came in a few days later. His chosen solo item posed no problems, so we sat and discussed our little duet. Well, the whole thing worked fine and John went away feeling very happy and leaving us likewise. We'd decided to call our little offering 'Variations on a Theme from Morningtown Ride'.

That was the first of many visits which John was to make over the years, and like the flautist James Galway, he admits that his first excursions into light entertainment, or *variety* as it's often called in the television world, were a turning point in his career, strictly from the point of view of his relationship with the general public.

During that first week he appeared with me, back in 1966, John happened to read in the trade press that the show was getting the viewing figures I previously mentioned, of eighteen and a half million. He had been, at that time, travelling through the United States giving guitar recitals at various concert halls, many of them housed in that country's colleges and universities. He came into the studio one morning armed with a quite alarming statistic which he'd worked out over dinner the previous evening.

'You know, Val,' he said casually, as we sat tuning up our guitars, 'I've worked it out, that in order to reach the same audience in concert, as I'm about to play for tomorrow, I'd need to do a concert every evening for the next eighty-eight years.'

There's food for thought there, you know. The message in my opinion is loud and clear: *if you're going to put your professional reputation on the line by accepting television, then you'd better be sure you've got it right.*

Whatever else may be said about my efforts on television back in those days, I certainly seemed to be 'getting it right' as far as the public was concerned. My contract was renewed and my professional life was nicely rounded off with the news that the Variety Club of Great Britain had honoured me by selecting my name as BBC Television Personality of the

Year. The celebratory lunch and presentations followed a month or two later, giving me the privilege of sharing the top-table honours with such established stars as Michael Caine, Anna Neagle, Frankie Howerd, Virginia McKenna and David Frost. Those occasions are made all the more special by the knowledge that your name has been chosen by fellow members of your profession.

Lynn completed the year, as far as our personal life was concerned, by presenting the Doonican family with a brand new baby daughter, Fiona Catherine. My standing at the box office was by now beginning to show signs of improvement. I was already signed up to do my own show in Great Yarmouth in the summer of 1967, and was to be joined by Arthur Askey. What a pleasure our partnership turned out to be, not just for that year, but also for 1968 and 1969.

Arthur was a joy to work with and I thank him for all he taught me during our time together. His stagecraft was quite superb, as I'm sure all my colleagues who have shared the stage with him will agree. He gently guided me through some of the subtleties, like *where to stand, when to move, where to look,* and in general *how to behave when sharing the stage with other people.* He certainly knew where the laughs were in a routine and demonstrated the art of how to make the most of them. In spite of all my years in the business I somehow became aware that I had entered a part of the first division where I hadn't played a lot, and I'd found a great coach. It's lovely to look back on those hundreds of evenings when I'd listen to him singing away to himself in the next door dressing room as he prepared for the first house. I remember his neatly laid out dressing table with all his personal bits and pieces. There was always the smell of throat pastilles in his room. One of his little idiosyncrasies was to have with him at all times a tin of Meggazones – he'd cut one into several slices and 15 minutes or so before curtain-up he'd pop a piece in his mouth. Meggazone fumes will always remind me of singing a duet with Arthur. Five minutes before the overture he'd breeze into my room looking like a little Burton's dummy and bubbling with enthusiasm. 'Come along, son,' he'd say, 'I don't think that poor audience can bear to wait for me any longer.' He really did love his work, and showed it. He was an inspiration to all of us.

I said to somebody shortly after his death that 'Arthur was always a hard act to follow on stage, but for sheer professionalism in his career he was impossible to follow'. I'm so glad I knew him.

We were at the Wellington Pier for our season at Great Yarmouth. The business turned out to be quite amazing. We both stayed at the Carlton Hotel just across the road from the pier, our rooms looking out on to the seafront. As the weeks went by we fell into a kind of ritual which we carried out like a couple of overgrown schoolboys who had just come into the business. Each day, if we weren't out playing golf, we'd have a beady eye on the front of the house across the road watching the crowds standing in line to get their tickets for that evening's shows. Time after time we'd spot one of the box-office staff emerge into the sunlight carrying that coveted piece of theatre equipment, the 'house full' sign. Whoever spotted it first would dash to the phone and ring the other, when we'd both chant in unison, 'We've done it again, playmate!'

Our opposition in town was again very impressive: Morecambe and Wise, Mike and Bernie Winters, Mike Yarwood, Rolf Harris, Ruby Murray and a host of others. Arthur's show-business anecdotes were inexhaustible. I was to learn virtually every word ever uttered by the legendary Eddie Gray of the Crazy Gang. Arthur idolised Eddie's humour and said on many occasions that he thought him to be the funniest man he'd ever met. I feel it is a great shame that Arthur never got around to writing a book about his old friend. I feel sure it would have been quite a classic, and a valuable record of two great comics.

Playing to packed houses was a new experience for me. The only times I'd known it previously was when somebody else was Top of the Bill. My name was now up there and it felt good. In fact, 'being good box office' is one department of the popularity stakes which has always been a bit of a mystery. Some people seem to draw the crowds pretty consistently year in, year out while others who appear to be just as popular can't do it. Everybody, of course, however good, blows hot and cold as the years go by, but as with making hit records, you never know for sure if you can make it work again next time around. That's why this is such a great business: no matter how long you're doing it you never cease to feel that old choke chain.

By now, I was taking my own backing group wherever I went, its modest complement forming the bulk of my entourage. They were, of course, part of my show at Yarmouth, eliminating all extra rehearsals with the pit orchestra, so much part of my life until that time. Having your own group of backing musicians, with all its inherent problems, is truly one of the most comforting of perks enjoyed by the more successful entertainers. When the pressure of other commitments makes it difficult for you to attend rehearsals, you really have no need to worry, secure in the knowledge that, should you not turn up until just before show time, the lads will know your every requirement.

Long summer seasons, sometimes extending to four months, can, however, bring their own problems as far as the individual members of your company are concerned. Their personal domestic situations can make it extremely difficult, especially if a young family is involved. They may also have other business commitments needing their attention; they're unavailable for other work, such as recording sessions and broadcasting work, and this can damage future prospects. For all or some of those reasons a change of keyboard player was required before our Yarmouth season. The replacement, a young bearded lad in his mid-20s, arrived for our first rehearsing session. Neither of us could possibly have conceived what a permanent fixture he was to become in my working life. For over 40 years now, Roger Richards has been the mainstay of my musical support, having taken over as musical director in 1969. In the mid-1970s, he married Maureen, one of our then backing singers on stage and television. During all our years together, I can honestly say that I've never appeared professionally in a musical capacity without Roger's invaluable support. It's hard to believe that since that first rehearsal at Great Yarmouth he has never missed or cancelled a performance for any reason, in spite of all the colds, flu, tummy bugs and other ailments he has chosen to overlook in the line of duty. Quite apart from catering to my own musical needs, he became musical associate for hundreds of TV shows and recording sessions. Looking back, it's even harder to believe that in all that time there has never been a cross word or any hard feelings between us. His contribution to my career has been enormous, and something for which I am truly grateful.

Looking into my diary for the autumn of 1967 was quite daunting. Apart from the television series, there was the exciting prospect of appearing in my very first Royal Performance. My latest single, 'If the Whole World Stopped Lovin'', was among the top five hit records, and then, of course, there were many club dates on offer.

This was a period when the theatre clubs around the country reached a quite phenomenal degree of popularity that was to last for years. Large fees were available to the more popular stars of the television and record industry if they were versatile enough to perform effectively in cabaret. Some of these establishments were very large, catering for some 1,500 or more people each evening. Dinner or light meals were served at some, while others were nothing more than huge drinking clubs. In an effort to justify the hefty salaries paid for the entertainment, some of the smaller ones crammed so many people in as to make it almost impossible for anybody to enjoy themselves.

I remember an occasion when there really wasn't room for the band and myself on the minute stage or bandstand. If one of us so much as moved to adjust the amplifier controls, it invariably meant knocking over a music stand, and causing chaos trying to retrieve the scattered contents. Roger, facing the stage, his back to the audience, was perched precariously on his adjustable piano stool, inches from the edge of our raised podium. On three sides of us people were packed like sardines around the scattered tables, the men in shirt sleeves, their ladies fanning themselves with anything to hand.

Nevertheless, the show was a resounding success, the audience enjoying themselves, their reaction everything we could wish for in the circumstances. As we neared the end of our allotted time, I noticed a very fat man laboriously make his way between the tables and head in my direction.

''Scuse me Val,' he puffed. 'Will you do me a favour, mate?' I leaned forward, trying not to fall off my bit of the stage. 'My wife Doreen would love you to sing that song "Scarlet Ribbons" – it's her favourite.' I honestly didn't feel the occasion was right for that particular song, but after what the poor chap had gone through getting to the stage, what could I do?

I signalled to Roger, who nodded his approval and began the gentle introduction, music-box style, high up on the piano. A hush came over the room as I quietly dedicated the song to Doreen. After a gentle ripple of applause, you could have heard the proverbial pin drop, so I began. All went well for the first verse, which ends with a kind of rallentando, or slowing down. At that vital stage the tinkling piano suddenly stopped, its music-box effect replaced for a second or two by a dull thud, then the whole place burst into raucous laughter. 'What the hell is going on?' I thought, looking over my right shoulder in the direction of the silent piano. Roger's head and shoulders had completely vanished from behind the keyboard, but were quite remarkably replaced by his feet, waving about in the air like some strange antennae. The room by now was in uproar, and I stood dumbstruck centre stage. Then, quick as a wink, the legs were gone. Seconds later a red-faced musical director, hair standing on end, came slowly clambering back to his original position.

It appears that Roger's amazing multi-purpose collapsible stool had done precisely that: it collapsed. He went into a kind of Fosbury flop off the stage, landing flat on his back in the middle of an adjacent table, his long legs flailing about overhead. Well, you try following that with the second verse of 'Scarlet Ribbons'. Even Doreen had had enough by now.

Like the seasoned campaigners we're supposed to be on such occasions we simply made the most of it, Roger, taking bow after bow and yours truly promptly getting into our final routine.

The chap who ran the place thought the whole show was wonderful, and kindly invited us to his private office for a drink. Believe it or not, he later whispered to Roger, 'Damn good entertainer, this man, isn't he? Knows how to keep the audience happy – although I'll be honest, I don't think he needs the gimmicks, like your somersault off the piano stool. Out of character, I thought.'

Roger has never done it since. Shame really!

I shouldn't knock the fact that there were so many people in the club that evening. Overcrowded though it was, I'd choose it any time in preference to performing before empty tables and chairs. There really can't be anybody in our profession, however pampered by the trappings of stardom, who can honestly deny having suffered those occasions when, for one reason or another, the public didn't turn up.

Back in my radio days I was engaged to appear for one week at a restaurant down in Plymouth. The place itself was nice enough, but unfortunately the public weren't interested in going there. I turned up one evening, only to be told that not a single customer had booked for dinner. The manager, the resident quartet and myself sat and tried to use up some of the coffee they had made, while licking our respective wounds. Assuming the evening was a lost cause, I rose and slipped on my overcoat, ready to enjoy my freedom. Just as I approached the door, it opened, and in walked a family of four, mother, father, daughter and son-in-law. I looked back towards the manager as if to say, 'Surely you don't expect me to...' He looked at me in turn as if to reply, 'It's not my fault, mate,' then he ushered the rather self-conscious foursome to the best table.

Fifteen minutes later the musicians played a half-hearted fanfare, and on came the 'star of the show'. I must have looked pathetic – I certainly felt it. Finishing my opening song, I bowed in the direction of my audience of four, then to my great surprise the head of the family rose to his feet and waved in my direction. 'Why don't you bring your guitar and stool over and join us in a glass of wine?' What a relief.

The following encounter couldn't have been more unexpected. It seems that the mother loved my morning radio show and had specifically requested a visit to the restaurant to see me work. So I sat on my stool, guitar in hand, and without the aid of a microphone sang all the songs she wanted to hear. The band, feeling redundant, retired to the bar, while I stayed with the family for an hour or more.

If you happen to have a well-known face through television or films it's quite common for people to inform you that somewhere in their private world you've got a 'double'. I've heard it happen so many times through the years, but on the few occasions when I've come face to face with the evidence I've been quite puzzled as to why anybody should see a resemblance. One particular occasion that comes to mind was when a Sunday newspaper contacted my manager, telling her of some chap who had come to their attention.

'They say that the man has come into their office, and that the resemblance is quite uncanny,' Eve told me over the phone. 'What they'd love to do is get the two of you together for a photograph for next Sunday's edition.'

Anyway, I agreed to meet them at a London hotel. When I got there they eagerly welcomed me and took me to a private room where their photographer was waiting. A few minutes later my 'double' arrived and we shook hands. I was convinced, once and for all, on that meeting, that you most certainly never see yourself as others do. The man looked a bit like me, I suppose, but what all the fuss was about I just couldn't understand. When the paper came out that weekend everybody I spoke to was as surprised as I was at what little similarity there was. However, the whole thing gave me an idea for my show.

One Saturday night during the series I talked about this whole business of 'doubles', and was fortunate enough to get a few good examples on photographs. Putting the pictures away I then said quite seriously, 'Now the reason I've brought this up tonight is that very recently I did see something that quite stunned me, so much so, that I thought somebody was playing a joke on me. Now I won't tell you too much about it, I'll simply introduce a special guest and leave you to judge for yourselves.' The lights went very low on the set and the spotlights were trained on the stage entrance at the side. There was a rather dramatic roll on the drums and I announced, 'Ladies and gentlemen, from Sevenoaks in Kent, may I introduce Mr Martin Harris.' The audience, filled with anticipation, were on the edge of their seats as they waited. Then, rather nervously, into the spotlight walked Dave Allen. His hairstyle had been completely changed for the occasion, and he wore a heavy sports jacket and corduroy trousers. There were a few seconds of shocked silence, followed by wild applause mingled with Ooohs and Aaahs of approval. 'Good evening, Martin,' I greeted him, 'and thank you very much for joining us tonight.'

He shook my hand and nodded in a kind of shy acknowledgment. 'Hello, Val,' he said quietly in a very well disguised accent, and sounding very 'county'.

After one or two questions and answers, however, we couldn't kid the audience any more. They began to jeer and giggle, and pretty soon Dave and myself could keep it up no longer and joined in the laughter.

Some five or six years later I was checking into a hotel in Hong Kong.

The young Chinese girl behind the reception counter looked up. 'Hello, Mr Doonican,' she said smiling. 'Welcome to Hong Kong. We're enjoying your shows at the moment.' She told me that a series was currently being transmitted on Tuesday nights. I checked into my room and my travelling manager, Mickey, and myself sat down to a cup of coffee. I noticed a copy of the Hong Kong *Television Times* on top of the set in my room and flicked through it. I looked at Tuesday night and there, as the girl had said, was my show. The whole thing was written in the local language, of course, with the 'English subtitles' underneath. I wondered how old the shows were, and thought I might be able to tell by the guest list, so I read: 'THE VAL DOONICAN SHOW, with special guests the Smothers Brothers, the Edwin Hawkins Singers, and *Martin Harris*.'

'Who the hell is Martin Harris?' I said out loud; then turning to Mickey, 'Have you ever heard of Martin Harris?'

Mickey looked up. 'Martin who?' he said with a shake of his head. The problem went unsolved for the moment at least. The next day we flew to New Zealand. Halfway through one of the countless meals, Mickey leaned over and gently tapped the back of my hand with the handle of his knife. 'Martin Harris was Dave Allen's double.'

'Brilliant,' I said, 'have a glass of champagne on me.' I'm no fool – Mickey was teetotal, and besides the drinks were on the house, or should I say 'on the plane'.

Chapter Seventeen

A s with my case of mistaken identity, or should I say unmistaken identity at that tobacconist's on the A40, it's good for all of us in the public eye to find ourselves, from time to time, with egg on our faces. I recall one rather special occasion when I really got a plateful.

A very posh luncheon party was laid on by ATV at a time when they boasted a formidable stable of successful television stars. The function in question had been arranged so that some special accolades could be awarded to a chosen few. The famous faces making up the guest list were so impressive that the old cliché 'anybody who was anybody' just about fits the bill. I might, for the purpose of my story, inform the reader that Val Doonican was one of the lesser lights and not in line for any of the credits.

A very distinguished gentleman in a dark suit, sporting a red carnation in his buttonhole, made the closing speech and sat down to warm applause. He had mentioned in passing that he had a further appointment and asked us to forgive him if he slipped away once his duties had been performed. In fact, as we got back to our conversation, coffee and cigars, he quietly left the top table and began to shuffle his way between the others, nodding farewells to those who caught his eye. He paused at our table and said hello and goodbye, then to everybody's surprise he turned in my direction and extended an open hand.

'May I just say a special hello to you, old boy,' he said beaming. All eyes were on me as I stood up to take his hand. 'You've been a great favourite with my family,' he kindly told me. 'So may I thank you for all the pleasure you've brought us.'

'Thank you for saying so,' I said, 'I'm flattered.' I prepared to sit down, but he turned to all my famous colleagues.

'My dear mother thinks this man is the cat's whiskers,' he told them, 'and it's not just a passing fancy, she's followed his career right from the start when he had his first records like "My Old Man's a Dustman".'

He waved goodbye as I slowly slumped into my chair. 'Congratulations, Lonnie,' somebody said. Well, you have to laugh like everybody else!

My summer season for 1969 was in Blackpool. It was nice to be back there after three years, especially since I was starring, not at one of the smaller theatres as previously, but at the prestigious No.1 venue, the Opera House. The show was to run twice nightly, Monday through Saturday, from mid-June right through till early October, when the illuminations were finally switched off.

Arthur Askey, once again, occupied the dressing room next to mine, while the lovely Moira Anderson joined as the show's leading lady. The bill also included a dynamic vocal and instrumental group from Greece, the Trio Athene, and the indispensable Des Lane.

The staging by Ross Taylor was truly lavish, by any standards, and I'm glad to say the business throughout more than lived up to expectations.

The family and I took up residence for that summer in a house at Lytham St Anne's, a few blocks from the famous champion golf course of the same name. As luck would have it, Royal Lytham Golf Club were hosts to the British Open Championship that same year, an unexpected perk for the golf enthusiasts among the visiting entertainers. Practically all of the other Blackpool courses were reserved during the previous week to enable the hundreds of hopefuls not fortunate enough to gain automatic entry to the championship proper to get through the pre-qualifying rounds. This gave many of us the opportunity of visiting the 'tented village' at Royal Lytham, and of watching the 'big boys' at practice. We were not to know at that time, of course, that this was to become one of the most exciting British Opens of all time from a British point of view. Having feasted on the action all week, both on the course and in the comfort of our sitting rooms, we had to content ourselves with savouring those final breathtaking moments on Saturday evening from our theatre dressing rooms, just around show time. It was unforgettable to hear Henry Longhurst describe the historic closing scenes as Tony Jacklin brought the ultimate golfing accolade back to Britain after so many years.

Playing that great course over the following months was to take on a new meaning for all of us golfing fanatics.

Another 'veteran' of the music hall was in Blackpool at the same time as Arthur Askey and myself: his name was Billy Tasker. A delightful gentleman he was, with an impish personality. He and Arthur were old pals and spent quite a bit of time together on the golf course. They didn't consider themselves to have the same staying power as the young bloods and were more inclined to slip away for nine holes or so when the coast was clear. On occasions, however, we did join forces and it was great fun. If a fairly good player went off the tee and smashed a long drive down the fairway, they'd look at each other and plan their strategy.

'Now, my old friend,' Billy would say to Arthur, 'do you think you can outdrive him? I know I can if I really want to, it's just you I'm worried about.'

Arthur would size up the situation, tee up his ball, then winking at Billy would say, 'Tell you what, I think I'll hit a bad drive on this hole [which was more than likely] 'cause I've got a terrific idea for my second.'

It was such a joy playing with fellows who didn't get too serious about it, which so many of us did, probably spoiling the fun for others. I played quite a bit with two lads who really drove other golfers mad. They argued all the time over little things like the giving of short putts, or whether one moved while the other was playing, causing him to slice or hook. Things got so bad one afternoon, that having had a five-minute slanging match on the tee, one of them slammed his driver back into his golf bag, and threw it over his shoulder.

'I'm sick and tired of playing with you,' he stormed. 'It's one ****ing thing after another, this game is supposed to be for ****ing pleasure, so play on your own, I'm ****ing off.' And so he did. All alone he marched off the tee and headed for the clubhouse, about a mile across the course. We stood and gaped for a minute.

'What do we do now?' I asked. 'We've played twelve holes, the match is all square, and you've got no partner.'

'Oh bugger him,' said the wounded one, 'let him go, we'll play on and start a new game with three of us.' He teed up his ball. 'Anyway, he won't be able to open the car, I've got the keys, so let him wait for a lift home.'

With all the resentment and frustration accumulated over the previous few minutes transmitting itself to the golf club, he walloped the ball. It veered off to the right, going like a rocket. To our horror, we watched the white dot flying, as if guided by some kind of homing device, in the direction of his homeward-bound partner. 'Fore,' we shouted in unison, but our sulking prima donna refused to budge. Our second chorus was too late. The ball smacked him on the back of the neck, and we saw him stumble under the weight of his clubs, falling forward on to his knees as if he had just been shot by John Wayne. 'Jesus,' we shouted this time and, as if released by a starting pistol, set off at a sprint in his direction.

He was scrambling to his feet when we got there, and positively seething with rage. He pushed us aside.

'Clear off and leave me alone,' he bellowed. 'Don't touch me.' The final bit sounded like a line Elizabeth Taylor would come out with when her drunken lover tried to apologise. He flung his golf bag over his back, almost spinning himself out of control. Then came a classic line that I shall never forget. Turning to his guilty-looking partner he yelled, 'You! You did that on purpose, you rotten bastard.'

Now, I ask you, especially if you've ever tried to play this impossible game of golf, to consider the probability of such a thing. His partner, like most of us, found it difficult enough to hit the fairway, or a green 50-foot wide, but hitting a fellow's neck from about a 130 yards? Well, that could certainly be called Target Golf. However, they were back playing together a few days later, arguing as before, each one completely sure that it was the other fellow who caused all the bother.

It takes a lot to deter golfers: they play with backache, toothache, colds, coughs or anything else. They play in flaming hot sunshine, freezing cold weather, rain, hail and snow, always somehow convinced it will all change for the better any minute.

I played with some friends of mine in thick fog one morning. The whole thing was quite ridiculous on reflection. We could barely see the end of the teeing area, and there we were slamming the balls into oblivion, then setting out like a search party in the hope of finding them, only to repeat the exercise ad infinitum. When we eventually found our way to the clubhouse bar, one member of our expedition related a great story.

We were, at the time, touring on the music halls and were all pros.

It was on just such a foggy morning that he and three fellow members of the cast made their way to a local course, convinced that the fog would soon lift. There wasn't a soul about the place as they enquired about paying green fees.

Entering the clubhouse, they found a lone member of the bar staff cleaning some glasses while a cleaning lady started her chores in the men's lounge.

'You're not going out in that, are you?' the barman jeered.

Rather embarrassed, one of the lads replied, 'Ah well, it might not be too bad, once we're out there. Can we pay some green fees?'

'You pay them at the pro's shop,' the barman told them, 'but he's not in yet, he's not as daft as you lot.'

The lads awkwardly stood about looking at such interesting things as photographs of past captains and presidents adorning the walls. They didn't like to ask for coffee – somehow the conditions weren't right. The barman, carrying a large tray of clean glasses, walked across the lounge. As he reached the door he paused, 'If you want to go ahead, gents, you can pay the green fees when you get back, that's if you ever do get back.'

The four said thanks and went in search of the changing rooms. The fog seemed even more dense when they reached the first tee, and they were relieved at not being visible from the clubhouse windows, just behind them. The first man to go off the tee stood there as if blindfolded, wondering just where the hell the fairway was situated. 'Here goes, lads,' he sighed, as if going off the high diving board for the first time. He didn't have the cheek to say 'Keep your eyes on this for me', as golfers often do. 'Crack', went the drive. They all gazed into the fog, but not for long. The sound of the club against the ball was almost immediately followed by the sound of shattering glass, coming from the direction of the clubhouse. The culprit stood dumbstruck, and then slowly turned to his friends.

'What the hell was that?' he said.

One of them almost whispered, 'How could the ball get back there?'

The driver shrugged his shoulders in disbelief. 'Did I do that?' then, endeavouring to look even more invisible than they already were, they picked up their bags and slunk into the gloom.

You can just imagine the conversation that took place on their way around the course. 'Well, let's just say it certainly wasn't us. They can't prove anything, can they?'

'Who else could it be, there wasn't another golfer round the place for miles.'

'How about saying we found our ball up the fairway? It couldn't be us.'

'Suppose the ball finished up in the men's lounge – what then?'

'Let's just get in the car and slip away.'

'No, they know we're at the theatre, they'd have us for not paying green fees as well.'

'Surely they must be insured against things like that. Do you think so?'

'What? Insurance wouldn't cover four lunatics playing in thick fog.'

One thing is certain, not much concentration was given to playing golf over the next few hours. By the time they had made their perilous journey down the 18th fairway, the fog had completely gone, and they were able to see the clubhouse quite clearly. Any moment, they expected to see the daunting figure of the secretary in blazer and grey slacks approach them, but no. In fact, it wasn't until they walked off the final green that they came face to face with the result of the early morning's disaster. A large sheet of some kind of transparent paper had been fixed temporarily over a huge gaping hole in the plate-glass window of the main lounge. 'It wasn't a dream,' they thought. 'What now?' They changed their shoes, donned their jackets and ties, took a deep breath and headed for the bar. One or two members were sitting chatting over some drinks. The barman was the first to speak. 'Ah, the men of the moment. Your ears must have been burning this morning. The lads couldn't believe anybody could play in that weather. You deserve a drink.'

That wasn't a bad start, anyway. They graciously accepted the offer, and sat chatting with the members, and their new-found friend the barman.

'Actually it was very enjoyable after the first few holes, we had quite a laugh,' one of them lied. Then he bought everybody a drink.

'We didn't have a laugh when you went off the tee,' the barman said. 'Didn't you hear that window go?'

As one voice, and looking as harmless as four altar boys, they chanted,

'Window, which window? What happened?' while at the same time looking at every window in the room except the right one.

'The plate glass, down there,' the barman pointed. 'I'm amazed you didn't hear the almighty crash it made.'

'Goodness me,' one of the lads gasped, 'how the hell did that happen?'

'This is it,' the others thought, 'how much money do we have on us?'

'Poor old Flo, the cleaner,' the barman said, shaking his head and pouring a pint. 'Got the flex of the damned Hoover caught up under a stack of chairs, tipped them over and bang, right through the window. She was so shaken up, bless her, that we had to let her go home.'

The four lads swapped glances, not daring to smile. 'Poor Flo,' they thought, 'maybe we should have a whip-round.' But they left well enough alone, said their goodbyes and thank yous and sought out the pro's shop.

'Are you the fellows who played in the fog?' he asked as he opened the green fee book. 'You deserve some sort of medal.' They felt as though they'd earned one.

But back to that summer season at the Opera House – various representatives from the Bernard Delfont office in London (who were responsible for promoting the show in Blackpool) paid us regular visits, each of them leaving us in no doubt that everybody was very happy with the results. One such visitor was Leslie McDonnell, the managing director of Moss Empires Ltd. He watched the show, after which he took Arthur, Moira and myself out for a late-night meal at a local hotel restaurant, which was very popular with the show-business fraternity. His enthusiasm for our performances, plus the subsequent results at the box office, was evident from the start, and we spoke of very little else while we enjoyed our meal. The main reason, however, for his visit was to confirm, what up to then had been merely an idea, that the show 'en bloc' should open the following summer for a six-month run at the London Palladium. One small problem remained, however. Arthur Askey was booked to appear there for the forthcoming 1969 pantomime season, and it was felt, understandably enough, that he couldn't very well follow one season at this world-famous theatre with another. A replacement had to be found. Meanwhile, my sights were set on more immediate commitments, namely my 1969 television series.

By now, my producer, John Ammonds felt that maybe it was time to move on to something different, so it was mutually agreed that the reins should be handed over to a young producer who had worked for a while as John's assistant. His name was Terry Hughes. Terry (now working very successfully in Hollywood) worked on the show for two years, before going on to create many BBC hit shows, not least *The Two Ronnies,* eventually forsaking his producer/director role to take on the mantle of BBC Head of Light Entertainment.

When the 1970 London Palladium season came around, Arthur's role was very successfully taken over by Norman Vaughan. He and I were to work together quite a lot throughout the show, one very enjoyable duo being a golfing number which I'd written in partnership with the late Ronnie Taylor. It was called 'Put Down a Ball, Pick Up a Club, and *Swing!*' It was along the lines of the classic Crosby song 'Straight Down the Middle', and was to be sung by Norman and me while I shot imitation golf balls out into the auditorium. We set the number up in a way which suggested that the theatre was a golf course, which we were both playing for the first time. The opening hole was straight ahead, the second, a short hole into one of the boxes, while the third was on to an elevated green supposedly up in the circle. The patrons, of course, had no idea what to expect as we smacked the balls in their direction, the result being much audience reaction, which is precisely what we wanted.

On the first night, however, it was the opening duet that stopped the show. Norman, at that time, was very much linked, in the public's mind, with the promotion of Rose's Chocolates, his catchphrase being 'Rose's grow on you'. This phrase, you may well remember, was accompanied by the spectacle of roses growing all over his jacket, ending with a rose popping out of his hand while he made a thumbs-up sign accompanied by his famous 'Ooh'.

The idea was that when I first introduced him, at the top of the show, he was to enter covered in roses. I would then act as though I didn't understand the reason for it, never having seen the TV advert. Then our conversation went:

NORMAN: Oh, come on, you don't mean to say that you've never seen me wear this on TV?

VAL:	Never.
NORMAN:	Well, ask the audience about my catchphrase.
VAL:	What catchphrase?
NORMAN:	Ask them, if they met me in the street wearing this jacket, what would they say?
VAL:	OK. *(To audience)* What would you say if you met Norman wearing this jacket in the street?
NORMAN:	*(To audience)* One, two, three!
AUDIENCE:	Rose's *grow* on you.

As so often happens on opening night, things didn't quite work out as planned. Norman entered, rose-covered, to great applause, and everything was fine until:

NORMAN:	Ask them, if they met me in the street wearing this jacket, what would they say?
VAL:	OK. *(To audience)* What would you say if you met Norman wearing this jacket in the street?
VOICE FROM GALLERY:	Piss off, you silly sod!

Well, I don't need to tell you what that did to our opening routine. The audience laughed for a good couple of minutes, leaving Norman and me so hysterical that we found it almost impossible to go on. In the circumstances we decided to rephrase our script slightly to avoid repeating the indignity.

Our little golf routine worked very well indeed and, like the opening spot, brought its share of surprises.

One particular Saturday night we were thoroughly enjoying the reaction of an exceptionally responsive audience, as we cracked the polystyrene golf balls into the darkness of the auditorium. When the time came for me to direct one of my shots at the box situated on the left of the stage, we both looked up to see a group of smiling people leaning over the edge, as if daring me to hit them. Norman shouted 'Fore' but they persisted, knowing the possibility of my getting the ball anywhere within feet of them was remote. He then moved in their direction and, addressing a bespectacled man in the middle of the group, said, "'Scuse me, sir, but I do hope those are not your best glasses. This man is deadly accurate. I would remove them if I were you.' The gentleman laughed heartily, but removed his glasses nevertheless, as if taking Norman's advice seriously.

One of the spotlights slowly moved to one side, gradually illuminating my target and all went quiet. I took a few preliminary waggles at the ball, then *wham*. To our amazement, and indeed everybody else's, it went like a rocket off the centre of my club head, and absolutely dead on line for the box. Our good-natured customer stood his ground, still smiling until a split second later it caught him, exactly where Norman had predicted, on the bridge of his nose. As one, he and his party jumped to their feet and cheered their appreciation. The whole theatre joined in the spontaneous ovation, while I modestly took bow after bow.

When all the excitement had died down, I thought I should apologise to the gentleman, just in case I'd caused him any discomfort. 'Not at all, it's quite all right, old man,' he said. 'Worth it just to see such a wonderful shot. I'm bringing a whole party of friends here next weekend, we'll look forward to seeing you do it again.'

We were doing 13 shows a week, including three performances on Saturday, which meant spending something in the region of 40 hours a week backstage. But we took it all in our stride, as entertainers do, the adrenalin which flowed with the success of the show far outweighing any weariness we may have been feeling. There was also the fact that we were an extremely happy company, everybody looking forward to each performance, and all enjoying each other's company.

Chapter Eighteen

A select group of British entertainers were, in the 60s, making variety shows for the ATV company, run by Sir Lew Grade. Notable among them were Tom Jones, Engelbert Humperdinck and Des O'Connor. Then one day, my agent, Eve Taylor, was approached about the prospect of my name being added to that list. We were in no doubt whatever as to the enormity of the decision facing us. On the plus side, I was to be guaranteed a series of 13 one-hour shows of my own to be transmitted all over America, as well as being sold to most English-speaking countries around the world. It did, however, mean my severing a long-standing and very personal partnership with BBC Television, putting my whole popularity, as far as the British public were concerned, in a pretty vulnerable position. There was no way of knowing how the new mid-Atlantic shows would turn out, of course, and this was at a time when the British viewing public had a certain scepticism about artists leaving the BBC to work on 'the other side', for what they always judged to be monetary reasons. I don't think the suspicion is quite as prevalent today, since it is difficult to keep track of the comings and goings between so many channels. But back then, however, you were either with BBC or ITV and somehow, to many people, the two didn't mix.

My own instincts told me to stay where I was, but then, as I have already said, I've never been all that ambitious, but simply happy to enjoy what I'm doing as long as it's working well, and I feel it's as good as I can do. But as far as my overall career was concerned, I was being made an offer which I couldn't and really shouldn't refuse.

Having severed my contractual ties with BBC Television, and facing a kind of interval before tackling the international series, I thought it would be a good idea to flex my muscles, so to speak, in my new environment. Eve arranged with the ATV company that I should make a Christmas special for the commercial channel (my first ever starring TV show that didn't carry the BBC name). I suppose it was only to be expected that everybody concerned would be pulling out all the stops to make it a success – after all I was the much publicised new boy, even to the extent of having my own private parking space, identified by a special name plate, outside the front entrance of the studios – a luxury never extended to me either before or since.

The set for the Christmas special was one of the most impressive and elaborate I've ever known in any show. It was built along the lines of the interior of a rather imposing country mansion. Entrance hallway, library, study, bar, lots of beautiful woodwork and beams, a huge log fire burning in the grate, the whole thing festooned with decorations, including, of course, a magnificent Christmas tree shimmering with lights and baubles. It really was a breathtaking piece of design. My guests included Sandie Shaw, Jimmy Tarbuck, Ronnie Corbett, Henry Cooper, Eamonn Andrews and Graham Hill. It was one of those shows that had such genuine atmosphere, that from the very start it was a sure winner. Messrs Tarbuck and Corbett were superb: I can't remember when I've seen the whole cast of a TV programme laugh so spontaneously throughout a show, as on that occasion. One of the sketches included in the show was supposedly happening during a Christmas party. I'd been given a magical crock of gold which, when rubbed in the manner of Aladdin's lamp, would fulfil one's most fantastic wishes.

The action began with Ronnie Corbett wishing that, just for once in his life, he could be a big man. This was followed, with the aid of trick photography, by Ronnie's transformation into Henry Cooper. Next came yours truly, wishing that, instead of being so laid back and slow, I could be the fastest man in the world. Val then becomes Graham Hill. Both Henry and Graham were 'surprise guests'.

The sketch was concluded by my asking Tarbuck what his dearest wish would be. He began to rub the crock of gold, his eyes gazing at me.

'I hope you won't find this embarrassing, Dooners,' he began, 'but all my professional life, I've had a great hero. He's Irish, he's suave, he's handsome, he's got a lovely voice and is everybody's favourite, so just for one moment, please may I be my hero?' His touching speech is followed by the predictable flash and transformation, but to everybody's surprise Jimmy becomes Eamonn Andrews. What we didn't know, however, was that Jimmy had secretly tutored Eamonn in the art of putting his thumb and forefinger of each hand into his waistcoat, à la Tarbuck, and endeavouring to tell a gag in the most dreadful Scouse accent. It was one of the funniest situations I can remember in any show I've done and helped to make the show a very painless experience.

My opening dialogue made special reference to the set, indicating that it was to be my home for the Christmas holiday. I even went so far as to say, 'Sorry I can't take you up the grand staircase to have a look at the bedrooms. In fact, the other side of that partition is where Tom Jones is rehearsing his show.'

Even after that, in came the letters: 'My goodness, what a lovely home you have, a long way from your little place in Ireland'. 'Thank you for letting us see your home. I live quite near you, and I must say that it looks nothing like that from the outside'. 'What a chore for your dear wife, having all those workmen about the place putting up lights and things. Hope you didn't have to keep making tea and coffee for them.'

The proposed series of shows on the horizon was to be bought and screened by ABC Television in America, as well as being transmitted at home by ATV. A London-based representative of the American company was pretty familiar with what the *Val Doonican Show*s were all about and must have been impressed enough for the deal to have gone so far towards finalisation. Word got through to me, however, that a further entourage was coming in from the States to see me work.

Naturally, my being at the London Palladium was about as good a shop window as anybody could want, and put me at a distinct advantage. Working at the world's leading variety theatre, in what was by now a well-established stage show, doing what I did best, was as much as I could hope for. Well, to paraphrase an old saying, they came, they saw, they contracted, the result being an invitation from Sir Lew Grade to Eve and me, asking us to come to his office for the signing of the agreement.

Once again, the whole deal was splashed all over the newspapers, the accent, of course, being on the amount of money I was allegedly being paid. Headlines announced VAL SIGNS ON DOTTED LINE FOR FIVE MILLION POUNDS. The five-million figure was a lie, I'm afraid. If the show ran five years, and was sold to all the potential markets open to such marketing, then maybe it could eventually reach something in that region. That, however, is not in any way meant to undervalue the whole thing, it was a dream come true for any television performer such as myself, hosting his own show. So we signed up and kept our fingers crossed.

A producer and director were flown in from Hollywood and two American writers were contracted, while on our side, we had a co-producer and writer keeping an eye on the British side of things. One of the ingredients vital to the show, according to the American team, was some British comedy, preferably something which could be resident, as it were, throughout the series. Great interest was focused on a comedy series running on ATV at the time, starring that very talented comedy actor Bernard Cribbins, assisted by the equally gifted Sheila Steafel and Bob Todd. It was decided that their contribution would be based in a London pub called the Flying Ducks.

It was virtually impossible to choose a weekly array of guests which would have equal appeal on both sides of the Atlantic, but we all worked very hard on the shows, and I must say, no expense was spared.

When finally we had 13 hours of material 'in the can', I was asked to travel to the United States for a promotional trip. Eve, Lynn and I flew to New York, where we were booked in at the St Regis Hotel. During the following 10 days or so, I was to be faced with an exhausting succession of radio and television appearances, coupled with endless newspaper interviews and photographic sessions, in an intensive effort to promote my name to a brand new audience.

In fact, the only familiar face I was to see throughout was that of David Frost. His very highly rated talk show was running at the time, and he spared no effort to make my appearance an enjoyable and indeed an effective one. Then there was the Dick Cavett show, the Mike Douglas show in Philadelphia, and many more.

My sister Nancy had emigrated to America as a GI bride way back in my youth. Since she lived in Philadelphia, she and her family were in the audience as I appeared on the highly successful *Mike Douglas Show,* and for me it was a memorable experience. She had never seen me work before, even though she had naturally followed my career with great pride. After the show we had a meal together and talked endlessly of our respective lives since our last meeting. Lynn and I stayed on in New York for a few days and managed to see a few Broadway shows. All in all we had a wonderful time and both felt that come what may, the experience was something we wouldn't have missed.

I waited with baited breath for the reaction on both sides of the Atlantic when screening time came around.

There is no doubt in my mind that the folks back home didn't like the shows, for the simple reason that they weren't the same as they'd always been. The sketches and lavish production somehow disarmed people who had become so accustomed to my many series from the BBC Television Theatre. I actually had many letters from 'dyed in the wool' BBC viewers who watched, simply to see what I was up to 'on the other side' as they put it. The letters said, 'We think you have spoiled the shows, and don't think we'll be watching again, but good luck anyway.'

The reaction in the States was mixed, my reviews ranging from very enthusiastic to indifferent.

Remarkably, several reviewers came to the same conclusion as I did myself: that the shows somehow did not seem to match my own television personality as my previous ones had done. The American producers and directors had not seen me work prior to their arrival in London, and simply built a show around me from their experience of working with other people, not through knowing what had made me popular in the first place. It was a shame they didn't know a bit more about my work to start with. But then, that's show business, as they say. By the end of that year and after much soul searching, Eve and I agreed to call it a day and return to making shows for the British market. We will really never know why the thing didn't work better.

Maybe I was just not right for the American TV public. Maybe I was doing the wrong kind of show for them, or, as Jimmy Brennan from the Queen's Theatre in Blackpool would have said, 'Maybe there was a Catholic procession in Buffalo.'

Tucked away in the drawer of my desk at home is an object that serves as a constant reminder of autograph hunters, and one in particular. I have no idea who she is, or where she is, or what she looks like, but she will always remain in my memory.

My manager Eve and I had a battle year after year, arguing about what songs we should release as single recordings. She would choose one and I would shake my head, then I'd suggest a track I'd just recorded and she in turn would 'pooh pooh' the idea as being ridiculous. Well, shortly after I'd had a very big hit with a song called 'What Would I Be' written by singer Jackie Trent, she very excitedly told me of a new song she'd heard. I sat obediently in her office and listened to a demonstration recording of it, and predictably enough, couldn't see anything in it. After endless coaxing and cajoling, Eve could see that I was not going to be convinced. 'Listen,' she said, hand on heart. 'I don't often ask you to do something just for me, but I know I'm right, love. Now, for once take my word and do it.' I surrendered, and promised to include it in a forthcoming recording session.

'It's fabulous,' she shouted on hearing the playback at the recording studio. 'You won't regret it.' A few months later it came out, had every bit of promotion available, and disappeared without a trace. Shortly afterwards a little package arrived at my home. The attached message read: 'From your know-it-all lady manager, sorry, I was wrong, but I still think it was lovely, Love Evie.' Inside was a superb solid gold matching pen and pencil set bearing the simple inscription 'Val'. It really was a lovely thing for her to have done and I was very touched by it. Since I am one of those all-time losers as far as personal possessions are concerned – keys, pipes, lighters, glasses, wallets, money clips (and full ones at that) – Lynn absolutely forbade me to take the things out of the box, and there they lay for ages. Then, while I was making a special appearance at the Palladium, and having lost my other pens, I took the gold ballpoint from its padded cell and popped it in my pocket.

An enormous crowd awaited the artists outside the stage door after the show, autograph books were being passed from one person to another, and cheap plastic pens, of course, were changing hands. At one point I found myself penless as a nice lady said, 'Please sign this for me, Mr

Doonican.' Reaching into my pocket, I produced my solid gold, specially engraved heirloom and wrote my name with a flourish. 'Thank you so much,' she said, smiling as I handed her the book and the pen, as I had been doing to dozens of people previously. Too late I discovered my folly and frantically searched with my eyes through the sea of people in the vague hope of seeing that gentle face. But the lady was nowhere to be seen. I've never forgotten her, though.

Many of the guests I had on my ATV series came in from the States, since most of our entertainers, apart from the occasional pop groups, weren't all that successful over there. People like Eddie Albert the actor, Burl Ives, Howard Keel, Jerry Reed the country guitarist, Ray Stevens of 'Everything is Beautiful' fame, Petula Clark and many more joined me for the series. Most of them were unknown to our daughters who, at that time, were very young and much more impressed by our own internationally or nationally known names – the Beatles or Basil Brush.

We sat round the breakfast table one morning prior to my leaving for the studio. I used to drop the girls off at junior school on my way. They were happily munching their Rice Krispies or Shreddies.

'Dad,' said Fiona, speaking with her mouth full. 'Who's on your show this week?' I mentioned somebody. She wasn't impressed. 'Who else?' she asked. I mentioned the remaining guests, finishing with the name Phil Harris. 'Who's he, Dad? Is he a singer?' There was no point in mentioning 'Darktown Poker Club' or 'Woodman Spare That Tree' to a four year old, so I gave it some thought. Then I had a brainwave.

'You've seen *Jungle Book*?'

'Yes.'

'Well, you remember Baloo the Bear?'

'Yes, he scratched himself all the time.'

'Well, Baloo the Bear was Phil Harris singing "The Bare Necessities".'

'Was he really, Dad? Have you got a bear on your show then?'

'Not exactly, but it was Mr Harris who did the voice.' I knew she wouldn't understand. 'Baloo himself was just a cartoon.' That was a bit like saying there was no Santa Claus! I changed the subject, asked her to get ready for school and went to get the car out of the garage. Lynn saw them both into the back seat, and we headed for school. When I dropped them at the gates and was just about to say cheers and be on my way, Fiona handed me a crumpled brown paper bag.

'What's that, darling?' I asked.

'It's for Mr Harris, it's a present.' They ran into school, shouting greetings to their young friends, while I got back in the car. Before pulling away I sneaked a look in the bag – it contained a banana. Phil Harris was tickled pink!

Some years back I told a story concerning Fiona, while appearing on a chat show. She was at a girls' convent school at the time. Despite many years having elapsed since the actual incident occurred, she got quite a ribbing from her young lady classmates, and made me promise I wouldn't repeat the indignity. Now that she's got children of her own, the worry of embarrassment has subsided and she gives her blessings to the following paragraphs.

The setting, once again, was our breakfast room. The background noise, as before, was the munching of breakfast cereals.

'What will you be doing at school today?' Lynn asked, pouring her a drink.

'Oh, I'm not sure,' she said between slurps, 'probably learning numbers,' slurp, 'singing,' slurp, 'painting, and maybe we'll play *When Suzy was a baby*.'

'What's *When Suzy was a baby*?' Lynn enquired.

'It's a very good game, Mummy, I like it.'

'But how do you play it?' I said.

'Well,' she blurted, settling herself in her chair and rolling her eyes towards heaven, as if asking for guidance. 'Ah...it's all about Suzy you see, first she's a baby, ah, then a schoolgirl, ahm, then a teenager, then ah, she gets married.' This went on until poor old Suzy gave up the ghost, died, went to heaven and goodness knows what else.

'But how do you actually play it?' I insisted.

'Well,' she rolled her eyes again. 'We *actually* play it when we stand and hold hands – then we all sing:

When Suzy was a baby,
A baby Suzy was,
She went Umh Umh, Umh Umh Umh.

The first two lines were accompanied by a kind of communal hand-clapping, while the final Umhs were executed with the thumb being sucked, signifying the baby. She took a break here and had another mouthful.

'And then?' I urged.

'You'll give her indigestion,' Lynn said – mums always say that!

'And then?' I repeated.

She went into the second verse.

When Suzy was a schoolgirl,
A schoolgirl Suzy was,
She went, 'Hey Miss, I can't do this.'

This time, the final line suggested Suzy's trying to attract the teacher's attention by raising her hand aloft. She picked up her spoon, at the same time smiling at me, knowing what was coming.

'And then?' I shouted, this time.

She laughed and gave the eyes another roll.

When Suzy was a teenager,
A teenager Suzy was,
She said, 'Ooh aah, I lost my bra,
I left my knickers in my boyfriend's car.'

There was a sort of temporary paralysis for a few seconds, except for Fiona, who got back to the cornflakes.

'She said what?' Lynn asked, her eyebrows raised an extra inch or so.

Without even batting an eyelid, Fiona gave a repeat performance:

She said, 'Ooh aah, I lost my bra,
I left my knickers in my boyfriend's car.'

'Are those the proper words?' Lynn's voice had also gone up a bit by now.

'Oh yes, that's what we sing,' said the young innocent.

'And do the sisters hear you sing that?' I joined in.

'Oh yes, Daddy, the sisters all know it!'

I looked at Lynn and trying not to laugh, was unable to resist the temptation. I said, 'Those are funny words, I think..."Ooh aah, I lost my bra, I left my knickers in my boyfriend's car." I don't understand them – I mean – what would Suzy be doing, taking off her knickers in her boyfriend's car?'

The eyes gave a few extra rolls this time – she'd obviously given no thought whatever to the lyric before. Then, slowly and thoughtfully, she said, 'Ahm, I don't know what she was doing really – perhaps she was changing for ballet.'

One of the unique things about these little 'out of the mouths of babes' stories is that, somehow, they can't be written by scriptwriters. They must simply happen.

Many years back, I was involved in the making of a special album, the proceeds of which were to be given to the charitable organisation UNICEF. As part of the promotion, it was arranged that the first copy was to be purchased by, and presented to, the prime minister. Mr Edward Heath held that office at the time, and a visit to No.10 Downing Street was organised, complete with the usual batch of press photographers. We were asked to go as a family, so naturally the girls were dressed up for the occasion. On arrival we were ushered into one of the large reception rooms used for those functions. It was beautifully furnished, and the floor was covered in a magnificent Persian-style carpet. The two girls, who were aged about five and six at the time, had strict instructions not to touch anything, so while waiting for the arrival of our very special contributor, they began to play a kind of 'hopscotch' game with the designs on the carpet. When Mr Heath eventually came in, he greeted everybody very courteously, giving extra attention to his young guests.

'Do you like our nice house?' he said to them. Once again everything was brought back to the basics, they smiled their approval and then Sarah issued a challenge to the prime minister.

'I'll bet,' she said, pointing to the carpet, 'that you can't get from here to there without treading on the blue bits.'

Needless to say, he didn't try it at that moment. In fact, he was preparing to meet a deputation from the Miners' Union immediately after our visit, so a much more complex game of hopscotch was on the horizon.

Chapter Nineteen

I n 1970, I had the pleasure of being one of the chosen subjects for TV's *This is Your Life*. I can honestly say that I didn't have a clue until that fateful moment when the little book was pushed in front of me, and those now famous words were addressed to me: 'Val Doonican, tonight, this is your life.' Unbeknown to me, the planning stages of the whole thing had been going on for ages beforehand. I truly suspected nothing, although after the deed had been perpetrated, I found myself putting all kinds of two and twos together.

The first question the organisers put to Lynn was, 'How can we be sure to catch him?'

'On the golf course,' she assured them. 'Organise an attractive game of golf with people he likes to play with, and come hail, rain or snow, he'll be there.'

That year was a very special year for me professionally. I was now booked in my own show for a period of six months at the famous London Palladium. All kinds of plans were in the melting pot.

The family and I had just got back from holiday in Barbados, when I received a call from my agent. It appeared that Leslie Grade's office, who were responsible for staging the Palladium show, wished to talk to me about organising a special photographic session. The resulting photos were intended for the theatre souvenir brochure. I rang Leslie Grade who suggested I might like a round of golf with the famous Ryder Cup captain Dai Rees. A photographer, of course, would be in attendance to take some suitable shots. This all sounded very plausible to me, since my golfing routine with Norman Vaughan was well known.

The golf match was planned for a few weeks hence, and naturally I looked forward to it very much. Now, believe it or not, only days before my golfing appointment, I had a phone call at about dinner time (Lynn was sitting, looking at a magazine, waiting for the food to be ready). The voice on the other end sounded very Irish. Frankly, I thought it was somebody trying to be funny. The conversation went something like this:

ME: Hello.

VOICE: Can I speak to Val Doonican?

ME :   Speaking, who is this?

VOICE :   (a very Irish name).

ME :   Sorry, how did you get this number [which is ex-directory]?

VOICE :   Oh, I'm with the *Irish Times* – we had it here in the office.

ME :   Is that you, Tarbuck?

VOICE :   Mr Doonican, could you tell me what you're doing next Wednesday?

ME :   Next Wednesday? Why do you ask that? I'm playing golf actually.

VOICE :   With Dai Rees?

ME :   Yes. How did you know that?

VOICE :   Actually, somebody tipped us off that it was Dai Rees's *This is Your Life*. He's being set up!

ME :   Well, if he is, nobody's told me.

VOICE :   I see, well, thank you very much.

I put the phone down, still wondering what the whole thing was about, and not suspecting a thing. Lynn looked up from her book.

'Who was that?'

I shook my head. 'No idea, says he's from some paper, asked me if next Wednesday is Dai Rees's *This is Your Life*.'

Lynn put down her magazine. 'Potatoes are ready,' she said, disappearing into the kitchen. The whole thing disappeared from my mind. My friend Mickey rang me the next day, offering to take me to South Herts Golf Course on the Wednesday. I wondered why he'd want to come along, and consequently asked him.

'I'd love to meet Dai Rees,' he said convincingly, 'maybe get a picture of him.'

He picked me up on the Wednesday, with lots of time in hand. 'I thought we'd leave early,' he said, 'the traffic is pretty awful today.' In fact, we were just approaching the golf club, with about half an hour to spare, when Mickey suddenly said, 'I'll take you down this way, there are some fantastic houses in this road. We've plenty of time anyway.'

I said that I wouldn't mind being early. 'Give me a chance to hit a few shots and loosen up.'

Undaunted, Mickey showed me all the houses as if he had just become an estate agent. He'd obviously been told to get me there at a certain time, in order to avoid my seeing any scanner vans from Thames TV which were secreting themselves in the vicinity of the clubhouse.

Dai was his charming self, the photographer was eager and ready, so things began to happen. We made our way to the teeing ground and our round began.

Once again, it was easy to deduce, in retrospect, that Dai had been asked to have me on the 18th green at a certain time. At the time, however, I was covered in confusion. We'd played some nine or ten holes when he casually suggested that we cut across the adjacent tee and play back towards the clubhouse. 'Looks as if it's going to pour down,' he said, looking up into a pretty rainless sky.

Anyway, we'd had quite a few pictures and I thought maybe the great man had better things to do and had given quite enough of his valuable time.

Soon we were playing our approach shots on to the 18th green. In fact, I played quite a good one, which was followed by Dai's shot, on this occasion not quite as close to the flag as mine. (I'll elaborate on this in a moment.)

The 18th green is quite elevated at South Herts, and as we popped our heads above the hill approaching it, I noticed a man standing by the flag, wearing a golf hat. 'What's he doing there?' I thought as I approached my ball, then like a bolt from the blue, I recognised Eamonn Andrews. 'Eamonn!' I exclaimed. 'What the hell are you doing here?' Then, as if struck by a thunderbolt, I thought, 'My God, it *is* Dai's *This is Your Life.*'

Dai, Mickey and myself gathered round Eamonn, and I waited in antici-pation for Dai's shattering surprise. Then it came:

'Val Doonican, tonight, this is your life.'

It really was a wonderful night. The only occasion in about 35 years when the entire Doonican family (with the exception of my father) were gathered together in one room. Some of my dearest friends came from far and wide, together with some special people from show business, in particular the late Dickie Henderson, and Moira Anderson, who was appearing in the Palladium show.

One lovely surprise brought very special memories of my boyhood back in Ireland. When I was very young, in common with most other boys, I longed for the weekly treat of Saturday at the pictures. I just loved cowboys – one of my favourites being Gene Autry. Lynn knew that I had written to him when I was about six years of age, asking for his autograph. Sadly, I never had a reply. Well, halfway through my evening of surprises, there on film, direct from his home in America, was the legendary Mr Autry himself.

'Howdy there, Val,' he greeted me, while leaning on a corral gate. 'Gee, I'm sure glad to have this opportunity of sending my greetings to you, and to apologise most sincerely for not answering your letter.'

That was followed by a short extract from one of his movies. 'And that,' said Eamonn, 'was what you and Mickey paid your precious fourpence to see way back in those early days.'

'Jesus,' said Mickey, 'we were robbed.'

Well, as I've said, it's easy to be wise after the event, and think 'I should have twigged that something was going on'. For example, during our West Indies holiday, Lynn had about four long-distance calls from London, making up all kinds of stories as to who they were from; there had been that strange phone call from the phantom Irish man, Mickey's sightseeing trip around South Herts, and Dai's ending the round of golf so quickly.

Two memorable remarks were made at the party afterwards. I told Eamonn that I took great exception to his opening comments on film, spoken, incidentally, over the arrival of our two balls on to the 18th. Since we were not in view, you simply saw an empty green, then a ball pitching on. As I've said earlier, my ball arrived first, quite close to the flag. 'Oh, that'll be Dai,' says Eamonn's voice, then Dai's ball appeared, not quite so close. 'Yes, that'll be Val.' The cheek of the man.

The second story came from an ex-member of the Four Ramblers. I hadn't seen Tommy Burns for about 15 years, but he'd been flown across from Dublin. It so happens that my family were on the same plane. My mother, however, was travelling incognito, using the name Mrs O'Reilly (this was just a precaution in case anybody noticed that there was a Mrs Doonican on the plane, and mentioned it to me). My old partner Tommy, however, had known my mother for many years and recognised her, but wasn't sure if she'd remember him – after all, she was then 82. As they disembarked in London, some representatives from Thames TV greeted them. As they were all going to spend some time together as a party, introductions were considered advisable. Tommy was just about to say hello to my mother when somebody said to him, 'Oh, Mr Burns, have you met Mrs O'Reilly?' He was a bit lost for words, and remarked to me later: 'I had no idea your mother had married again.'

In 1972 I signed a new record contract, this time with the Phonogram Company, better known as Philips. I'd previously been with the Pye label, and before that, under contract to Decca. Since, as I've told you, all my previous recordings remained the joint property of Eve and myself, we were now able to pass them on to Phonogram for the duration of our contract, to do with as they wished. They immediately set about releasing several compilations of previously released tracks, including a six-box set marketed by the Readers' Digest Company.

Having spent the summer of 1971 working on the American TV shows, it was back to summer season again in 1972, the venue on this occasion being the Winter Gardens in Bournemouth.

I joined Parkstone Golf Club for the season, and enjoyed my free time with friends and members at this very hospitable club. My own golf reached its peak around that time and I was quite proud of myself for acquiring a handicap of four. I know that this kind of information means nothing to the non-golfer, but for me and my hobby at the time, it was everything.

Speaking of non-golfers, I came home from Parkstone Golf Club one day, having played in a match and returned a score of level par. I was absolutely elated as I walked through the kitchen door.

'Hi, love,' I shouted.

'Hello,' Lynn answered from the lounge. 'Have a good morning?'

'Good morning?' I asked mockingly. 'A good morning? Do you know that I played in a match this morning and I *had a par round*?'

She went on with whatever she was doing. 'Bully for you then,' she said, 'is that good?'

'It only means that I didn't drop a single shot.' I thought that was bound to get some kind of recognition. I waited.

Finally she spoke. 'Oh, by the way, love, the office rang. Will you give them a buzz before five?' and that was that. If our marriage could survive that, believe me it could survive anything!

Later that year I did my first home-grown series of shows, as well as a Christmas special, for ATV, and enjoyed myself much more. Looking through my diary for the year that followed makes me realise what energy and enthusiasm I had in those days. The sheer weight of my commitments had little or no effect on me at the time as far as I recall, which confirms the old saying 'amazing how time slips by when you're enjoying yourself'. The year began with a trip to Holland, followed by a season at the then famous Coventry Theatre in preparation for a long summer show at the ABC Theatre in Great Yarmouth. This was to be followed by a further eight weeks at the Prince of Wales Theatre in London, which, in turn, was followed by another television series. Many, many further entries clutter up my date book, all contributing to what surely must have been one of my busiest years.

I knew that my television shows were being sold to various English-speaking countries around the world. Like many British-based artists, I was attracting interest from a lot of them, in particular, Australia and New Zealand. The extent of the shows' popularity, however, was a bit uncertain. I just knew that people were seeing them, and for this I was grateful. It was also helping record sales abroad.

Enquiries began to come in as to the possibility of a tour 'Down Under', but while my success at home was still relatively untapped, Eve kept putting it off. I simply didn't have the time to take on any more engagements. By the beginning of the 1970s, the time appeared to be right, so a tour was arranged, beginning with some 20 or so appearances in New Zealand, followed by five or six weeks in Australia.

The summer prior to the tour saw me in summer season down in Bournemouth. One of my golfing partners during the engagement was Max Bygraves, who was also working there for that particular season and lived there on a permanent basis. Max, one of the most experienced of all our top entertainers, had by that time undertaken several tours of the Antipodes, so I asked him what he thought my prospects might be.

'Oh, you'll love it, mate, and you'll do fine,' Max assured me. 'They're a smashing audience. You might get the odd heckler when you work the clubs. They can quite enjoy having a go at the Poms, but don't let it worry you, each time you go over there you'll find it gets better and better.'

How right he was. I've been 18 times now over the years, and it's gradually become like a second home to me. The larger clubs over there, by the way, are mainly in the state of New South Wales, the only state where poker machines are legal. You'll find thousands of them throughout the clubs, their income being the main source of subsidy for the more expensive cabaret acts. The management of the more successful establishments come in three categories: League Clubs, run by the big Rugby League teams. RSL Clubs, meaning Returned Servicemen's Leagues, and The Workers' Clubs.

They can be quite huge concerns with thousands of members, their facilities appearing to know no bounds – two or three restaurants, catering for different tastes, indoor bowling greens, swimming pools, squash and tennis courts, discos for the young set, several bars, snooker rooms and, of course, a large cabaret room/concert hall, seating up to 1,700 people.

Engagements in the other states – Queensland, South Australia, Victoria, Western Australia, Northern Territories and Tasmania – are mainly confined to straightforward concerts. Personally speaking, my heart has always remained firmly devoted to the concert stage. So, through the years, my promoters have tended to book me more and more in that direction.

Well, with this exciting prospect on the horizon, my musicians, singers and I boarded a Qantas 747 at Heathrow, and embarked on our 12,000-

mile journey. The flight took us through the Middle East, then Hong Kong, and finally the last leg of the trip towards Australia.

Very weary and cramped, we made a brief pause in Melbourne, in the state of Victoria, and were escorted into the VIP lounge for refreshments. My travelling manager, Mickey, and I sat sipping a coffee, when a man sitting in a nearby chair caught my eye.

'G'day,' he said, winking. 'I think maybe I know your face.'

'You could be right,' I said, hoping he was not mistaking me for somebody else.

'Aren't you that "Val Something" fella who sings on the television?' he asked.

'That's right,' I told him.

'My wife watches you a bit,' he said, rather grudgingly. 'Are you over here for a holiday?'

Hell of a way for a holiday, I thought to myself. 'I'm on my way to New Zealand,' I explained, 'to do some shows.' He looked at me a bit taken aback.

'You're not thinking of working here in Oz, are you?' he said, almost threateningly.

I was tempted to say no, and end the conversation. I didn't like the sound of it, but I told the truth.

'As a matter of fact, yes, I am, in a couple of weeks or so.' I waited.

'Well, you're a brave man I would have thought,' he said. 'I can't imagine you being popular enough for that.'

Well, there's nothing like a bit of encouragement at the start of a new venture.

My eventual arrival in Auckland, New Zealand, turned out to be a memorable occasion. In spite of my physical exhaustion, and longing for a comfortable bed, great celebrations seemed to be in progress as we disembarked near the arrival terminal. Huge crowds of people were gathered, waving and cheering, and a group of young people in some kind of traditional costume sang and danced on the tarmac surface adjoining the airport building. All my company and I wondered what the occasion could be, and looked around for a clue, never thinking for one moment that the centre of attraction was, in fact, myself. As we walked from the aircraft, the crowd's enthusiasm became even more pronounced, while on closer investigation the traditional costumes worn by the young dancers turned out to be Irish.

This was a totally new experience for me as my career up to that time, and indeed since, had gone along at a steady, but low-key pace.

Inside the terminal block, hordes of waiting people greeted me with warm words of welcome, before I was whisked away to my hotel for a press conference. All my tiredness and jet-lag seemed to fade with the sincerity of the hospitality extended to me over the next couple of hours. When at last I retired to my hotel suite, I slept for goodness knows how long.

The tour was to be a remarkable one in my experience. Each evening, the packed houses, the crowds awaiting my arrival at the concert halls, not to mention those waiting to see me afterwards, continued to amaze me. I simply had no idea of the extent of my popularity in this little country some 12,000 miles from the BBC Television Studios in London.

I recall a visit to a local radio station where I was to do an interview. I discovered that only with a police escort could our car get into the street where the station was situated. Until that time, I'd associated such public reaction with young pop idols such as the Rolling Stones or The Beatles, but never with a middle-aged family entertainer such as myself.

Well, the tour lived up to all expectations, with not a single seat available at any one of the 20 or so performances.

This happened, by the way, during a period when my working attire was mainly confined to what Lynn liked to describe as elegant casuals. The habit of my being dressed in a well-chosen wardrobe of knitwear was something, which, like the rocking chair, had crept up on me, so to speak, eventually becoming an integral part of my television personality.

Since the climate in Australia was not the ideal one for such stage wear, it was decided that we'd have some custom-built lightweight casuals made by a well-known London men's store. (I might add that I never intended, at any time, to wear casual clothes on stage. They were strictly a TV idea, originally chosen for their design rather than colour, since the first four or five series I did were in black and white. However, the popularity of the idea was such that had I not made some effort at following it through on stage, the audience, somehow, would have felt a bit cheated.) It was recommended by the makers of these specially designed pieces, that they should be very carefully hand washed, something which became quite an issue during a hectic tour of one-night stands. There was a memorable occasion when we played a concert at one of the large venues, which was followed by a well-earned day off. The only problem facing me was that my stage wear needed to be washed and cleaned, but our day off happened to be a Sunday.

Our audience for the Saturday concert included a party of sisters from a local convent. My manager, Mickey, on having a word with them, discovered that several of them originated from the vicinity of our home town in Ireland. After the show, we invited them backstage for a chat. An unusual occurrence for them, I feel sure. They admired my stage sweaters, which prompted Mickey to mention our cleaning problem. Without the slightest hesitation, they enthusiastically offered their assistance, suggesting that they should take the sweaters away, promising to have them all clean and ready by the following afternoon. The only condition facing me was that I had to agree to go to the convent the next afternoon for tea, while at the same time collecting my laundry.

Well, they gave us a wonderful welcome the next day, and a sumptuous tea was laid before my associates and me. As so often happens on these kind of visits, a guitar eventually appeared from behind a sofa, and was discreetly moved in my direction. An hour-long sing-song with a strong Irish bias was to follow.

The sisters, armed with their personal cameras, took endless souvenir photographs of our enjoyable visit, copies of which, I feel sure, were to make their way across the Irish Sea during the following weeks.

My stage wear never had such devoted care and attention, or smelled as clean and wholesome as after it had been looked after by the kindly laundresses. A delightful footnote to the occasion was later passed on to me by one of the girls in our group. It appears the sisters had some second thoughts about their generous offer while returning home after the show.

'Suppose they were stolen from the clothesline behind the convent,' one of them said. 'What on earth would we do? They couldn't possibly be replaced.' They obviously viewed the possibility quite seriously, too, as the upshot of their concern was a decision to take turns at a kind of sentry duty. Their vigil went on until the clothes were dry. For the remainder of the tour, my stage attire became affectionately known in our group as 'Doonican's Habits'.

So, I was sad indeed to say goodbye to the people of New Zealand. We boarded the plane and waved our farewells, hoping deep down that Australia would not turn out to be something of an anticlimax.

We stopped off at Sydney, en route to Melbourne, where our first Australian concert was to take place. We then planned to return to Sydney, where I was to appear at one of the top clubs for a month's engagement. The entertainment manager of the club in question kindly met us in Sydney, simply to say how much he was looking forward to our visit and happily to inform us that the entire month's engagement was sold out.

The Australian section of the tour was just as exciting an experience for the company, and we all looked forward to the prospect of being invited to repeat the trip.

Chapter Twenty

In common with so many of my fellow 'workaholics', I've never been all that enamoured by the prospect of going away on holiday. I've loved it from the family's point of view, of course, and look back on our trips when the children were younger with great affection. Now, as I get a little older and the pressure of work has greatly decreased, I find that my attitude towards going away for a break is fast approaching what it should have been all along. Up to the time when Lynn and I got married, I'd never really bothered to go on holiday at all. I suppose I thought my work was like a never-ending vacation.

It has been suggested to me on occasions, that perhaps I never found the right kind of holiday for me personally. Who knows, maybe my 'ideal' is waiting somewhere out there and we simply haven't got together. I should clarify the situation by saying that I love just staying at home, using the time to catch up on my hobbies.

My initiation into the more exotic kind of holidays came about in the mid-1960s through some friends of ours. The husband had achieved quite exceptional success with the company for which he worked, and was invited by them to spend some time in the West Indies as their manager there. Before leaving, the family kindly invited Lynn and me to come out and spend a holiday there as their guests, whenever we felt like it. Since we were busy settling into our new home at the time, we felt the idea to be a bit out of reach financially. Fortunately, my career was coming along in leaps and bounds, and pretty soon we began viewing the idea as a real possibility.

The following winter found us both enjoying the warm sun of Jamaica, not to mention the warmth of hospitality extended to us by Terry and his wife Bobbie, and their young family. After that initial introduction we made regular visits to both Jamaica and Barbados, sharing the joys of the Caribbean with fellow members of the entertainment world, like the late Sir Harry Secombe and sports commentator David Coleman and their respective families.

One sunny morning Harry, David and I went on a deep-sea fishing trip. An elegant cabin cruiser with a crew consisting of two young lads came and picked us up from the beach adjoining our hotel.

'Well, Val, old son,' I thought climbing over the side, 'this is a hell of a long way from the piece of string, bent pin, and tin of worms. This is the real stuff.'

The young skipper, inviting us to make ourselves comfortable, began pouring three very generous beakers of rum punch. Dressed in floppy sun hats, swimming shorts and little else, we settled down, sipping our local brew and wishing the folks at home could see us. Meanwhile our three fishing lines, baited and cast over the stern, were being made secure in the special housings which allowed them simply to get on with their job, as we headed seaward.

Each line has a little of its slack taken up before cast off. This is held securely by a kind of clothes peg device. At the first signs of tension on the line the slack is suddenly released, accompanied by a warning 'crack' as the peg snaps shut, signifying 'a bite'. That's usually the signal for novices such as myself to leap out of their seats, running madly about the place wondering what to do next. Then follows a most fascinating piece of theatre in my opinion. The young expert, with great enthusiasm, grabs the line and having invited you to jump into the work-seat to which your personal rod is attached he slowly and skilfully brings your fish home. All the time you're acting as a kind of willing helper, and sharing in the excitement. The job completed, he pats you on the back and shouts, 'Well done, sir, you got him and he's a beauty, too.'

It's a wonderful morale booster, especially later as you stroll up the beach, a large kingfish slung over your shoulder.

I knew that Harry had done it all many times before, so deep down I said a little prayer that the fish would pick him first, then I could sit and watch.

Goodness knows how many rum punches later Harry held the floor, or the deck, with endless stories of his days in the forces and his years with the Goons. Suddenly, we heard the warning click and one of the lines took up its slack. It was Harry's. He leaped into action, assisted by one of our young experts.

'Take it easy now,' he said. 'Don't rush him.'

A huge kingfish leaped from the water, some distance from the boat, only to disappear again into the depths, while David and I watched, and shouted our encouragement. Well, whether it was a case of Harry doing all the right things, or the fish's being a bit of an amateur, I don't know, but in no time, we were pulling the gleaming catch on board. He was a beauty indeed, and I must say I felt a bit sorry for him as he thrashed about there on the floor in the stern of the boat.

Harry must have felt that sense of guilt also, because no sooner had the kingfish shown signs of ending his struggle, than Harry took him by the fin and started apologising profusely.

'I'm sorry, my old lad,' he told him. 'It could have been any of them out there, you were just passing at the time. Nothing personal, you understand.'

The fish showed no sign whatever of accepting any excuses, but just lay there motionless. Then came Harry's final tribute to his victim. Holding the blue-coloured tail between his palms and gazing out to sea, he burst into song in that rich tenor voice: 'Your tiny hand is frozen, let me warm it into life.'

His familiar tones echoed across the beautiful blue carpet of water with just the odd fish popping its head up to see what the hell was going on. David and I were busy laughing with Harry, never thinking for a moment that this was anything unusual for Mr Sea-goon. Our laughter turned to hysterics, however, as we turned around and caught sight of our young 'captain and mate', and the look of total bewilderment on their faces. You can well imagine, two youngsters who didn't know Harry from Adam, standing there thinking he must have lost his mind.

'Who is that man?' one of them asked, smiling. We smiled back, reassuring them that he was quite sane and did this sort of thing for a living. One of them turned to Harry and said, 'What's your name, sah?'

'Secombe,' shouted Harry.

'Where you come from?' the lad asked. I knew what was coming next and couldn't wait to see the lad's face.

'I come from Wales,' Harry told him.

'Where?' the boy said, looking puzzled: he'd obviously never heard of Wales.

'Wales,' Harry repeated, 'Wales, boy.' Then slapping his huge torso with the palms of his hands he said, 'With a figure like mine, I couldn't very well have come from Sardines, could I?' This was followed by the typical Secombe laugh and a raspberry. The young boy looked at all of us with a blank expression.

It's a very interesting study, actually trying to analyse how well certain types of humour will travel. Like wines, some will be acceptable on arrival, while others will just die in transit. Being Irish, and having been weaned on my own native humour, I've lived through countless examples of 'one man's humour being another man's blank look'. Phrases or sayings which were so much part of my early life, can, when casually introduced into a conversation, bring a snigger of approval from some, or nothing more than a puzzled look from others.

I appeared on television some years ago with a very successful international star. Part of our preliminary conversation was to be on the subject of poetry, and the art of writing lyrics for popular songs. I had mentioned, during a script meeting, that when I was a young lad, our prize chestnut was as follows:

There was a young man from Tralee,
Who was stung on the neck by a wasp.
When asked if it hurt,
He said, 'Not at all,
He can do it again if he likes.'

The Americans present had never heard it before, thought it funny, and suggested that I include it in the chat. At rehearsals that afternoon I recited it in passing. One or two of the floor crew laughed out loud, but the star of the show just looked at me amazed. 'You're not going to say that are you?' he asked. 'It doesn't make sense, I mean, it doesn't even rhyme!'

The summer of 1975 found us back in Torquay, and what a happy time that turned out to be. I was appearing at the Princess Theatre, while Ronnie Corbett starred at the Festival Theatre in Paignton, just down the road. Another friend, comedian Jerry Stevens, was staging his own show at one of the major hotels. Ronnie, Jerry, my friend Mickey and I made up one of the most enjoyable golfing partnerships I can remember. Just about every morning of the week we made our way to Newton Abbot Golf Club, known to most people as 'Stover', to enjoy a four-ball match followed by a snack lunch and a drink. The club made us very welcome, as indeed do most golf clubs around the country.

Ronnie's daughters Sophie and Emma were about the same age as Sarah and Fiona, which was fortunate. Lynn and Ronnie's wife Anne took them to the beach on many occasions while we were at the golf club, or having an afternoon nap prior to our two evening performances. A mutual friend of ours named Mervin Saunders had the use of a very nice boat and frequently took us out as a family. Complete with picnic lunch we travelled along the coast enjoying the sunshine, at the same time getting a welcome respite from the bustle of the busy holiday town. One Sunday, the Corbetts and ourselves were returning from such a trip when the children's attention centred on a huge oil tanker, standing off the bay some distance out to sea. 'Could we go and have a look at it?' they asked. We tried to explain just how far away it was, but they persisted with their request.

Both the dads were quite adamant, however. It was our friend Mervin who finally brought the subject to a head.

'Oh come on,' he said, turning the wheel seaward, 'it's not all that far.' Well, it was 'all that far', but worth the trip. I'd never believe that a vessel could be so huge, and, never having experienced one so close to, I was very impressed. We did a couple of circuits of the ship and headed for home.

By strange coincidence, I attended a cocktail party the following week and was introduced to someone who was very much involved in the world of oil tankers. He was, however, much more fascinated by our world of summer entertainment.

'How many shows a week do you do?' he enquired.

'Twelve,' I told him. He looked surprised.

'Gosh, twelve shows a week, for how long?'

'About four months, I suppose,' I said.

'What?' he gasped. 'That's...Let me see...Crikey, almost two hundred shows. You must be positively knackered at the end of that lot.'

I tried to explain that it's just a job of work, and you get used to it.

'You must have one hell of a holiday when you've finished it,' he said, shaking his head.

'Just a couple of weeks, in fact,' I admitted, 'then I start work on a TV series.' The expression on his face was such that I began to feel ashamed.

'Two weeks is no damn good.' He was more or less telling me off now. 'You should have a month or two.'

I laughed out loud. 'I haven't had two months off for as long as I remember.'

'Well, you should have,' he said, beginning to sound like my family doctor. 'You can't possibly recharge your batteries in two weeks.' Then taking me by the arm, he guided me towards the window overlooking the bay. 'See that tanker out there,' he said, pointing towards the horizon. I nodded into my glass of wine. 'Well, you and I are no different from that monster. It takes ages really to get it moving, but it's even harder to bring it to a complete stop. You can switch off everything, but its own impetus will take it on for miles.'

'Miles?' I said, with an air of disbelief.

'Miles,' he repeated. 'And the first of those miles is about the same as your two weeks' holiday. You haven't even come to a halt when you're back to your TV series or whatever.'

I've thought quite a bit about that gentleman's words of wisdom. I think he's got something!

The daily rounds of golf were just what I needed that summer. Apart from the sheer joy that game brings anyway, I was both mentally and technically preparing myself for a very important game. I had been invited, some months previously, to take part in the very successful television series *Pro Celebrity Golf* at the beautiful Gleneagles Golf Club in Scotland. When the great day arrived I was picked up early in the morning from our temporary home on the outskirts of Torquay, and taken by road to Exeter airport. A small private aircraft was awaiting me there, and within 10 minutes of my arrival, I was being whisked away in a northerly direction. Happily, the weather en route was glorious, so I just sat there enjoying the view and wondering what joys or disasters lay in store for me. The whole series of *Pro Celebrity Golf* is usually played over a couple of weeks, the promoters endeavouring to put two nine-hole matches 'in the can' per day. The pilot drew my attention to a tiny grass airstrip up ahead, or should I say down ahead, a long tidy row of similar aircraft to our own lining either side of it, rather like a guard of honour. Some black limousines stood by the modest reception buildings indicating that I wasn't the only one arriving at that particular time. In fact, as I said hello to one of the representatives from BBC Television, standing by the cars, another plane lightly touched down. 'That'll be Mr Crosby now,' I heard somebody behind me say, causing my ears to prick up. One of my great personal ambitions had long been to meet the man I always considered to be the finest pop singer of all time. I felt sure the opportunity was at hand, knowing we were both heading for the same destination.

A minute or two later, I was ushered into one of the waiting cars, and just as I climbed aboard, a voice said, 'Oh Val, have you met Bing?' I turned, and there entering the car parked alongside was The Man Himself.

'Hi there Val, how'ya doin'?' he reached out of the car and took my hand. 'I believe we're playin' a bit of golf together today.' Till that moment, of course, I had no idea who my playing opponent was to be. Just as our respective cars were pulling away, he opened his window and called out. 'Let's have some lunch together before the game.' We did just that within the hour, and then made our way to the golf course. Bing, as most golfers will know, had been an extremely good amateur golfer, and even now, in his early seventies, he still played well. It was indeed a day I shall never forget, made even more memorable by the young Scottish lad I told you about earlier, who had no idea who the great Mr Crosby was when he asked for my autograph during the round.

I was to return to Gleneagles the following summer and have the pleasure of seeing Mr Crosby once again. It wasn't so long after when we heard the sad news of his sudden and fatal heart attack on a golf course in

Spain. I know it's been said by many people, but it's so true nevertheless, that I doubt if he would have chosen any other place on earth to say farewell than on a golf course.

I've never appeared in pantomime as a solo artist. I specify 'solo artist', since I did appear many times while with the Ramblers, and found it great fun. Offers have come along, of course, but somehow, the idea of playing an Irish Robin Hood or Buttons just didn't appeal to me at all. During my season at Torquay in 1975, I was invited to appear in a Christmas entertainment at the Opera House in Manchester. The show was never intended as any kind of pantomime, but simply a festive season variety show, scheduled to run for about eight weeks. In fact, the show was virtually the same as our Torquay bill, with the exception of one extra act, which had to be found.

My musical director, Roger, rang me one evening at home, saying he'd just been watching the show *Wheeltappers and Shunters* and had seen an act on there which he felt would be ideal for our purposes, providing, of course, he was available and interested. During the following week, our show's producer, Maurice Fournier, put out some feelers and managed to get a video of the act concerned. We all thought he was a great entertainer and ideal for our show. Fortunately, he was both available and interested, agreeing to join the show for rehearsals prior to our Manchester opening.

He was, as it turned out, a great asset to the show (his first ever theatre engagement, by the way), and was to appear with me for summer seasons over the following two years, in Scarborough in 1976 and Bournemouth in 1977. The man I'm referring to is Paul Daniels, and from that first meeting in Manchester, somehow there was never any doubt he would achieve the success we've seen him enjoy since. Paul is a very inventive man with enormous drive and ambition. Then there's the talent and personality to make it all come together and work. I've really enjoyed watching his rise to the heights.

Having said all that, I must admit that the season at Manchester was not what I would call a hit. First and foremost, the audience didn't turn up in the kind of numbers I'd grown accustomed to seeing, and so again we get back to the argument as to why? The next season we did was everything

I could ask for, so as I say, why? Maybe the show was not 'Christmassy' enough. Maybe the theatre was not the right venue for it. Maybe it was because Tommy Steele was having enormous success with his Hans Christian Andersen presentation just up the road at the Palace Theatre – or on the other hand, maybe there was a Catholic procession in Bristol. I don't know the answer, and neither does anybody else. It was just another tug on that choke chain, and didn't do me any harm at all.

My television shows at ATV were entering their fifth year and, in my estimation, needed an injection of fresh ideas. Strangely enough, it was a time when the shows, which were being aired at 7.30pm each Tuesday, reached their highest ratings ever, having, for one week at least, reached the No.1 spot for the first time.

Then, one day in London, I bumped into Terry Hughes, one of the BBC producers I'd worked with previously, and now Assistant Head of Light Entertainment at the Television Centre. To my astonishment, he gave me the impression that I would be welcome back at the BBC, providing we got the right shows together. The reason for my surprise at the prospect of returning was that, as I had left there in 1970, after so many happy years, the BBC may have felt that they'd had my 'best' years. Terry rang Eve within a week or so, saying that Bill Cotton, then Head of Light Entertainment, would like to see me. An appointment was arranged, and after a long sojourn 'on the other side', I entered the BBC Television Centre again.

Bill, Terry and I sat in the office for an hour or so, chatting about the prospects of doing more shows, and reminiscing about the early days, and my first shows there.

'I think we should try a series in the New Year,' Bill said, 'and with a bit of luck, I think we might get five more years out of it.' Well, we did, and many more.

Just as I was about to leave the office, Bill said, 'Maybe you should do one special, in the meantime, just to get the feel of the place again.' He then suggested that Yvonne Littlewood might be the person to produce and direct the shows – another wise decision. 'One last thing before you go, and this is the sixty-four thousand dollar question...'

'Go on,' I said.

'How would you feel about doing them live on Saturday nights, like you used to in the old days?'

I accepted gladly, we shook hands, and I left.

I've always loved doing live television. Many of my fellow artists could never understand why. 'Why put that pressure on yourself?' they'd say. 'Nobody notices whether it's live or not, so why bother?' Well, the explanation has always been an elusive one but – it just feels different. There's an urgency and excitement about knowing that this is your one and only chance to get it right. Maybe it's different for me, having done so many live series in the past, and having become accustomed to the stimulation. It could be, in fact, that artists who entered the television world during the pre-taping years have never known what live TV feels like, whereas I know what they're missing from where I stand. I'm sure it's very much a personal thing anyway.

Chapter Twenty-One

My return to Saturday nights live on BBC was just the injection needed for me at the time, and it breathed new life into my career. Yvonne Littlewood, a very talented and conscientious lady, with a formidable record as far as musical TV shows are concerned, was at the helm throughout. We both endeavoured at all times to present a format which covered a broad spectrum of varied music, from pop and country, through to jazz and big band nostalgic sounds, and classical. It was quite common to discover as my guests on Saturday nights such contrasting talents as country singer Charlie Pride, jazz virtuoso of the harmonica and guitar Toots Thielemans, and flautist James Galway. In fact, when looking back through my old scripts for research, I'm very proud indeed that in this day and age when survival can depend so much on blatant commercialism, we managed to maintain our integrity for so long. It has also stretched me vocally, encouraging me to tackle duets, both vocal and instrumental, with a wide range of artists. Imagine my pleasure on hearing the news of Yvonne's inclusion in the 1986 Honours List. Her receiving an MBE for her contribution to television is something she richly deserves.

By now, Eve Taylor was showing signs of having had enough of the business. She'd been a hard-working agent and manager for as long as I could remember and her track record was very impressive indeed. Eve always was a highly strung, excitable lady, and I was not at all surprised when the stresses and strains of the entertainment world began to take their toll. Her friends and associates noticed the change in her long before she became aware of it herself.

Finally, it happened. Returning from a short holiday in America, she rang me up, asking me to drop into the office later in the week.

'I don't think I can take the strain of this business any longer, love,' she told me as I sat across from her in the office. It was easy to see that apart from anything else, she was, in fact, losing interest in the whole thing. 'I really can't be bothered with the hassle and the rat race [her favourite description of the world of theatrical management].' In spite of my knowing that I was about to lose my manager of 20 years' standing, I couldn't but agree with her that this was her only suitable action. It was time to retire.

We were both of one mind as to her successor, a mutual friend named Bernard Lee. Bernie had long experience since starting out as an office boy in the Grade organisation many years ago. He'd worked very closely with the late Brian Epstein in the heyday of The Beatles. He'd then gone on to handle many of the major stars, while working as a partner in the famous London Management company. However, most important of all, he was a friend. He knew me and what was important to me both professionally and personally. My business affairs were transferred to Bernie lock, stock and barrel and as far as I know, dear Evie breathed a sigh of relief.

Bernie was in complete agreement with my decision not to take on any further summer-season shows. He also confirmed my reservations about doing any more club work, not that there was all that much available by this time. The club circuit which had enjoyed such an enormous boom through the 1960s and 1970s was beginning to show signs of coming to an end. People were not coming in anything like the same numbers, which meant smaller profits or, indeed, no profits at all. As the old music hall some 20 years earlier had changed over to bingo halls, so the clubs became discos, or simply drinking houses.

As often happens, one trend replaced another, and so a new field catering for the public's needs slowly emerged. Civic centres were appearing in more and more towns and cities, attracting an increasing number of established artists to appear for one or two nights. Much of the 'family' type audiences, starved of theatre life and not attracted to the clubs, began to reappear. Many of the towns, in fact, were now inspired to reopen their old theatres, refurbished to look alive, well and above all welcoming. For somebody such as myself who had worked at these places before their demise, it was a real thrill to return. The Opera House in Belfast (where I'd last appeared in 1955), the Darlington Theatre, the Grand Theatre Swansea and many more, together with the new breed of entertainment centres, meant a whole circuit of very attractive venues.

The pressure of 12 shows a week during the summer was replaced by two or three nights a week, giving both the entertainers and the theatres a pretty good chance of success. It's good to note, of course, that most of the major summer resorts continue to present long-running shows, while the less successful ones, no longer able to support a resident company in the summer months, take advantage of those artists available for just one or two nights. As I've said, the theatre has always been notable for its survival, moving with the times and in my experience, invariably for the better of all concerned. It's easy indeed for people to say, 'Oh it's not like it was in the old days, they shouldn't have changed this or that', but those changes have so often been part and parcel of the theatre's survival, and a result of things no longer working 'as they used to be'.

Having been fortunate enough throughout my long career to have worked through the various phases of the big band era, the music hall, the club or cabaret period, and of course, the television phenomenon, I can honestly say that the one-night concert pattern now in vogue for such as myself is undoubtedly the most enjoyable I can recall. People accustomed to seeing some of their favourite artists on television can go along and see them in what I certainly feel to be the most advantageous light.

Through the early 1980s, my annual TV series contained a weekly-filmed segment, mainly located in Great Britain and Ireland. These filmed inserts enabled us to introduce a bit of outdoors into an otherwise live studio presentation. They also gave us the extra challenge of finding weekly settings for a specially selected song. During the weeks, we tried sailing, travelling the canals by barge, horse riding, gliding, cycling, visiting country gardens, taking my audience on a visit to my home town, and on one occasion, dashing about above the Norfolk countryside in a twin-seater autogyro, a tiny flying machine with no outer body, looking for all the world like a three-wheeled tandem with no handlebars.

Some months previously I had happened to see a BBC documentary film about the autogyro and its creator, Wing Commander Ken Wallis, and found it quite fascinating. I only had to mention this to Yvonne, of course, for the wheels to be set in motion. The video of the show was delivered to her office where we could watch it at our leisure. A few days later, everything was arranged with the Wing Commander, who was most enthusiastic about our idea.

Our proposed film sequence was planned over two days, on location up in Norfolk near the Wing Commander's home. The opening segment of my song took place in a nearby hangar, where I viewed some wonderful vintage aircraft, my lyrics inviting the viewers to take to the air. Then, strolling outside, I discovered the tiny autogyro and climbed aboard.

It was a very chilly afternoon and I think the entire crew were somewhat relieved as we prepared to finish for the day. The actual flying sequence was scheduled for nine o'clock the following morning.

'Do you think you'll feel scared tomorrow?' Ken Wallis asked as I dismounted from the flimsy machine. Even though I'd done some flying in various light aircraft and gliders, I felt this was something quite different.

'I honestly don't know what to expect,' I told him. 'We'll just have to wait and see, won't we?' I was beginning to remove my headgear when Ken reached out a hand and stopped me.

'Tell you what,' he said, smiling wickedly, 'why don't we have a little trial run right now? You're all dressed up, the machine is ready – so what do you say?'

Before I had time to answer, Yvonne jumped into action. 'Just give us some time to set up,' she requested. 'We might get some good stuff in the can. Who knows, it could be chucking it down tomorrow morning.'

Later, as we sat warming up for take-off, Ken turned and shouted through the roar of the engine. 'Tell you what, I'll go up about fifty feet and hover a bit. If you feel that it's too scary, just give me a sign and I'll come straight down again, OK?' I laughed out loud, thinking to myself, 'Yeah, suppose I do chicken out, what happens tomorrow? We can't just pack up and go home empty-handed. I've got to like or lump it.'

At last we took off, in a cloud of dust, rising almost vertically to 50 feet or so. In fact, it was very exciting, if extremely cold. Leaning forward, I gave Ken a very professional-looking thumbs-up sign. I gasped for breath as we climbed to 200 feet or so, then came diving down to zoom past the waiting camera. Tears streamed from my eyes as the cold wind bit into my face. It was such a strange sensation to gaze down at the airfield below, with nothing to break my view but the sight of my shoe on the footrest.

Yvonne and our cameraman were delighted with this unexpected bonus, so it was a satisfied company that made its way to the hotel for hot baths and dinner. I slept soundly that night, happy with the prospect of more flying in the morning. Our location next day was, in fact, at the Wing Commander's home, where he has a short, grass-covered take-off strip. We also had the added pleasure of visiting his mini-hangar, housing some 13 autogyros, including those used in the famous James Bond movie *You Only Live Twice* for which he did all the flying. We nicknamed it his Gyrobank.

On the actual night of the show, Ken agreed to come along to the studio, complete with his flying machine. It gave our audience and viewers at home the opportunity of seeing exactly what it looked like.

As anybody involved in outdoor filming in Britain will confirm, the unpredictability of our climate can make life very difficult, and much of the time downright impossible. With that problem in mind, it was suggested that we could do some filming immediately following my 1984 tour in Australia. It seemed a good idea for a number of reasons: I was already there, the weather was pretty certain to be warm and sunny most of the time, and the whole area was photographically untapped, as far as my show was concerned. We looked forward to a fruitful venture. As the concert tour came to an end, Yvonne Littlewood arrived to organise things. My locations were selected in many contrasting areas – sailing on Sydney Harbour; sightseeing in the Blue Mountains; visiting a reconstructed old mining village called Sovereign Hill, near Melbourne, and a tropical island off the Great Barrier Reef; making a trip into the outback to Alice Springs and Ayers Rock; and much more. The musical tracks for my songs had, of course, been put on to tape while I was still in London prior to my tour. These were relayed to me on location, while I simply mimed to the lyrics. Quite a fuss was created over my visit to

Ayers Rock, which, as you may know, is a sacred site to the Aboriginal people. Our application to film there was handled by the Australian Tourist Authorities in London, but sadly, permission was refused at the last moment. We accepted the decision, naturally enough, but the Northern Territories Tourist Board thought it unfair and interceded. When the newspapers got hold of the story it became quite a national incident. Headlines in the major newspapers announced: VAL BARRED FROM THE ROCK IRISH SINGER BANNED NO ROCKERS AT THE ROCK. Smaller headlines were to be found in the papers as far afield as London and New York. I should mention that we had no intention of going on to the Rock. This, we knew, would be out of the question. We simply wanted to film the unique landmark in three different lighting conditions, dawn, afternoon and sunset, the lyrics of my song relating these to stages of our lives.

Anyway, we were finally invited to go there and everybody gave us a great welcome, including the Aboriginal guides who were there to oversee our efforts.

While the storm was raging in the newspapers I was constantly being called by the media and, of course, being stopped by people in the street.

One evening, while doing some night filming in the heart of King's Cross in Sydney, I was intercepted once again. I was actually being filmed, singing the verse to a song, indicating my disillusionment with city life and my longing for the open spaces. The idea, in fact, was to mix the film through to my tropical paradise on the Great Barrier Reef. Since the location was a busy street corner, and the time was rush hour, the sound of orchestra and voice were being transmitted to me with the aid of a tiny mike, similar to a hearing aid, which was neatly placed in my ear. In other words, nobody would ever detect that I was, in fact, singing my heart out. The camera had been strategically placed across the street. Suddenly, as I reached the climax of the song, a complete stranger walked up to me with his hand outstretched.

'Good God, look who we have here,' he said smiling, and obviously glad to see me. He was now standing directly between me and the camera, completely unaware of his intrusion. 'My wife and I are great fans of your TV shows.' His voice was barely audible through the noise of the traffic and the 30-piece orchestra blasting into my ear, not to mention my own voice.

'Thank you,' I said, shaking his hand, then, pointing to the camera perched on its tripod across the way, I told him, 'Sorry, I'm filming at the moment, as you can see, so could you stand aside for a few minutes?'

Like so many people on these occasions, he looked at the camera, smiled his acknowledgment of the situation, apologised, then continued to talk.

'You know, we wouldn't miss one of your shows – and what about all this Ayers Rock business, eh?'

By now, one of the crew was urging him to let me get on with things, but he was in full flow.

'My wife and I watch the papers every day; we haven't missed a word about it. I see you're going there after all.'

'Yes, thank you,' I said once again, this time gently pushing him out of shot. 'Say hello to your wife for me.'

That was all the encouragement he needed. 'You can say hello yourself,' he told me, grabbing my arm. Then moving his free arm in the direction of an adjacent shop door he yelled out, 'Hey Mavis, Mavis, come over here a minute! You'll never believe who's here, it's what's his name on the telly – you know…Andy Williams.'

A few minutes later, I was back to work, my hearing aid in place, trying not to look at any of the gang, who were still laughing. The filming turned out very well and made a welcome change in the make-up of the show.

My early visits Down Under were, as in the case of many visiting artists, limited to the main centres – Perth, Adelaide, Melbourne, Sydney and Brisbane, any extra engagements consisting of cabaret appearances in the clubs of New South Wales, since, as I mentioned, I felt much more at home in theatres and concert halls.

I've been both a personal and a professional friend of Rolf Harris and his wife Alwyn since way back in the 1950s. One evening, while discussing my forthcoming trip Down Under, Rolf asked: 'Why do you confine your bookings to the same venues every time? There are so many lovely dates outside the main cities, which you really should include. Australia is a hell of a big place, so take this opportunity to really see it.'

He then took the trouble of writing a long list of the best theatres in each state. My promoters came on board and we began to consider the many fine civic theatres and concert centres in towns within easy reach of the main cities. It opened up quite an extensive tour, which from the work-satisfaction point of view is right up my street.

There's always been a fear among some artists that if you play anywhere other than the large, more prestigious centres, people might think you are slipping, or losing your grip, or that you are over the hill. Frankly, I've never been able to see this argument. People are people, towns are towns, and as long as the theatre is nice and has the facilities, I can't see anything wrong with it. Maybe that comes from the fact that I was born and brought up in a small city of some 30,000 people, and I loved it when visiting artists included our town on their itinerary. The family have joined me for some of the trips and share my enthusiasm for the place. Between us, we must have seen more of Australia than most Australians!

The number of working hours that were crammed into the making of my 'live' Saturday night shows back in the UK would, I'm sure, amaze the casual viewer. Planning the whole thing, choosing and learning duets with guest artists, not to mention the memorising of seven or eight songs a week, plus the script, took all the hours available. Yvonne Littlewood, Roger and myself tucked ourselves away in a small basement room in the bowels of the BBC Television Centre week after week for about three months a year, often not finding time for a lunch break, simply to get the thing ready for Saturday nights.

In 1982 I was to meet a musical 'soul mate' who for two seasons at least shared his vast musical knowledge and experience with our resident group. I'm speaking, or writing, of Ray Charles. (As he himself would immediately add, 'No, not that one, I'm the other one!') Ray spent some 35 years of his life attending to the musical requirement of Mr Perry Como, the Ray Charles Singers becoming, in the process, one of the most famous of choral ensembles since the late 1940s. He was already known to Yvonne, who had previously produced and directed some of Perry Como's work. Ray was visiting Britain as musical adviser to the Muppet Shows, then in production at ATV Studios at Elstree, when I first met him.

Yvonne, Roger and I had by this time completed some six series of music shows, so a fresh team member warming up on the touchline was precisely what was needed. For two series, Ray turned our trio into an enthusiastic quartet, and very enjoyable it was too. He kindly described our hardworking group as 'the tightest ship' he'd ever encountered in his long career.

I know what a great privilege it was to have at our disposal a fine, 30-piece orchestra, boasting the cream of Britain's session musicians. An orchestra equipped to cater for the needs of varied guests such as Tony Bennet, Andy Williams, Rosemary Clooney, Dionne Warwick, John Williams and so on. All of them were placed in the capable hands of the conductor/arranger Ronnie Hazlehurst.

I became quite accustomed to these distinguished artists standing on the studio floor, facing the musicians and saying: 'Wow. Not many shows in the world these days can boast a backing group like this!' To this day, I look back and think: 'Thank you BBC!'

Sadly, Ronnie passed away a while back. The BBC held a memorial service for him at Broadcasting House. So many faces from the past were there representing lighting, design, sound and of course the members of the orchestra past and present. All had come along to pay their respects. My beautiful backing singers of yore joined the journey down memory lane. The lads from the orchestra set up on stage and it seemed somehow that it had never come to an end. I joined Terry Wogan and Cilla Black in words of respect for his quite remarkable career, composing the theme tunes for countless successful television programmes. I recall one day, many years back when I was rehearsing with the late John Denver. As Ronnie was leaving, he pressed a piece of paper into my top pocket and casually said: 'Have a look at this and see if it's of any interest.' It turned out to be a special lyric to his theme tune for 'Last of the Summer Wine,' which has run now for almost 40 years. I recorded it shortly after and sang it that day at his memorial service as a tribute and a farewell to Ron. What a stalwart he was for so many years.

A question often put to me these days, both by the show-business publicity machine and the general public, is 'Why do you think your popularity or success has lasted so long?' I find it virtually impossible to find any kind of intelligent answer; after all, it's not for me to analyse why people have enjoyed my work all these years. I just know that they have, and I'm deeply grateful for it, and thank the public sincerely for rewarding me so handsomely with their goodwill.

I think it was Perry Como who, in answer to that same question, replied, 'The secret of my many years of success is three-inch lapels.' When asked to elaborate, he went on, 'Well, when I first began to enjoy popularity, three-inch lapels were the fashion, so I decided to have some. They suited me down to the ground, so when suddenly everybody changed to four-inch lapels, then two-inch lapels, and even no lapels at all, I decided to stick with what I'd got and still have them today.'

Need I tell you that the moral of this little story is: 'When you find out what it is you do best, and what the public wants from you, then stick with it, and do it as well as you can.' Of course, you must send it for a regular service, keep it looking as good as possible, and most important of all, think very hard before trading it in for a new model.

Personally, I can't think of a better answer than that, when endeavouring to explain my years as an entertainer. I've been a small fish in the great big ocean of show business, but thank goodness the waters have remained reasonably calm for me and I've enjoyed every minute of it. There's no denying the fact that many of my colleagues would find the prospect of wearing three-inch lapels year in, year out very boring indeed. Well, that's very much a personal thing, depending on your make-up or personality. Some of my pals swap and change their golf clubs every time a new model comes on the market. In my experience, once the novelty wears off, your golf is much the same as before. It's the way we swing the club that causes all our problems.

Chapter Twenty-Two

By the late 1980s, we were honestly beginning to feel that we were squeezing the last few drops from our weekly music shows. My annual Saturday night series on BBC1 together with the Christmas special were now in their 20th year. Oh, the show was still very popular, but time was moving on and I suppose that fashions were changing. Having been in the business for so many years, I'd watched this happen before in the clubs and music halls.

The Head of BBC Light Entertainment at the time was James Moir. He was a friend and we had worked together for many years. I sat and talked to him about whether he felt that this particular type of show had run its course. His immediate reaction was a kind one, but he knew, from a professional point of view, what I was getting at. He suggested carrying on but consulted Michael Grade (then controller of BBC TV) about my concerns.

We all met up one day at my home. I was interested to hear Michael's views and thought it would clear the air. He did say it would be a shame to end such a long run (and he'd have to consider the problem of how to fill that Saturday-night slot). He suggested the possibility of changing the format a little, maybe introducing an element of comedy. My reaction was that through the years we had explored this, but had ended up with what myself and my producer Yvonne Littlewood thought was the best of all worlds.

I did agree, however, with the idea of filming a series of six special programmes back home in Ireland. These were to be transmitted early on Sunday evenings, a spot in the scheduling commonly referred to as 'The God Slot'. The chosen title for the shows was *Homeward Bound*. As ever, I was presented with a wonderful guest list carefully chosen to suit the contrasting locations.

The show turned out to be a very pleasurable mix of music, both modern and traditional, sacred and profane, as well as a chance to see my own country in all its finery. We made sure that the viewers were given a chance to see as much of Ireland as possible and to marvel at all the talent it has produced.

In Dublin, I obviously had The Dubliners to serenade me. A little further south, I was to spend the day with singer Chris de Burgh near his home in Dalkey. Then it was County Wicklow, where I joined my old friends, The Chieftains and followed that by some spectacular filming at Glendalough with The Fureys. Further north, I had the great pleasure of working with the acclaimed singer, Mary Black. From there, I travelled to one of Ireland's most historic landmarks, the Giant's Causeway. Close by, at the famous whiskey distillery of Bushmills, my special guest, James Galway and myself sat by a warm fire and shared an old Percy French song entitled 'Little Bridget Flynn' while a small gathering of locals sneaked in to watch. Later, with the Causeway as a backdrop, Jimmy talked at length of his young life in Belfast. An upbringing so different from mine and yet our love of music and our great mutual respect has never made such things an issue.

The film crew then headed west. This, for me, was the most memorable part of the trip. My very first visit to the Aran Islands, the small group of ancient monastic settlements was an amazing experience. The rain was pouring down and strong winds were blowing as we came in to land on the tiny airstrip. The whole place looked quite desolate and forbidding as we headed for our hotel, but all the gloom lifted in an instant as we dashed through the rain and were welcomed by the warmth and smells of home cooking.

My special guest for this particular edition of *Homeward Bound* was someone with whom I had worked several times and had become a family friend; the singer and harpist, Mary O'Hara. It so happens that Mary's husband, Pat O'Toole is a native of Aran, so I had the added pleasure of visiting his mother at her cottage. Both Mary and Pat are fluent Gaelic speakers and listening to them awoke memories of my early childhood, when I spoke our native tongue quite freely. I had to admit to them how rusty I had become as I tried to join in their conversation. I was forever asking them. 'What's the word for…?' Pat assured me that it was simply lack of practice. 'Tell you what,' he suggested. 'How about trying a whole morning on location where, apart from the script, English is not allowed.' I was given special licence to ask for occasional translations, but apart from that, I was a bit like a holidaymaker in Spain or France trying to hold a ham-fisted conversation with a taxi driver or waiter.

I continued to practise my Gaelic at our next location, which was up in Co. Donegal in the North West. We gathered at a lovely pub owned by the family of a young woman who had captivated the world with her unique style of music. Her name – Enya. We were welcomed there by her whole family, the other members happily pulling pints behind the bar. In their own right, they formed that haunting singing ensemble, Clannad. Their father was a fellow veteran of the Irish dance bands of the show-band era and we had a lot of memories in common. Now, that particular part of the north-west coast is very much a native-speaking area, so pretty soon I was back to my refresher course. I had the pleasure of strolling along a deserted beach, chatting to Enya with a camerawoman ahead of us, walking backwards. She spoke very lovingly about her grandmother, who loved such walks. Each time we were 'off camera' I'd revert to my pigeon Gaelic. Enya was very encouraging and through her influence I was later sent a Fainne, which is a brooch worn by members of the Irish-speaking community. So, all in all, the *Homeward Bound* trip was a wonderful experience. I treasure a small English-Gaelic dictionary given to me on leaving and still use it for the occasional practice.

Following the meeting with Michael Grade, my Saturday night show did run for a further two years and then we called it a day. On reflection, I'm quite convinced that my shows came to an end at exactly the right time. After all, I was then in my sixties and, as I've already said, television was changing in style and fashion. I had some important decisions to make, or as Fagin would say: I was 'reviewing the situation'.

I had no interest whatsoever in attempting some kind of chat show or introducing another musical format. I was truly 'spoiled rotten' for some 24 years, presenting a show which I loved and hopefully perfected. I simply didn't want to spoil all the joy I'd had by doing something with no real purpose other than keeping me on television.

A year or so after I finished making the television shows, I began to come across letters or articles in the newspapers and magazines asking, 'Whatever happened to Val Doonican?' I think it was the American singer Howard Keel who said: 'As far as the public is concerned, if you're not on television, you must be dead.' There's so much more to the entertainment world than TV, although it certainly plays a huge part in the public's perception of your work.

In the 1990s, though, the opportunity arose for me to make a couple of 'sell-through videos'. There was a huge market at the time for entertainment videos which were not made for television, but contained many elements of a traditional music show.

I heard from my manager that a production company had asked if we could make a special music video back in Waterford. I was invited to select a dozen or so songs that we would film in locations that had nostalgic associations for me. It was called *Songs from My Sketchbook*. My old friend Laurie Holloway agreed to take charge of the music and we started what was to be one of the most enjoyable undertakings I could remember.

Among the special moments were finding myself once again sitting at my old school desk, making a half-hearted attempt at glass blowing at the world-renowned Waterford Crystal Works. I also retraced the walks I took with my father every Sunday. A highlight was a specially arranged family gathering with as many of the Doonicans, young and old, as could be assembled, set against the musical background of the old Perry Como classic 'Memories are Made of This'.

Some years back, I had done a series of concerts in Ireland. Of course one of these was staged in my home town. After taking my bows, I was asked to return to the stage. There stood a man of about my age. Quite astonishingly, I could instantly recall his younger self from my Boy Scout days. Joe Farrell said a few words of welcome, then introduced his son. A young gentleman entered from the wings and said many kind things about my long career. He told me that he was one of the 'cutters' from Waterford Glass (the lads responsible for those wonderful trophies held aloft by so many sporting superstars). 'Well, knowing you were coming over,' he went on. 'I was given permission to make you this special item. A memory of Waterford.' Then from behind his back, he produced the most exquisite crystal rocking chair – a result of many hours' 'overtime'. It is a real treasure and reminds me both of my roots and of my great good fortune.

Sadly, Waterford Crystal has been one of the casualties of the recent economic slump – all the more reason for me to cherish the precious collection of unique pieces given to me over the years and wonder at the skill that went into making them. They have pride of place in my home.

The second sell-through video was entirely different. It was based on the notion that those of us who have made the decision to 'try their luck' on the fringes of the great big entertainment world were inspired to do so by those who came before them. In my childhood, the man who was 'all the rage' as the saying goes – was Bing Crosby. Tens of thousands of young hopefuls unashamedly copied every detail of his style because it was the popular way to sing at the time. Again, think of the impact The Beatles had almost 50 years ago on vocal groups, or the late Michael Jackson 20 years after that.

With this in mind, I decided to pay tribute to my musical heroes. The video and CD were called *Thank You for the Music*. My personal list of thank yous went to Crosby, Como, Nat King Cole, Peggy Lee, Les Paul, Burl Ives and many others. We filmed it all in the London area, but used locations, such as old ballrooms and parks that linked in with the songs we were performing. Filming 'Mississippi Mud' was great fun as it involved a bunch of local children jumping up and down in puddles in brightly coloured wellington boots. For the Matt Monroe number 'My Kind of Girl' cine film that Lynn had shot in the 1960s of our two girls as toddlers was spliced together in time with the music. It's a sequence that makes us laugh to this day. On that project, I also had the added pleasure of working with my daughter Sarah who was part of the production team and worked with me on the script.

When my 70th birthday was looming, Lynn asked the girls to put out a few feelers about what to give Dad for his big day. It was Fiona who brought up the subject. 'You're not the easiest person to buy for,' she said. 'So how about a few hints?'

The passing years had somewhat dampened my enthusiasm for golf and I was very much aware of the gap that it had left in my leisure activities. I've had a lifetime of dabbling in art, from oil painting to sketching. In fact, some years earlier I had completed a course at Amersham Art College in Buckinghamshire. 'Tell you what,' I said to Fiona. 'I've always had a soft spot for watercolours and I wouldn't mind having a crack at it before it's too late.'

That was all the family needed. Lynn popped into one of our local art galleries and set the ball rolling. Talking to the proprietor, she asked if there was someone locally who could give lessons to a beginner. He walked her around the gallery, pointing out the styles of various local artists. She paused at one particular landscape. She knew I had a great love for the countryside. 'I may be wrong,' she said. 'But I think he'd go for something like that.'

'Well, that's fortunate,' said the gallery owner. 'This artist lives about five minutes from your house.'

So, one afternoon while I was golfing, she slipped into my study, gathered up as many of my artistic efforts as she could lay hands on and headed for the home of the artist Denis Pannett. He looked at my work and agreed to give a course of six lessons to get me on the right track.

Well, it turned out to be a very special gift indeed. As the months went by I looked forward so much to each new challenge. Pretty soon, I was turning out watercolours with which I felt quite happy and sometimes even a little proud. In fact, a couple of years later, Denis suggested that I had some of my better results turned into greetings cards. With a smile, we refer to them as my O Levels.

Throughout my life, I have had a tendency to get sudden urges to try something I have never done before. The list of my 'flights of fancy' is so long, I won't bore you with all the details. My late mother, referred to such moments as a 'Figaery'. You would hear her say, 'For God's sake, what kind of Figaery did he have growing that awful moustache?' or 'She has had one of her Figaerys again. Look at the bleached hair!' It got me thinking, is there such a word? Well, a nephew back home looked it up on an Irish website – a kind of Gaelic Google – and there it was – Figaery: an impulse or whim. So now you know!

Among my 'Figaerys' have been woodwork, learning to fly both gliders and small aircraft, and learning to play a number of musical instruments. Towards the end of my TV years, in an effort to vary the guest list as much as possible, Yvonne Littlewood thought we should take advantage of the huge popularity of country music. Soon our cast included such stars as Glen Campbell, Don Williams, Charlie Pride and Crystal Gayle. When I heard that the renowned Blues Harp aficionado Charlie McCoy was to be a future guest, I felt a 'Figaery' coming on, and decided to learn to play this tiny version of the harmonica. Childhood memories of playing the mouth organ were stimulated and suddenly, there I was, visiting a music store to acquire the correct instrument. I found the challenge fascinating and pretty soon I was driving anybody within earshot mad with my stumbling efforts. I thought I would do my best before the arrival of the expert, and by the time he got here, I was making a reasonable stab at it. So much so, that he generously suggested that we share a brief duet on the show just for the fun of it.

One of his recorded tracks, called 'Stone Fox Chase' was the opening theme music for the BBC music programme *The Old Grey Whistle Test* for many years. This was to be our duet. In fact, the producer of *The Old Grey Whistle Test* used a clip of our duet in their next edition. I was very flattered, and I am sure that my family hoped that I had got the whole thing out of my system and would be quiet from then on! Little were they to know that John Williams and the band Sky were booked for a future show. I thought it would be fun to learn the tuba and join Herbie Flowers in a duet! It made an interesting accompaniment to my daughter's O Level revision.

Since I stopped recording my television programmes I have concentrated on developing my one man show that I continue to perform in theatres and concert halls all over the British Isles, as well as 18-concert tours of Australia and New Zealand.

My many loyal fans, who have steadfastly followed me throughout the years, are still a regular feature. Some were just children when they first came to see me, with their parents. I now have the great pleasure of seeing them bringing their own children to the shows. I can only admire their stamina for turning up so consistently and making my job so easy and pleasurable. I would like to thank them all.

In order to adapt to an audience, which is gradually less eager to go out in the late evening and get home past their bedtime, it has become very popular and extremely successful to stage afternoon concerts. I have enjoyed this very sociable schedule for some years in concert halls Down Under, where many rural fans are also facing a long journey home. Now, it has caught on here in the UK, and I always enjoy the easy family atmosphere that it has brought to my concerts.

As I write this, I'm in my early eighties and still doing what my family calls my 'occasional laps of honour'.

For many years, I have been privileged to be associated with one of the entertainment world's special charities. It's called the Entertainment Artists Benevolent Fund (EABF) and is the main beneficiary of the annual Royal Variety Performances. I have enjoyed being one of its vice-presidents since the 1970s. My late assistant, Peggy (she of the notorious 'green folder') was cared for at the charity's beautiful retirement home, Brinsworth House, when her health deteriorated back in the 1980s. She had lived alone at the time, so I was so grateful for the way they made her so comfortable.

On the occasion of my 60th year in show business, I was approached by the EABF and asked if I would like to front a special celebratory concert at the London Palladium to help boost the charity's funds. This was to be along the lines of a 'Variety Show' featuring a wide range of acts including speciality acts as well as a variety of musical styles, comedy and dancing.

This was to turn out to be one of the most exciting and moving events of my whole career. Not only was I surrounded by fellow artists, all of whom gave their time and talents so willingly, but the sheer emotional experience of reflecting on just how blessed I have been for such a long time. Colleagues and friends, such as Nana Mouskouri, Rolf Harris, John Williams, Bradley Walsh, Robert Powell, Frank Carson and so many more were there to lend their support. My great friend and former producer/director Yvonne Littlewood even came out of retirement to help oversee things.

There was much to reflect on, as I looked out from the stage into that famous auditorium. Sitting out there, among others, had been three ladies who shared so much working time with me in the past under the name of 'The Triangle'. They had sat, perched on stools, behind me on the stage, supplying the backing vocals for all the long summer seasons and overseas tours. Now in their seventies, they are all still great friends and are very much part of the extended family I have acquired over my career.

The greatest pleasure, for me, was to look up at the Royal Box and see my two grandchildren. I was very aware of how little experience they had had of seeing their grandpa doing what they had only heard about from older people. After all, they were not even born when I was a regular TV face.

You discover, as indeed I have, that the longer you survive in the entertainment world, the more likely you are to become a victim of the generation gap. By that, I simply mean that the generation of television watchers and radio listeners who grew up with you will grow old and simply disappear from your radar. At the same time, of course, a brand new and much younger audience will have latched on to the next generation of artists while having little or no knowledge or interest in what came before.

My granddaughter, Bethany, was asked once by one of her primary school teachers, 'Have you seen Grandpa on the television?' Bethany thought this over. 'No,' she replied. 'I've seen him on the sofa.'

Epilogue

I am often reminded these days of something that happened to me many years ago. I was visiting my home town of Waterford, and was just about to go into the graveyard of our old parish church. An old lady approached me, who I recognised as a friend of my late mother. 'Hello, love,' she said. 'Are you going in to see your mum and dad?' I told her I was. 'I've just been having a chat with your mum,' she said. 'Then I went to visit my brother.' She looked back over her shoulder. 'Isn't it awful?' she continued. 'Everyone you talk to nowadays is dead!'

At the time, I didn't really understand what she meant, but I am beginning to do so now.

It is lovely to look back now over the years and feel a genuine gratitude. Somebody recently asked me, 'What has been the greatest gift in your long life?' Without a doubt, I must answer, my family: my wife of some 47 years, Lynn, my two beloved daughters and, of course, our dear grandchildren, Bethany and Scott.

Sarah, herself an author, having had two novels published, has run her own writing class in London for many years. Fiona combines her work in marketing with being a wife and mum. Trying to tackle this volume over the past months would have been quite impossible without their help and guidance.

I hope that this ever-changing world will be as kind to my grand-children as it has been to me.

Well, hopefully, there is more of my story and my life remaining. I stress the 'hopefully', because it has been such a joy and I want to spend as much of life as possible with my very special family. For many years, it has been a little family joke that Lynn constantly says, 'Aren't we lucky?'

whether sipping a glass of wine after dinner, getting back home after a tiring day, or simply settling down to sleep at night. Sometimes, we have received phone calls from friends away on holiday, who simply say, 'We were just sitting here looking at the view and thinking "you know what Lynn would say? – Aren't we lucky!"'

Now that I have shared all of my 82 years with you, including the pleasure of 62 of those in the wonderful world of music, I will finish by saying, 'Thank God for whatever talents I was granted, and I sincerely hope I have never wasted any of them.'